GSD Platform 4

Harvard University
Graduate School of Design

www
.gsd
.harvard
.edu

PREFACE

The seventy-fifth anniversary of the Harvard University Graduate School of Design marks a particular temporal moment of a projective present. The works presented in this new volume of *Platform* are at once aware of their commitment to a certain set of experimental and forward-thinking ideas and cognizant of their relation to a long and consistent tradition of such ideas within the School and the University, which itself is celebrating a 375th anniversary.

Previous editions of *Platform* have helped to identify the GSD's major research and pedagogical preoccupations. In this regard, *Platform 4* is no exception. Like its predecessors, this book contains a structured presentation of projects, events, lectures, conversations, and exhibitions that are the hallmarks of the School's dynamic intellectual condition.

It has become customary for every edition of *Platform* to be coupled with an exhibition of the book's content. But this academic year, our first exhibition, "Dispatches from the GSD," curated in conjunction with our anniversary, is conceived as a celebration and an assessment of the School's historical contributions. There is of course always a benefit to reflecting on history, which in this case clearly helped us to select a number of critical events over the past seventy-five years that best encapsulate the School's achievements and its contribution and position toward particular domains of research and pedagogy.

More than anything else, this affirmation of the historical role of the GSD as the place for shaping the global discourse of design practice has helped not only to inspire but to form what we do today. This awareness of the historical continuity of the actions of our students and faculty renders even more deliberate our focus on specific and urgent areas of inquiry.

The global commitments and aspirations of the GSD go hand in hand with the diversity of its students and faculty. But even with this diversity, it is the coming together of the School's many constituencies under the symbolic umbrella of Design that provides the uncommon context for collaboration and cross-fertilization among the disciplines of architecture, landscape architecture, and urban planning and design as well as with the School's advanced studies programs. The seventy-fifth anniversary of the School is itself an important reminder that the idea of close proximity and connections among the various design fields was deeply imbedded in its founding.

The current volume of *Platform* is in one sense a document of a selection of the work and activities of the GSD from the past year. Yet in this anniversary year, it is also an explicit manifestation of the School's consistent commitment to the value of the singularity of the disciplines as well as to the productive consequences of our work across disciplines.

Mohsen Mostafavi
Dean. Alexander and Victoria Wiley Professor of Design

INTRODUCTION

On March 11, 2011, an 8.9 magnitude earthquake off the eastern coast of Japan sent 40 foot high waves crashing into the coastal city of Miyako, overwhelming the tsunami barriers and damaging the Fukushima Nuclear Power Plant. Meanwhile, at the Graduate School of Design, the spring lecture series, *A New Innocence: Emerging Trends in Japanese Architecture,* featured Toyo Ito, Kazuyo Sejima and Ryue Nishizawa, Junya Ishigami, and Sou Fujimoto. Set against the backdrop of national disaster and recovery, these architects presented their work and their personal accounts of the situation in Japan. The uncanny coincidence between the disaster and the lecture series was one of several moments this past year in which a world event found **deep resonance** within the GSD. Discussions provoked by the disaster made global events seem remarkably proximate.

The events in Japan shifted the discursive context at the GSD. Beyond a design school, the GSD is an immersive environment—a **dense atmosphere** saturated with creative and intellectual activity. The fourth volume of a series, *Platform 4* is more than a catalog of courses. It represents a selective sampling of the agendas at the GSD during the last academic year, revealing a diverse mixture of projects, research, and events. *Platform 4* attempts to place the reader "at the scene." On the steps of Piper auditorium when Jacques Herzog declared that, "architecture is like a love affair; it just is." Or when Peter Eisenman, in conversation with Rafael Moneo, differentiated architects that "have a project" from those that "have a practice." *Platform 4* documents both site and situation at the GSD—it is an **institutional index**.

Sorting through an immense database of content, the editorial team sought to organize the material through various thematic lenses. We asked ourselves, "What were the key debates of the past year? What were the critical questions asked? What was urgent? What was the chatter?" Initially described by key words and tag clouds, the content of *Platform 4* was mined for dominant themes that informed the eventual chapters. Four categories emerged, decanted from the mixture of topics: **Structure/Metrics, Rhetoric/Media, Type/Flux, and Situation/Agency.** Each chapter consists of a pair of words. The pairing is composed of two terms; the first, an existing design platform or methodology, the second, an emerging condition that re-qualifies the first. For example, the temporality of the term "Flux" modifies the continuity implied by "Type." The pairings create a conceptual space between terms, allowing them to interact and affect their individual meanings while expanding their capacity to contain the diversity of work between.

The Table of Contents organizes the book by location, type (Core Studio, Lecture, Thesis, etc.) and by theme. Thus, *Platform 4* becomes searchable in different ways. The network of linkages between the site, types, and themes produces a pattern of relationships and adjacencies—a visualization of the network of cross-disciplinary design agendas at the GSD.

While *Platform 4* records research trajectories from the past year, it also has the capacity to set agendas for future work. By framing a set of issues and topics, *Platform 4* focuses attention towards particular areas of interest, allowing individual work to build on and contribute to a larger body of disciplinary knowledge. In that sense, the themes within this book become **projective**. They provide frameworks for future inquiry, allowing *Platform* to become just that—a framework to build upon.

Eric Howeler
Assistant Professor of Architecture

STRUCTURE and METRICS place emphasis on the quantitative and performative while reflecting the contemporary currency of information in our data driven culture.

Powerful new tools for both simulation and measurement of natural phenomena have intensified current interest in **METRICS**. Quantifiable information about performance processes and parameters has empowered designers by allowing for a new functionalism of finely calibrated and responsive intervention. As design becomes increasingly tied to the analysis and transformation of complex environmental systems, metrics provide a means to measure performance requirements and their impacts. By establishing terms of evaluation, **METRICS** allows for verification; the critical step between theory and practice that validates theoretical assumptions.

Beyond consideration of load-bearing components in building systems, tectonics, and construction, a renewed interest in **STRUCTURE** has recognized the capacity of design to seek solutions in essential systems; in the organization of elements, the configuration of component relationships, and the disposition of material. Contemporary computational tools, coupled with structural and mathematical principles, allow Architects, Landscape Architects, and Urban Planners to work with greater precision and complexity. Rule-based design has also made structure and organization powerful new determinants of form.

Lisa Iwamoto and Craig Scott's option studio, *Material Systems/Structural Geometry: America's Cup San Francisco*, used research into structural systems as a generative design methodology. George Legendre's option studio, *Rising Mass 2*, looked mathematically at the tower type as determined by building codes and leasing conventions to develop new possibilities for high rise structures. Similarly, Eduardo Rico's lecture, *"Models, Cities, and Systematic Utopias,"* proposed urban scale design strategies based on computational data and mapping systems. **STRUCTURE** and **METRICS** place emphasis on the quantitative and performative while reflecting the contemporary currency of information in our data driven culture.

Structure /
Metrics

The course was framed by a general ambition to develop explorations in digital design, fabrication, and parametric tools that was informed and enriched by historical precedent while still maintaining a speculative and novel outlook. The primary focus of the course was the development of conceptual skills and techniques as well as technical understanding of the application of digital processes and tools in the development of tectonic and construction systems in architecture.

Students in this course completed projects that used a number of emerging and established digital techniques and processes to develop new prototypes for construction systems. These proposals took inspiration from and expanded on analysis of exemplary construction/tectonic systems. Existing system precedents were studied and reconsidered during the course to inform and inspire the development of each project. Students were encouraged to rethink existing systems in order to produce novel expression as well as performance.

A period of analysis and documentation of existing systems and their associative geometric and material relationships initiated the development of a rigorous analytical understanding of specific construction and tectonic systems, as well as a proficiency in applying this knowledge to construct associative/parametric digital models. These models constituted the tools to generate alternative variations of the analyzed systems. This informed a subsequent phase of prototyping using the fabrication laboratory's tools. The prototype fabrication exercise allowed students to gain knowledge in and explore the new potentials and capabilities of tools in the emerging field of digital fabrication. These digital design and parametric tools allow for the reconsideration and expansion of the potential applications of exemplary construction and tectonic systems today.

Brandon Cuffy, Jordan Mactavish, Ke Yu Xiong, Jing Zhang

(Re)Fabricating Tectonic Prototypes

Seminar | Leire Asensio Villoria

Manuel Diaz, Jungon Kim, Carl Koepcke, Azadeh Omidfar, Liwen Zhang

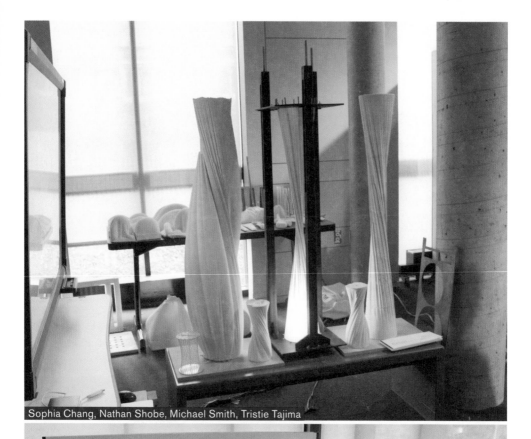

Sophia Chang, Nathan Shobe, Michael Smith, Tristie Tajima

Gonglue Jiang, Daekwon Park, Victor AP Perezamado, W Benjamin Tew

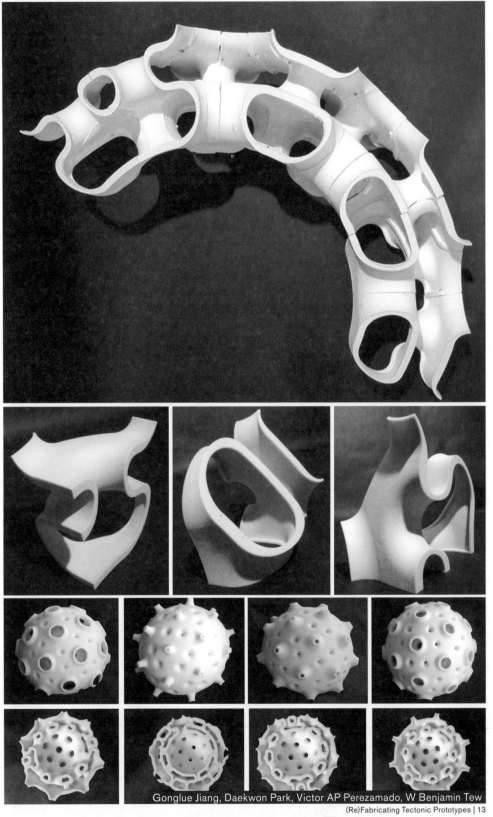

Gonglue Jiang, Daekwon Park, Victor AP Perezamado, W Benjamin Tew

In this studio, architectural conventions and typologies were taught by means of anomalies: extreme or exceptional conditions of space and form that elicit a heightened awareness of the norms that are customarily taken for granted. The aim was to bring architecture to heightened consciousness, and to confront it at a deeply conceptual level while learning the fundamental tools of the architect's craft.

The four projects were each conceived of as conundrums, seemingly impossible or paradoxical problems that demanded ingenuity and inventiveness.

Project 1: The Hidden Room. This project involved designing a group of five rooms, one of which appeared hidden from the other four. The program required providing a means of access to the hidden room while controlling the degree to which the room was vulnerable to disclosure.

Project 2: Elevator Intervention. This project asked students to insert the continuously extruded circulatory device in a building composed of remarkably interlocked volumes, passages, and staircases. Though the context could accommodate the extruded spatial element, the student was required to reconcile the conflict that necessarily ensued.

Project 3: Lodged House. The goal was to design a flexible space, capable of serving either domestic, work, study, or other private uses, in a new house to be located in a space between two existing, nearly identical houses. A problem to be solved was the likelihood that the proposal would create difficulties for the adjacent buildings, blocking several windows and making some rooms unusable.

Project 4: Lock Building. The project was about movement in time and space, actualized mechanically. The program was a building, parts of which were connected to and moved with the gate of a boat lock. The building was required to enable continuous pedestrian passage across the lock when the gate was shut, and nautical passage through the lock when the gate was open. The project was about the development of two crossing, mutually disruptive paths.

Architecture I

Core Studio | Preston Scott Cohen, Anna Pla Català
Ingeborg Rocker, Michael Wang
Elizabeth Whittaker, Cameron Wu

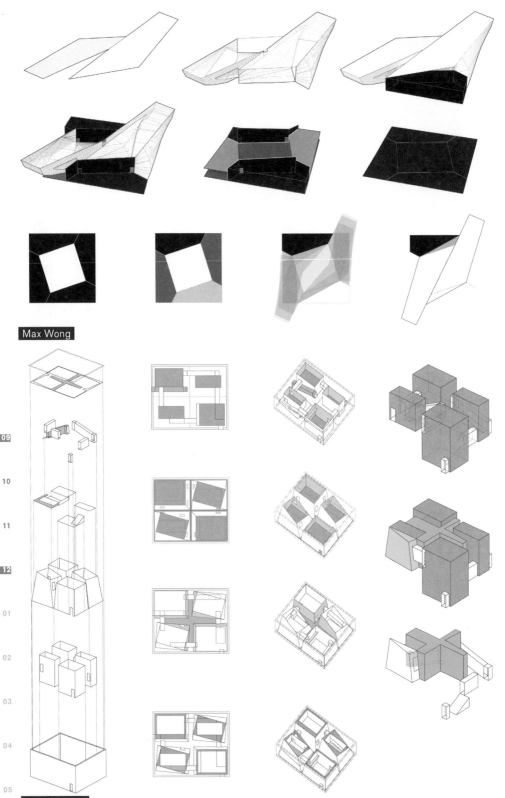

Max Wong

10
11
12
01
02
03
04
05

Sonja Cheng

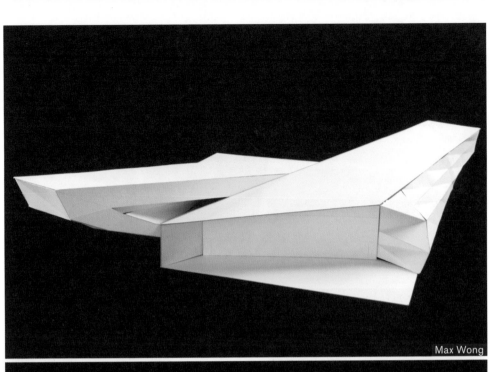

Max Wong

Sonja Cheng

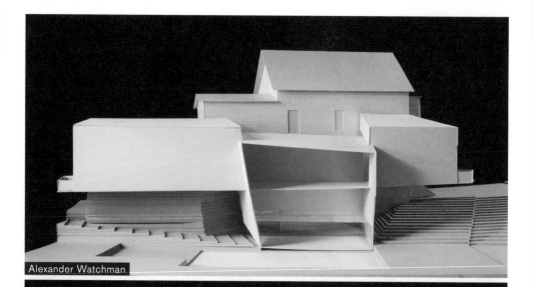

Alexander Watchman

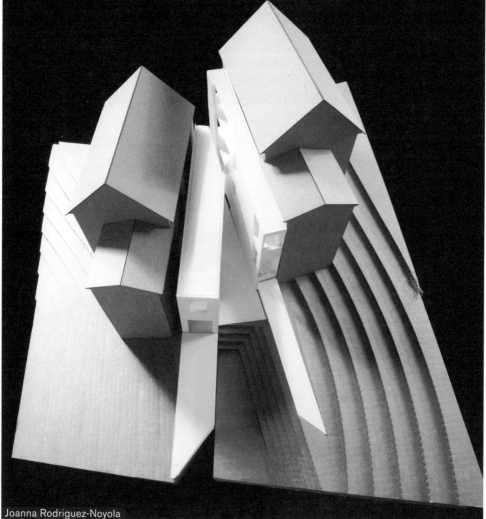

Joanna Rodriguez-Noyola

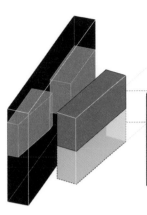
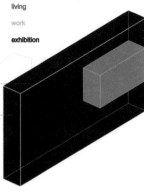

living
work
exhibition

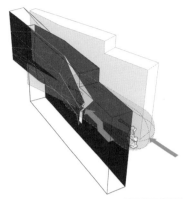

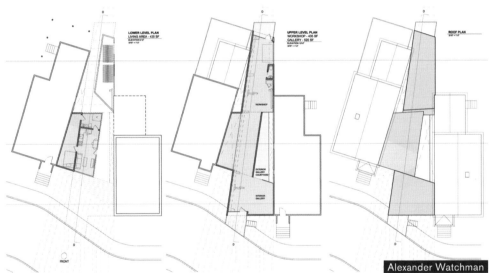

Max Wong

LOWER LEVEL PLAN
LIVING AREA - 435 SF

UPPER LEVEL PLAN
WORKSHOP - 435 SF
GALLERY - 520 SF

ROOF PLAN

Alexander Watchman

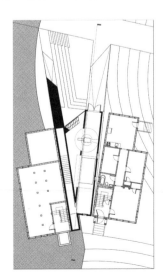
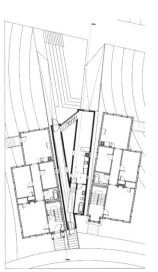
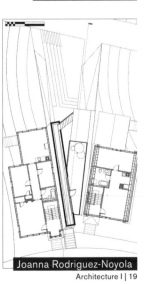

Joanna Rodriguez-Noyola

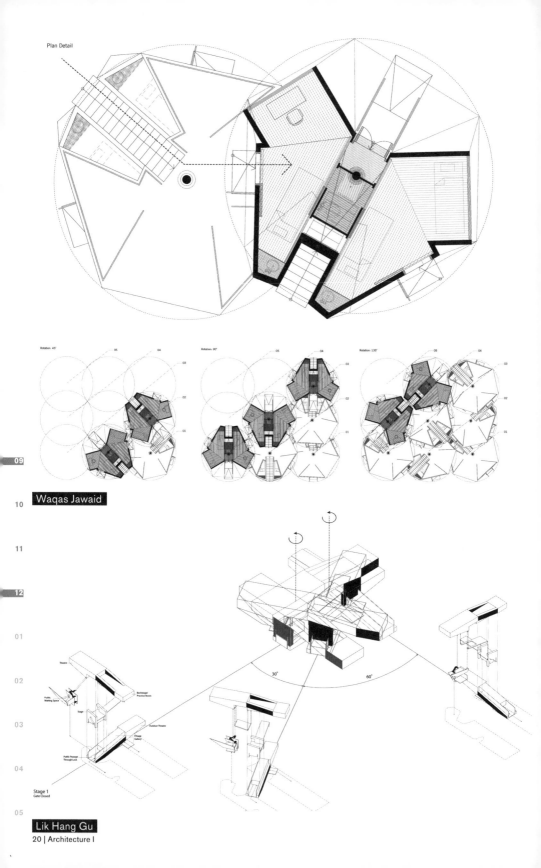

Plan Detail

Rotation: 45°   Rotation: 90°   Rotation: 135°

10   Waqas Jawaid

11

01

02

03

04

05

30°   60°

Stage 1
Gate Closed

Lik Hang Gu

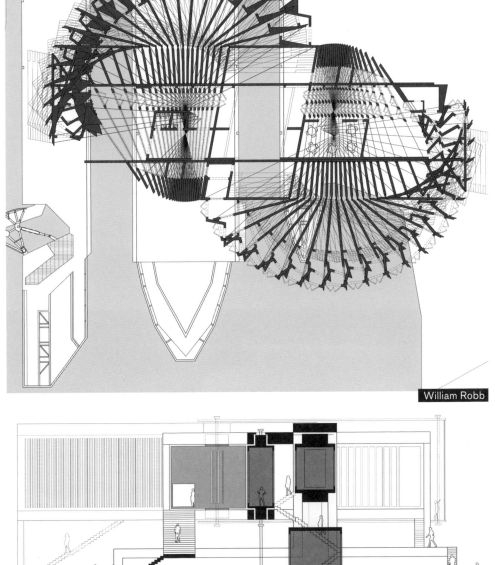

William Robb

Hyun Jung Joo

Sonja Cheng

Laura Siebenaler

Lauren Gerdeman
Architecture I | 23

Addressing the inertia of urban planning and the overexertion of civil engineering in the twentieth century, this third semester core studio focused on the design of large, complex, contaminated brownfield sites with a regional, ecological, and infrastructural outlook. Employing the agency of regional ecology and landscape infrastructure as the dominant drivers of design, the studio involved the development of biodynamic and biophysical systems that provide flexible yet directive patterns for future urbanization.

Through a series of contemporary mapping methods, field measures, case studies, readings, and design investigations, the course resulted in a series of collaborative exercises leading to a large-scale design project and future scenarios. Drawing from canonical case studies on regional reclamation strategies from across the world, the studio was further enhanced by a robust, regional representation program.

Focusing on the metrics of geospatial representation and remote sensing, two intensive workshops throughout the term of the studio didactically dealt with the interrelated subjects of regional cartography and site topography as operative and telescopic instruments of design across scales. Contributing to a complex, multi-layered profiling of the site as "system" and the reformulation of program as "process," the studio established a base platform for engaging an array of complex issues related to site contamination, biophysical systems, regional ecology, land cover, urban infrastructure, and economic geography.

Precluding conventional forms of urban development such as housing or retail development, the penultimate objective of the course was to explore and articulate the potential effectiveness of broader and longer range strategies, where biophysical systems prefigure as the denominator for re-envisioning public infrastructures and regional urban economies in the future.

09

12

01

02

03

04

05

Landscape Architecture III
Core Studio | Pierre Belanger, Niall Kirkwood, Julia Watson, Christian Werthmann

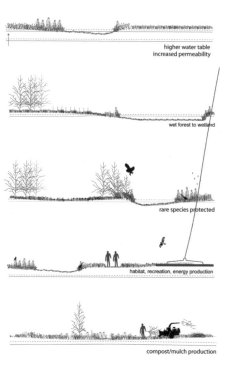

higher water table
increased permeability

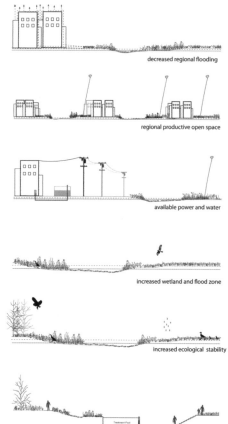

decreased regional flooding

wet forest to wetland

regional productive open space

rare species protected

available power and water

habitat, recreation, energy production

increased wetland and flood zone

compost/mulch production

increased ecological stability

establish management regime

increased recreation and outdoor edcucation

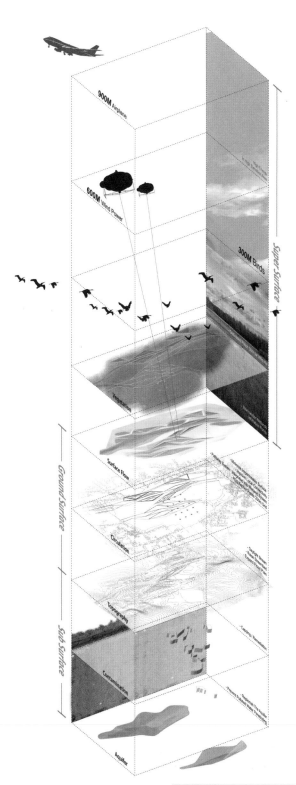

900M Airplane

600M Wind Power

300M Birds

Super-Surface

Vegetation

Surface Flow

Circulation

Topography

Contamination

Ground Surface

Sub-Surface

Aquifer

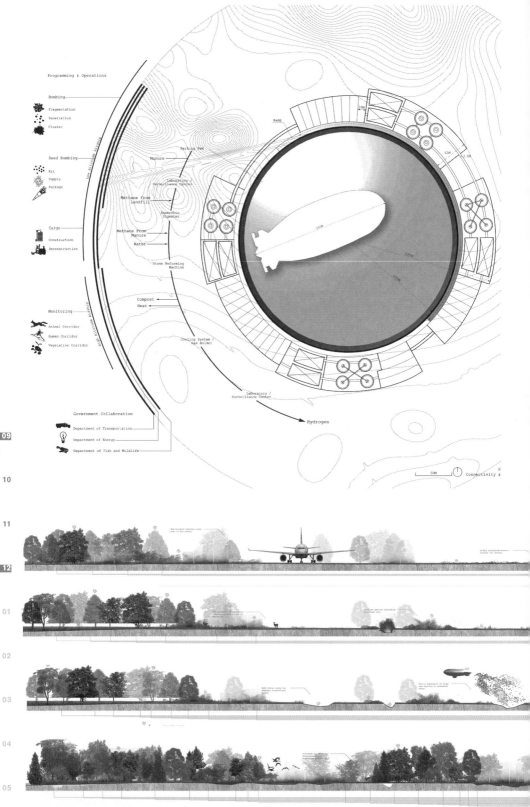

Programming & Operations

Bombing
- Fragmentation
- Penetration
- Cluster

Seed Bombing
- Kit
- Supply
- Package

Cargo
- Construction
- Deconstruction

Monitoring
- Animal Corridor
- Human Corridor
- Vegetative Corridor

Government Collaboration
- Department of Transportation
- Department of Energy
- Department of Fish and Wildlife

Low Altitude Airship

High Altitude Airship

Ramp

Manure

Parking Pad

Laboratory /
Surveillance Center

Methane from
Landfill

Anaerobic
Digester

Methane From
Manure

Water

Steam Reforming
Machine

Compost

Heat

Cooling System /
Gas Holder

Laboratory /
Surveillance Center

Hydrogen

Connectivity &

50M

09

10

11

12

01

02

03

04

05

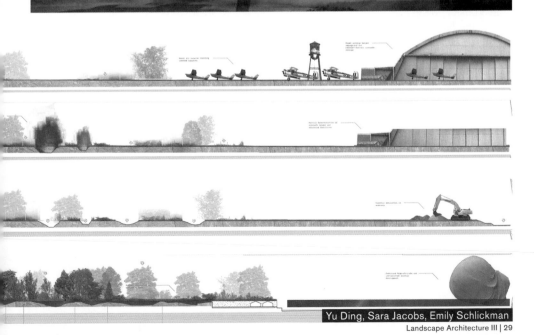

Yu Ding, Sara Jacobs, Emily Schlickman

Urban Planning I

The first semester core studio of the Master in Urban Planning program introduces students to the fundamental knowledge and technical skills used by urban planners to create, research, analyze, and implement plans and projects for the built environment. The studio operated in conjunction with GSD 3329: Core Urban Planning Workshop, which introduced students to spatial analysis through GIS; visual representation techniques; projections and forecasts in plan-making, including how demographic, economic, and market forecasts inform land use and infrastructure needs assessments; how alternative land use scenarios are constructed, including approaches to allocating land use, estimating carrying capacity, and build-out analyses; and evaluation of land use impacts through fiscal, economic, social, environmental, and transportation frameworks.

Urban Planning II

The second semester core studio builds on the concepts and methods of urban planning introduced during the first semester studio, when each student began to approach and think about urban circumstances and planning interventions. Of course, students learned that planners can, and must, approach problems in many different ways, because there are many different kinds of problems that an urban planner confronts.

Being aware of the idea that there is a single or overarching "planning method," beyond a sensibility that prioritizes the common good as it may apply to a particular scale of problem or a social milieu, is important.

Still, at the heart of most urban planning problems are issues pertaining to space and place: how to allocate and distribute space equitably; how to protect the qualities of existing places or guide their change; how to establish criteria for the intensity and character of use; how to use space more wisely relative to environmental and human resources; how to facilitate social interaction and propinquity; how to transport people and goods within and between places; how to fund the creation, renewal, or expansion of places; and how to make places useful, enjoyable, easy to negotiate, and beautiful for those who live, use or visit them.

For "place" one can substitute a street, a block, a square, a residential precinct, a park, a neighborhood, a development district, a "downtown," an entire town, or a metropolitan region. The studio was based on the conception of planning as a physically centered profession, dedicated to the organization and shaping of places for human occupation. Through the work, the semester emphasized an awareness of urban environments as complex physical organisms that in whole and in innumerable parts are subject to analysis, programmatic decision-making, plan formulating, and design interventions.

Students did not ignore the fact that the places we inhabit are products of complicated social, cultural, historical, economic, and political processes. The city, indeed any human settlement, represents the physical embodiment of all those processes. The studio focused on several of the roles that urban planners play in relationship to such processes in the creation of urban place.

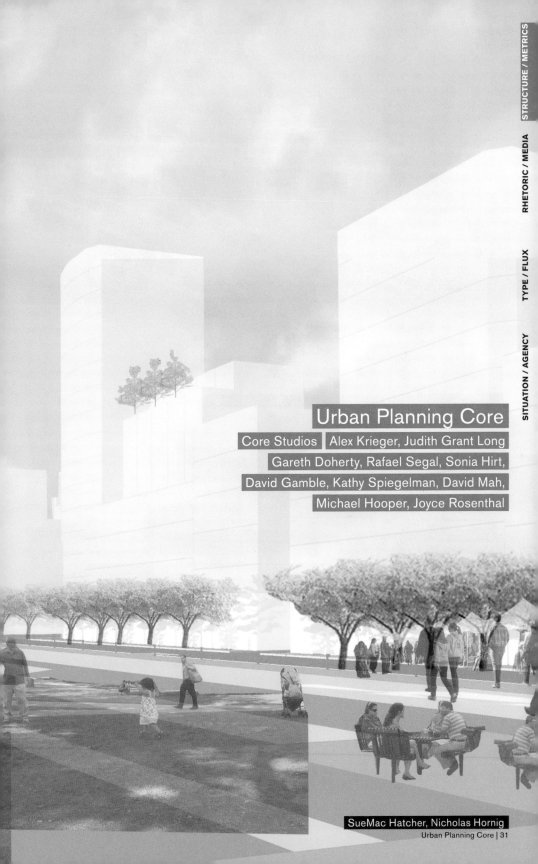

Urban Planning Core

Core Studios | Alex Krieger, Judith Grant Long
Gareth Doherty, Rafael Segal, Sonia Hirt,
David Gamble, Kathy Spiegelman, David Mah,
Michael Hooper, Joyce Rosenthal

SueMac Hatcher, Nicholas Hornig

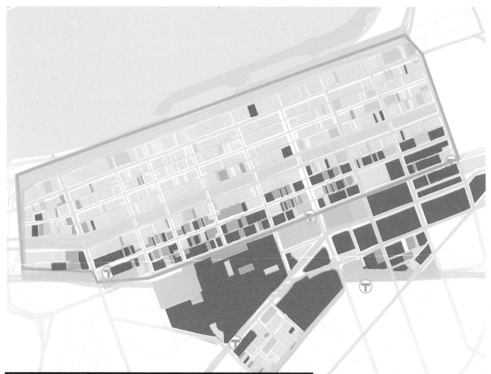

Renee Bissell, Sadatu Dennis, Emily Mytkowicz, Jessica Yurkofsky

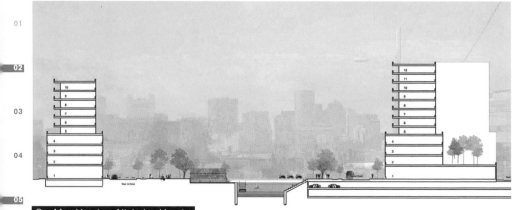

SueMac Hatcher, Nicholas Hornig

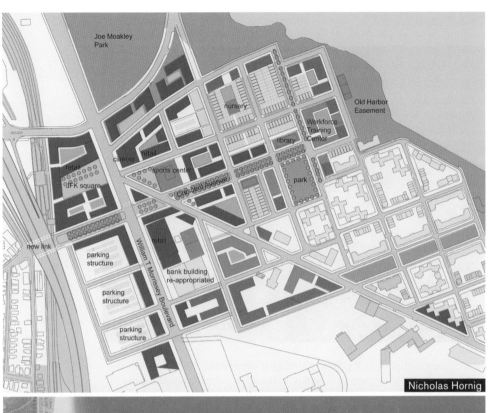

Joe Moakley Park

nursery

Old Harbor Easement

Workforce Training Center

library

retail

cinema

retail

sports center

Crescent Avenue

park

JFK square

new link

William T Morrissey Boulevard

retail

parking structure

bank building re-appropriated

parking structure

parking structure

Nicholas Hornig

Roger Weber

This course focused on the idea that spatial experience can be conceived, understood, and designed as a series of reactive computational events.

Computational architecture has evolved from focusing on form-finding processes and fabrication, to a current exploration of embedding systems and technologies that make architecture configurable, sensate, and active.

This course was open to graduate students of architecture at all levels with the goal of exploring the realms of theory, visualization, design, and production of augmented architecture. The claim of augmentation is not to apply sensor technologies to an inert object as a simple overlay, but to shape the entire design process with the idea of integrated systems as a determining factor. The intelligence of design, material, and sensor technologies and computation will therefore become combined.

The course engaged in a critical discussion on the impact that our daily digital experiences have on the perception and expectation of physical experiences. The students completed the course with an introduction to the application of responsive objects, their prevailing techniques in input and output, and their applications to the human environment.

Augmented Architecture

Seminar | Mariana Ibanez, Allen Sayegh

Elizabeth MacWillie, Daekwon Park, Benjamin W Tew, Corey Wowk

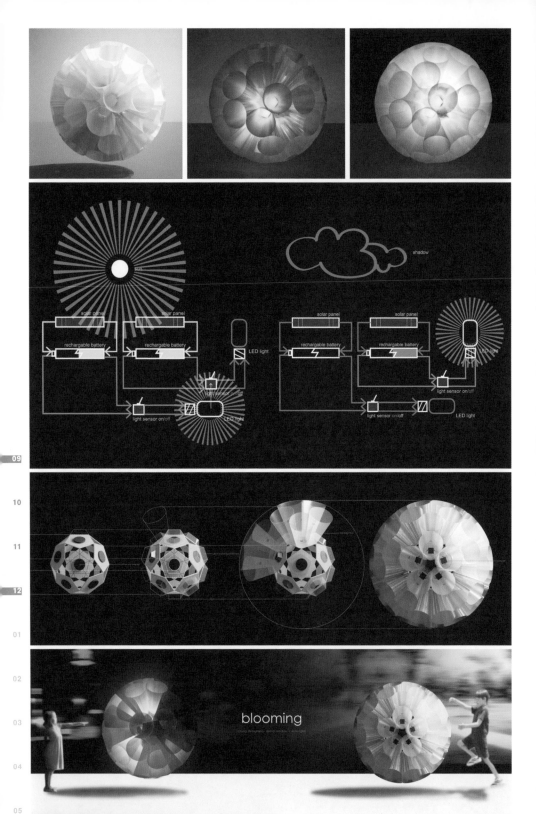

blooming

Hsiangheng Chung, Hsiao Rou Huang, Hungkai Liao

Melissa Chow, Helena Slosar, Yuichiro Takeuchi

This class explored the design and science of logical form making, examined through geometry, parametric control, algorithms, and digital tools. In particular, the field of investigation was the reciprocal relationship of topological experiment and controlled surface geometry. The point of departure was a cumulative sequence of fundamental topics and problems in design geometry that have recurring impact on the history of form. These problems provided a context and pretext for an introduction to parametric modeling, algorithmic automation, and the underpinning mathematical principles.

Ho Kan Wong

These logical and combinatorial investigations of modeling cultivated an objective approach to form that explored the application of parametric approaches that are both deductive (i.e. topological classifications, surface characteristics, and pattern logics) and empirical (i.e. material deformation and generative detailing). Thematically, the course fostered an integrated understanding of topics such as parametric geometry definition, surface geometry qualification, and the converse dynamics of packing and subdivision. The logical constraints of shape, including fundamental laws of material bending, modularity, and topological variation, became categories of analysis and design choice. The class also took a rigorous approach to the constraints of detailing complexity, as students used embedded rules and formulas to integrate design requirements directly into intelligent and adaptive construction details. Assemblies became not only formal propositions but objects of analysis, as the class introduced statistical methods and quantitative heuristics for the evaluation of form. Through case studies, students were introduced to the most contemporary methods of design analysis of geometry, as well as the implications of design decisions on time, budget, and feasibility. The class thus developed an informed understanding of the impact of complexity on the construction supply chain.

Ultimately, the class posited a new synthesis of specific geometric and technical knowledge that is relevant to contemporary designers and enables them to engage modern computation in a mathematically literate way. By deconstructing the mathematical underpinnings of digital tools and contextualizing them in a narrative of historical design problems, the class thus enabled the expansion of the formal range of architecture through objective design knowledge.

Topics in Parametric and Generative Geometry and Modeling

Seminar Andrew Witt

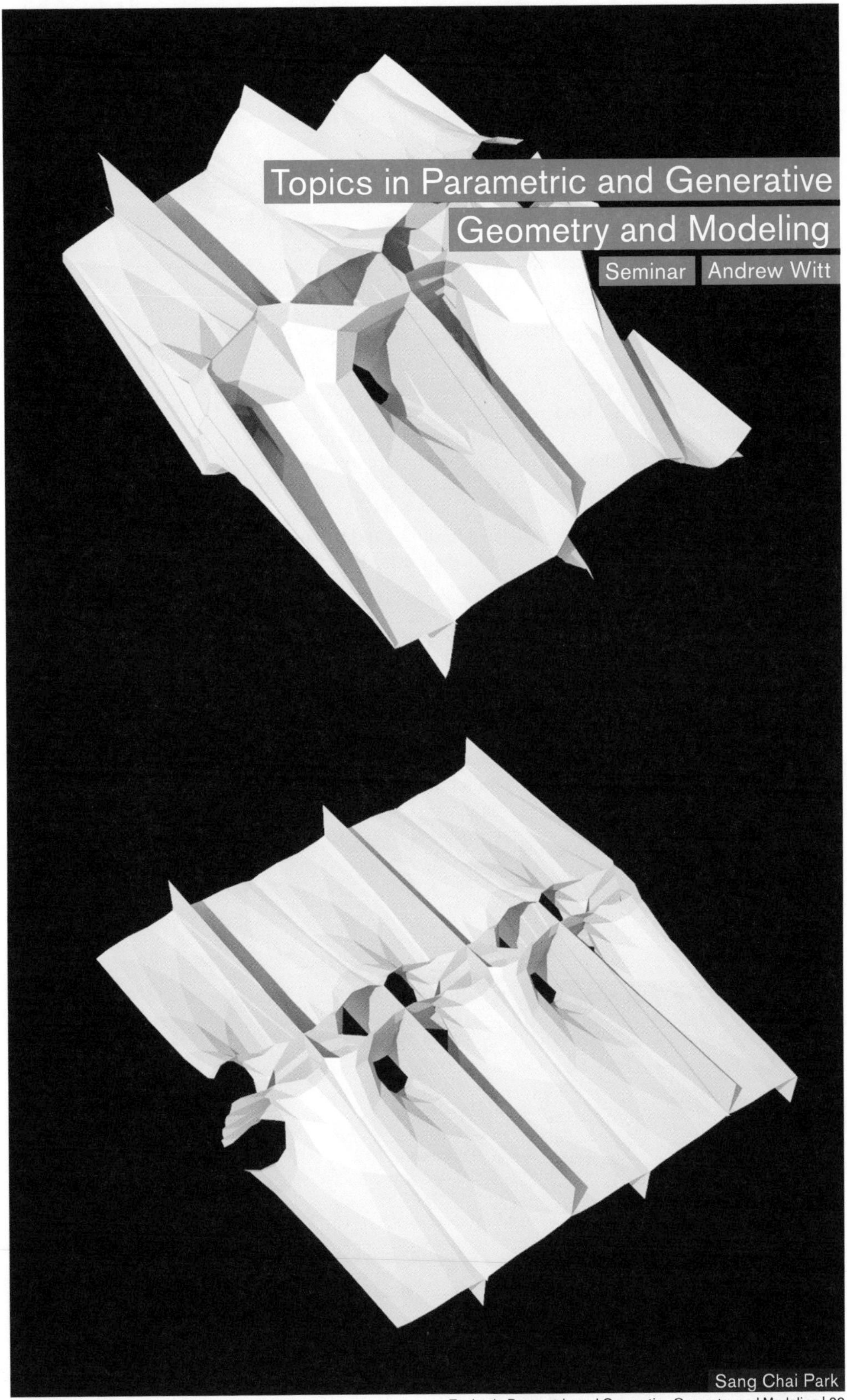

Sang Chai Park

The proliferation of architectural design focused on building form defined by modulated systems suggests the importance of finding evermore sophisticated modes of translation between material and building scales. This studio aimed to construct a hybrid methodology whereby material/structure becomes the synthesizing force that binds surface, space, form, and program.

Early- and mid-twentieth century experiments by architect/engineers such as Frei Otto, Felix Candela, Eduardo Catalano, etc., focused on form-finding to achieve structurally optimized building geometries where structure acts as an imperative that connects building material with form. Arches, vaults, domes, thin shells, tensile membranes, cable nets and the like intricately unite material with surface structure. Today, in contrast to such structurally pure models, computation has opened possibilities for intentionally blurring formal, structural, and material performance.

The studio project was to design the new America's Cup facilities, including the main pavilion, superyacht center, marina, and viewing spaces, sited on the piers of San Francisco's downtown waterfront. The oldest trophy event in international sport, America's Cup racing is driven by state-of-the-art sailing technology and design. The site the city has allocated for this significant architectural project is along the bayside edge of the city near other prominent public venues and infrastructure such as the Bay Bridge, Ferry Terminal, and SF Giants Stadium. As such, the designs considered not only the program of the America's Cup, but also what it means to build a new leisure and event space in this former working port, currently an urban waterfront landscape in transition.

The design research conducted here did not explicitly pursue a tectonic agenda, but rather attempted to achieve a synthetic outcome by negotiating a structural skin system's ability to adapt and transform in relation to material assembly, geometry and form, environment and space, program and site.

09

10

11

12

01

02

05

Material Systems / Structural Geometry: America's Cup, San Francisco

Option Studio | Lisa Iwamoto, Craig Scott

Paul Cattaneo

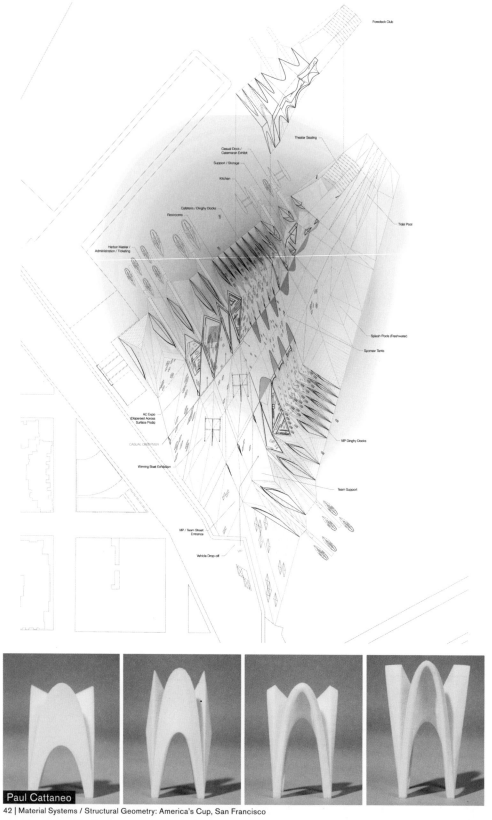

Foredeck Club

Theater Seating

Casual Dock /
Catamaran Exhibit

Support / Storage

Kitchen

Tidal Pool

Cafeteria / Dinghy Docks

Restrooms

Harbor Master /
Administration / Ticketing

Splash Pools (Freshwater)

Sponsor Tents

AC Expo
(Dispersed Across
Surface Pods)

CASUAL OBSERVER

VIP Dinghy Docks

Winning Boat Exhibition

Team Support

VIP / Team Street
Entrance

Vehicle Drop-off

09
10
11
12
01
02
03
04
05

Paul Cattaneo

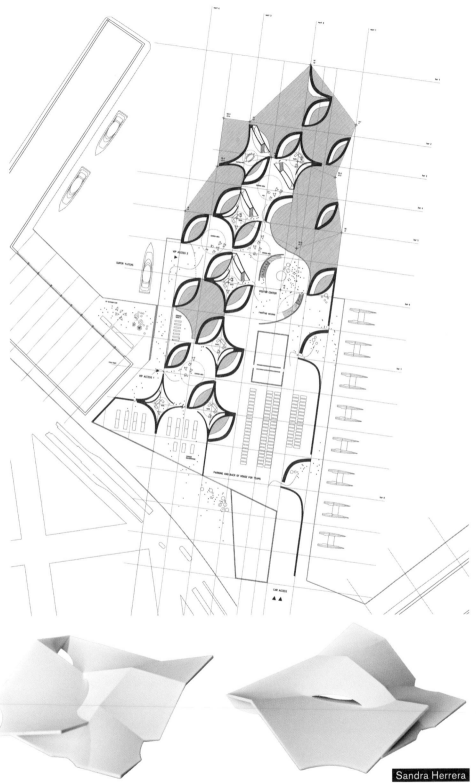

Sandra Herrera

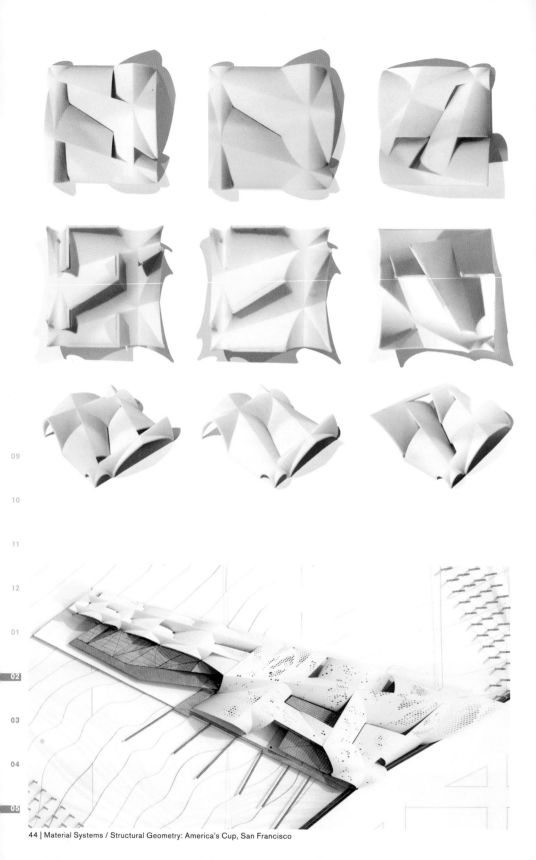

09

10

11

12

01

02

03

04

05

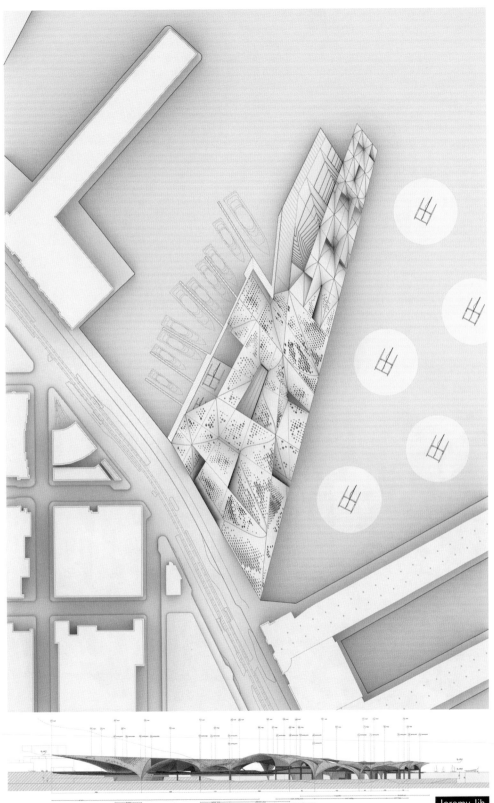

Jeremy Jih

Material Systems / Structural Geometry: America's Cup, San Francisco | 45

At the far end of the spectrum, this studio scavenged a fading trend of global academicism to formulate instrumental ideas in the context of what was, for a few years at least, the hottest academic undertaking: planning high-rise structures for the (now slowing) economies of the twenty-first century. But rather than simply aligning ourselves, even temporarily, with a topical problem, the studio took on frontally the apparent paradox posed by the high-rise type, circa 2000–2010: Why is the architecture of high-rises generally dominated by the structural expressionism of "iconic" tower design (to the extent that skyscrapers have now become in both East and West the ultimate refuge for signature design and the fulfillment of the architectural ego) when, historically, meeting the demands of the ruthless, semi-automatic technical and commercial demands on this brief ensured that high-rise buildings remained all but a sort of vernacular, a province of specialized craftsmen and consultants, an architecture without architects, as it were—much like the huts of rural Switzerland?

Tipped off by Alejandro Zaera Polo's excellent recent analysis of the workings of this artificial design ecology in "High Rise Phylum 2007" (*Harvard Design Magazine*, Spring/Summer 2007), this studio devised high-rise proposals that expressed the potentially "semi-automatic" mode of development advocated in "High Rise Phylum," as well as the particularities of personal desire.

Our site was in Manhattan. Unlike say, Frankfurt or London, where the themes of high-rise living, working, and development routinely undergo cyclical fortunes of infamy and rehabilitation, the Big Island has been quietly investing in the type for a century and is now witnessing the birth of its Nth generation of high-rises. In this it has been closely following the founding principles of the "Delirious" way: these include a fondness for "artificial" and regulated living; an enthusiastic acceptance of high-rise living (which of late includes "vernacular" adaptations linked to local residential practices); and the fundamental tenet that all programmatic fantasies must remain private, and outward expressiveness strictly banned.

Rising Mass 2
Option Studio | George Legendre

Richard Liu, Kazuaki Yoneda

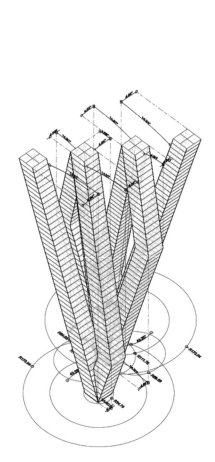
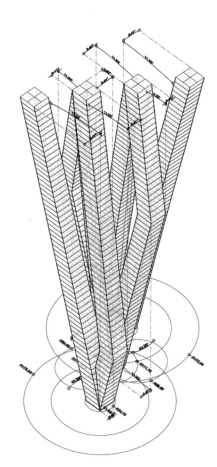

09

10

11

12

01

02

03

04

05

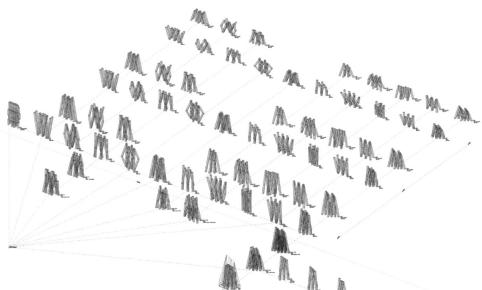

Richard Liu, Kazuaki Yoneda

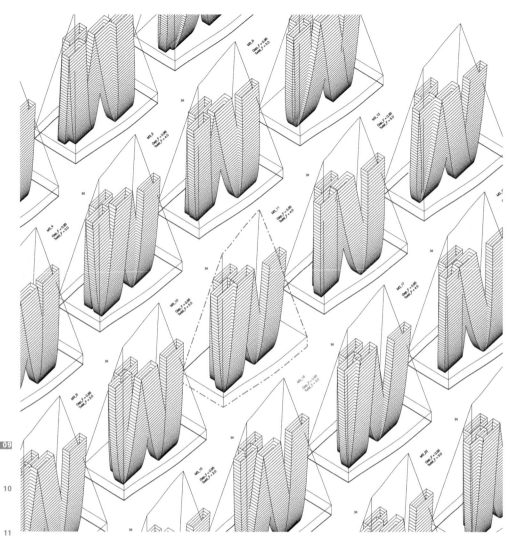

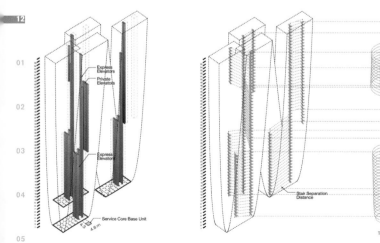

Jian Huang, Carl Koepcke

The Boston Botany Bay studio redefined the concept of the botanical garden for the twenty-first century. The archipelago of islands in the Boston Harbor became the field of experiment and a testing ground for new and stimulating ideas of how to celebrate, utilize, and research the wonders of plants. Nature activation, instead of nature conservation, was the focus of the studio. How can the botanic garden of the twenty-first century contribute towards new economical, environmental, aesthetic, and scientific demand? Can the botanic garden, the metropolis of plants, become a pretext for future urbanization? The aim of this interdisciplinary studio was to generate, test, and document contemporary notions of the botanic garden of the future. The studio focused on three complementary activities; research, strategy, and design. The strategy focused upon a long-term botanic vision for the entire Boston Bay, which was regarded as an integrated coastal zone; a unique morphology based upon a combination of natural phenomena and the interaction of man. As part of the strategy a series of prototypes was developed and tested as representative of the overall approach. These prototype projects operated as "agents provocateur" to initiate change. Finally, for the design stage each student addressed one selected island and produced detailed resolutions representing the botanic garden of the twenty-first century. Both research and strategy were envisaged as group work of the entire class, while the subsequent design of prototypes and separate islands were undertaken as individual assignments.

09

12

01

02

03

04

05

Boston Botany Bay

Option Studio | Bridget Baines, Eelco Hooftman

Fadi Masoud

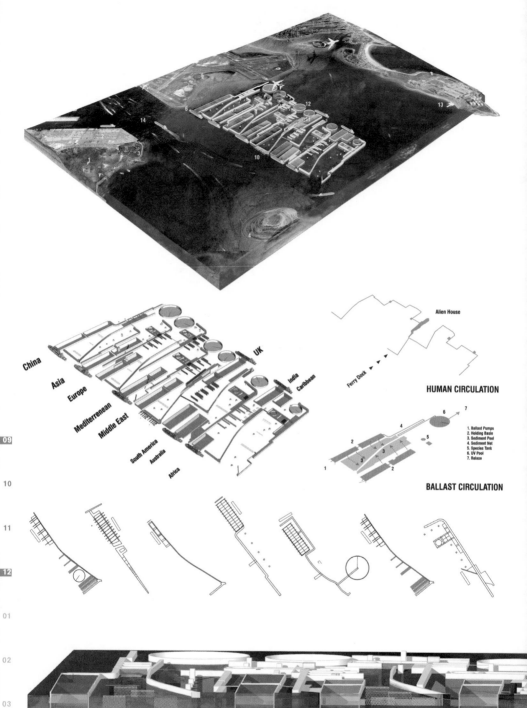

Alien House

HUMAN CIRCULATION

China
Asia
Europe
Mediterranean
Middle East
South America
Australia
Africa
UK
India
Caribbean

Ferry Dock

6
7
4
2
5
3
3
3
2
1
2

1. Ballast Pumps
2. Holding Basin
3. Sediment Pool
4. Sediment Net
5. Species Tank
6. UV Pool
7. Release

BALLAST CIRCULATION

09
10
11
12
01
02
03
04
05

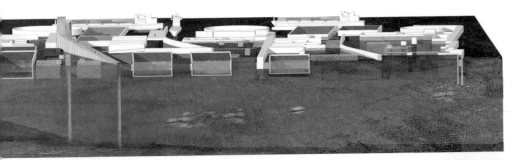

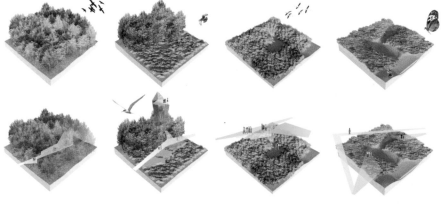

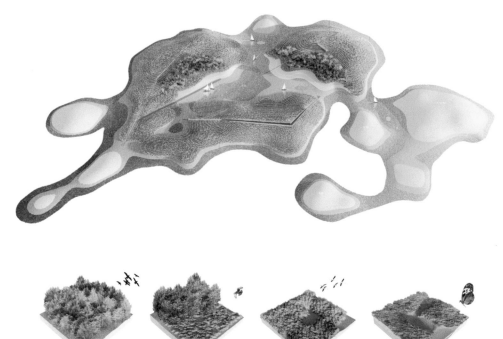

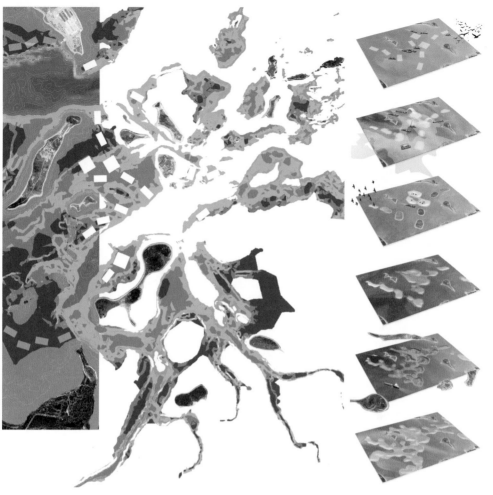

Chon Supawongse
Boston Botany Bay | 57

Overurbanism is the discipline that undertakes the project of radical typological integration in a single post-urban cybernetic universe: a large-scale machine with its own laws that propagates unpredictable organizations through paradoxical coexistence, radical inclusiveness, and mutual intensification. Overurbanism incarnates the ultimate meta-systemic megalomania: a plural organization made of a multitude of systems interacting in a synthetic field of competition and synergy. It is pure urban-territorial exteriority enveloped in a ubiquitous architectural interiority, a tightly self-contained system where the exponential discrepancy between the organizational complexity of the interior and the tightness of the containing envelope engenders an altogether unprecedented potential: the over-urbanity of anti-urban collectives.

Overurbanism is urbanism after the skyscraper: the form of urbanism that results of assembling anti-urbanisms. It replicates and supersedes the idea of the skyscraper as a condition that surpasses urbanity by swallowing its logics and multiplying them. If the skyscraper is a laboratory for new modes of collective life, which explodes the texture of normal life to offer an aggressive alternative reality that discredits all naturalistic urban realities, Overurbanism is the multiplicitous assembly of contemporary types, whose systemic integration engenders a manifold singularity, a monstrous globalized commune. It is an abstract medium that breeds higher forms of architectural value, fueled with the escalating vitality of a collective of collectives: a newborn ecology that withstands as a high, vigorous, and consistent life form.

If the skyscraper is the unconscious and self-evident medium for the thoughtless constitution of theories, architectural theory without representation, Overurbanism is the conscious and self-concealed medium for the courageous constitution of meta-rational models of ubiquity, architectural power beyond ideology. Restricted but plentiful, excessive but austere, stringent but magnanimous, abundant but severe, grand but veiled, ascetic but expansive, voluptuous but disciplined, Overurbanism is unbound of any dependence, any reliance, or even any care for reason, which it uses as a means for the propagation of its canon: brutal indifference. The straightjacket of redeeming urbanism, untied by the skyscraper through sheer congestion and intensive coexistence, is here reconfigured with the blunt force of an artistic invention.

The Overurbanism studio explored this renewed opportunity through the investigation of various forms of extraordinarily large contemporary development and the unfolding of new models of Overurbanism. Students were asked to engage case studies currently at work around the globe, and use them as the basis for the construction of a brief, a site, a context, and a normative, from which proposals developed a generative system aiming at the production of a differential prototypical lineage. The spectrum of architectural solutions, master-planning policies, urban regulations, and landscaping strategies embedded and more or less explicitly operating in these models, were recognized, systematized, exaggerated, and assembled in new developmental prototypes of "Overurbanism," the urbanism of post-systemic collectives.

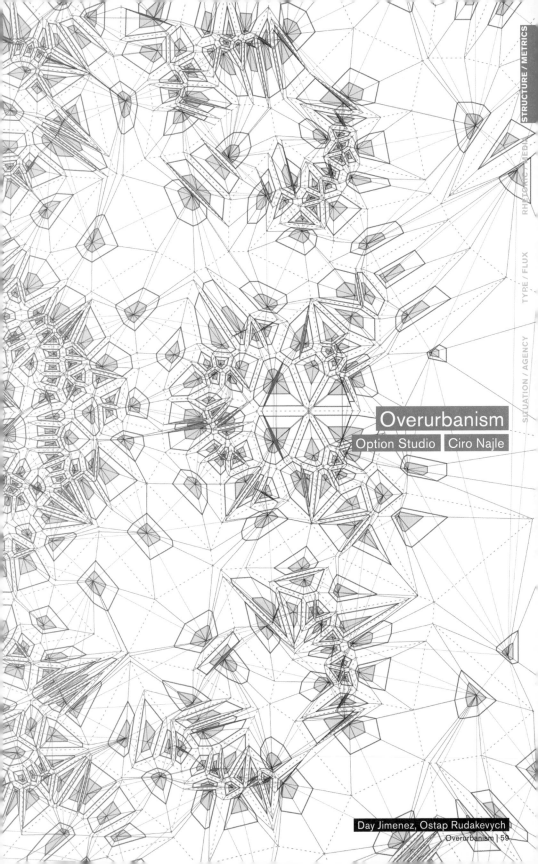

Overurbanism
Option Studio | Ciro Najle

Day Jimenez, Ostap Rudakevych

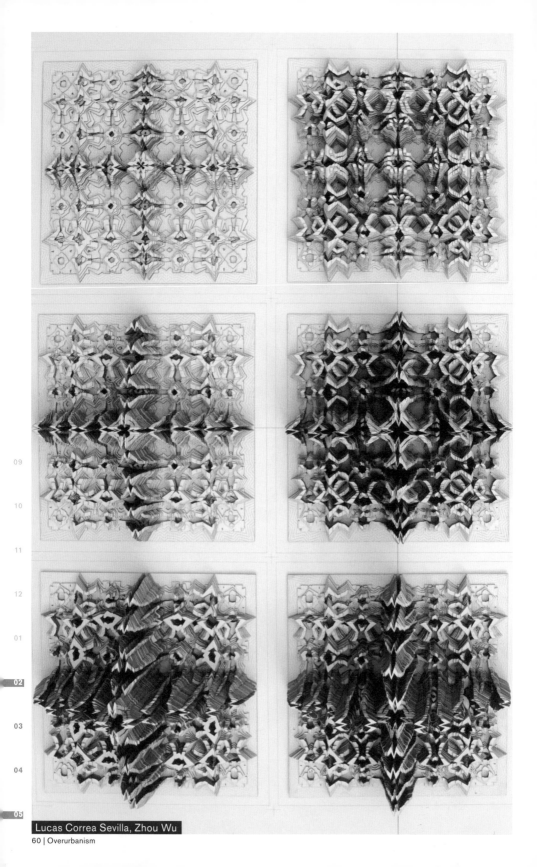

Steven Chen, Mariusz Klemens

Mohsen Mostafavi: Working for Zumthor, you were doing engineering but also architecture, and somehow there was also this kind of fusion with you to some degree, between the architectural issues and engineering issues. How did this experience actually change you as a structural engineer? What did you gain from this experience of working for seven years together with Zumthor?

Jurg Conzett: Well when I finished my studies, I was well-trained in technological knowledge in calculating structures, but during engineering studies in the 1970s it's really your memory talking about designing things. It was just something that was given to you as a problem to solve, and I felt this was a great loss and so I started as a practitioner in Zumthor's office. I remember him but I got to know him with lots of friends where he made a little transformation of an apartment in the old town of Kuhl and he just had founded his own office. We were together one evening and I thought he seemed to be an interesting person and I asked him if I could work with him as a practitioner. [He said], "You are an engineer, I have no need for an engineer." I said, uh, "Let's do not have that." I just calmly talked to him and discussed about money and what's going on. And so this was the start of this seven years working there, and as I said the office was very small and so they had a draftsman and two, four, five, persons and so, you realize everything that happens.

And for me it was like an extension of my education as an engineer. In a way that still today I think the methods of an architect can be that fruitful to an engineer. And mine though too, of course, but an architect's strength is usually in learning some basics about engineering, but on the other hand this still happens in a very small way I think.

And so for me this was an important experience. To learn how one can concede the [bedroom], which as I said is not so different from conceding [starts].

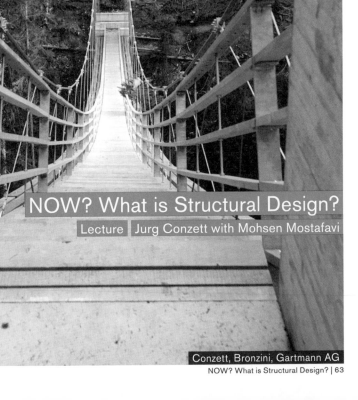

NOW? What is Structural Design?

Lecture | Jurg Conzett with Mohsen Mostafavi

Conzett, Bronzini, Gartmann AG

Shingle architecture in America is an unfinished project, still relevant today. Shingle architecture began as vernacular, was elaborated into what Vincent Scully coalesced into a style, and has been taken up by both modernists and post-modernists as a way of enriching rigorous architectural languages.

Latent in the most typical details of wood shingle architecture are elements absolutely relevant to the way we as architects can, and are often interested in, practicing today. Eyebrow windows become shreds.

Describing Bruce Price's addition to the West End Hotel at Bar Harbor, Mount Desert, Maine (1878–79), Scully uses a series of words invoking smooth deformations: "The building takes on the character of a stick style structure from whose mountainous roof a rich, wild, and naturalistic surface of shingles spills down its walls, splashes on its overhangs, and overruns its porch…awkward and disarming, its qualities arose from the hearty exploitation of its rough materials." Reading Scully's description one imagines a curving, flowing shingle surface. But Price's building doesn't look like that, not literally. Scully writes these terms in describing surfaces that are generally flat, angled, fragmented planes. The visual continuity is in subtle, though compelling, detailing, and while Price's work may be said to evoke Scully's description, it does not fulfill the promise of such fluid surfaces. It's probably best to say that the realm of architectural discourse when Price was working was quite different from the current realm. Contemporary invention expanded with the computer and, in turn, architectural discourse

has integrated the computationally curved, the modulated, and Scully's vision of continuous shingled form can be explored anew. Not that ideas of continuity are tied to contemporary computing, but certainly without computing ideas on continuity would be drastically different.

The rough deformations that can be read into the Shingle Style buildings are tied to a more plastic kind of deformation: a generic technique familiar to us from film. In Hollywood deformation is relatively easy, prosthetics are pliable. But when we as architects want to think about the same thing, we run into trouble right away—because something like a wood shingle pushes back. The materials of architecture have their own rules, their own ways of operating, and this is where we go from musing to method to try to figure out how to operate within the constraints of materiality.

As architects we commit to our own discipline, our own rules and ways of thinking. But architecture exists in a social realm and our work cannot rest on post-modern self-reference or it will remain on the level of meta-architecture. In this sense the gable is useful because the gable is both inside and outside of architecture. That is to say, the gable is an element that architects can treat according to the language of our discipline, but the gable existed before architecture cohered as a discipline, and it has associations that we as architects have difficulty controlling. Bringing the gable to interact with the method language of computer-generated forms is a way of talking about architecture and about the cultural context in which architecture operates.

09
10
11
12
01
02
03
04
05

Latent Methods:
Shingle Architecture in America

MArch Thesis | Eli Allen

Advisor | Cameron Wu

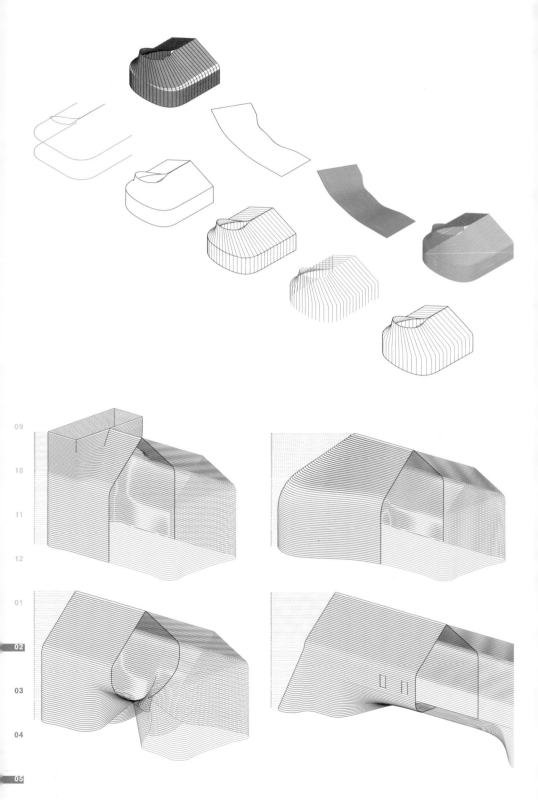

09

10

11

12

01

02

03

04

05

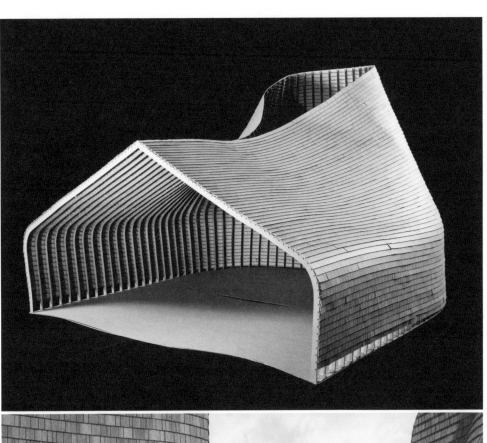

This thesis proposes a Figure | Figure typology that enables two disparate environments to intertwine into one existence and experience. This new duality reconsiders spatial hierarchies established by oppositional dichotomies such as figure-ground, solid-void, object-subject; where one condition inherently always supersedes another. Informed by the program for an aquarium, space here is not conceived as the residual background trace of the relationships between objects, but as an experience in reciprocity with the environment of water and marine life.

In mathematical terms, space does not exist. There are forms and objects, but space does not exist as an entity on its own. In contemporary architecture, the fascination with surface and its meanings, readings, image, and visual affect, have killed the idea of space. Figure | Figure is about inhabiting form as space(s). This reciprocity between water and human space reconsiders the relationship between the body, water, and architecture.

The paradigm of two congruent Figure | Figure continuums that do not mix is explored through the study of Triply Periodic Minimal Surfaces and Parametric Variants. Minimal Surfaces demarcate the two reciprocities and provide the structural and programmatic logic for the project. The transparency of the demarcation enables an immersive experience of water and marine life; multiple materialities, suspended gravity, layered transparencies, flows, views, and temporalities. The mediums of water and space articulate and envelop each other, contributing to the production of a new cultural, educational, and phenomenological experience.

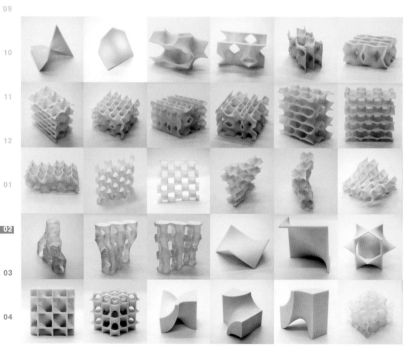

Curating the Aquatic Experience:
The Mediterranean Aquarium and Marine
Research Center in the Albanian Riviera

MArch Thesis   Alda Black

Advisor   Preston Scott Cohen

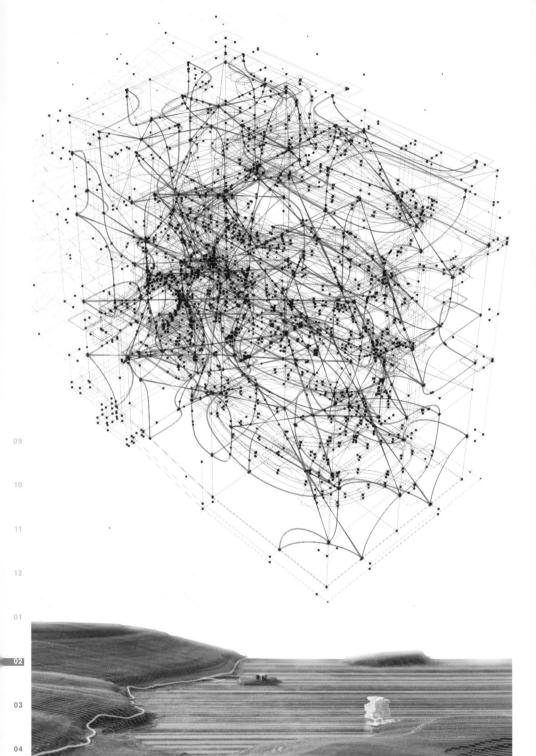

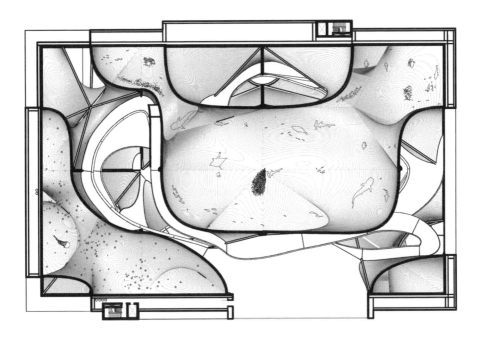

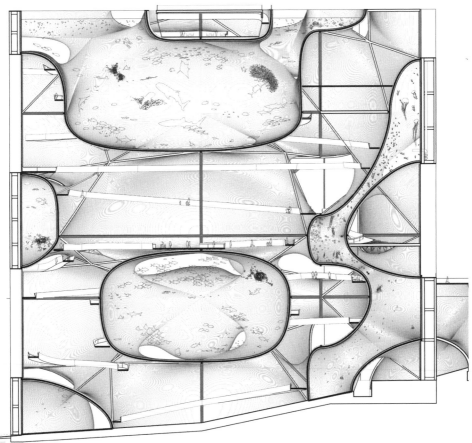

Modernist urban planning was born from two closely related concerns regarding the density and chaos of medieval cities: access to light and ease of movement. Ultimately, however, an obsession with circulation became the primary driver behind Modernist urban form, and improved light access was achieved only as a by-product of the low density and functional zoning enabled by pervasive transportation networks. But what if this had not been so? What if light access had been prioritized over movement? Today, much of the imperative behind these Modernist cities of circulation has been eliminated as digital information networks have supplanted their physical counterparts. The density and heterogeneity of the medieval city are now desired rather than condemned. And so we can imagine other possible Modernist strategies that would have addressed light access directly and used its requirements to organize the city.

This thesis project is one such alternative. It reimagines the city as an inversion of its extant self; rather than a diffuse distribution of building masses separated by a network of streets, this new city is a continuous and dense urban mass from which public access to light has been periodically excavated.

The rules for this kind of lighting are essentially an inversion of those celebrated by Hugh Ferriss in his Zoning Law drawings, but rather than limiting the extrusion of tall buildings, in this alternative version, light vectors define the mass surrounding urban courtyards. In order to ensure that a zone receives light, that zone must be defined within a hypothetical urban mass. Then, a period of time during which the zone will be illuminated must be identified. Annual light parameters control the northern and southern components of the light vectors, while daily light access controls the east-west axis, and the most extreme vectors combine to describe a volume that must be excavated from the urban mass in order to light the courtyard zone.

In order to test and demonstrate the potential of the solar courtyard type, two instances of this inverted urbanity are proposed here. The first is a new city located in a valley at 23 degrees north latitude, and the second is an urban reclamation scheme for the heart of Paris.

The first represents a relatively straightforward development of a system of solar courtyards, while the second takes on the challenge of adapting that system to the contentious surroundings of an existing city.

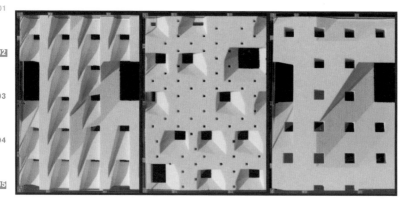

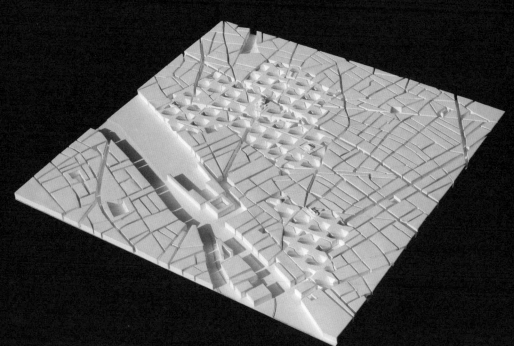

Typological Inversions,
or an Alternative Modernist Urbanism

MArch Thesis | Marcela Delgado, Mark Lewis
Advisor | Ingeborg Rocker

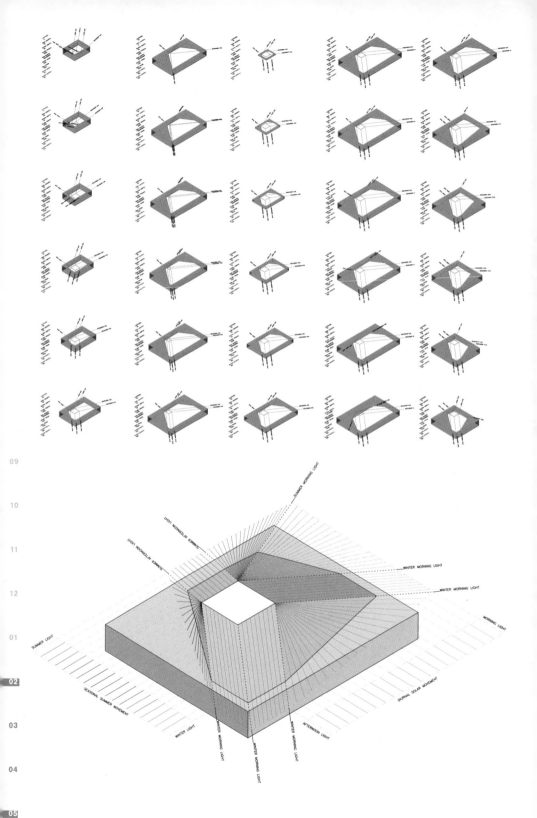

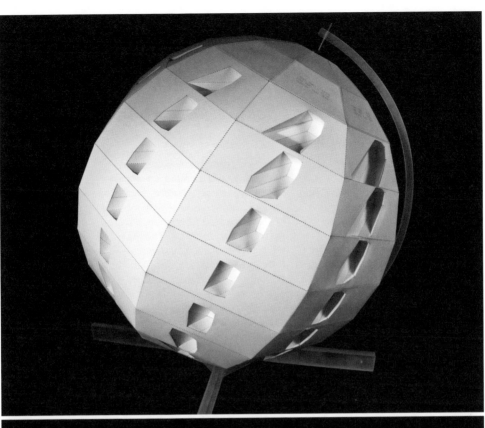

This thesis proposes a conceptual framework for applications of self-organizing logics in generative design systems. The methods introduced in this thesis are in an abstract and conceptual form that explores one possible future direction of computational design strategy. In order to explain the potential of this problem-solving direction, general aspects of what our contemporary practice in architecture and urban design is facing will be discussed in response to the increasing complexity in our culture. However, the main focus of this thesis is not on providing immediate solution methods to resolve any specific professional problems in contemporary architecture. Rather, the thesis investigates the emergent characteristics of this method that can potentially evolve new design solutions over time, and shows how tools employing the method can be used for design collaboration with humans, rather than simply as passive evaluation and analysis tools. The thesis foresees important potential for this new design direction inspired by self-organizing computation (SOC), and speculates regarding its potential areas of application in architecture and urban design.

In recent years, many scientists have started to gain the advantages of self-organizing systems in nature through their computational models in areas such as telecommunication networks and robotics. The main advantages of such systems are robustness, flexibility, adaptability, concurrency, and distributivity.

One of the unique characteristics of SOC is its non-reliance on any external knowledge. As with many conventional computational methods in architecture, imposing existing design patterns or transformation sequences is beneficial when one wants to efficiently derive what appear to be the subjects of our recognitions. However, reliance on a pre-existing template might preclude the possibility of discovering what original inputs naturally turn into.

SOC is a computational approach that brings out the strengths of the dynamic mechanisms of self-organizing systems: structures appear at the global level of a system from interactions among its lower-level components. In order to computationally implement the mechanisms, the system's constituent units (subunits) and the rules that define their interactions (behaviors) need to be described. The system expects emergence of global-scale spatial structures from the locally defined interactions of its own components.

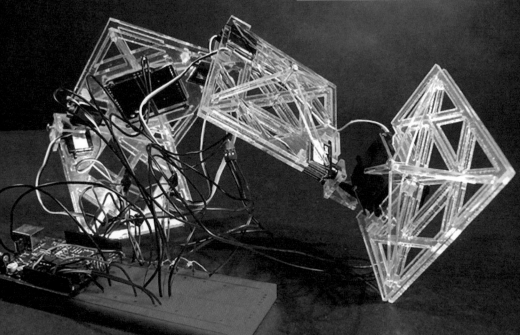

Self-Organizing Computation: A Framework for Generative Approaches in Architectural Design

DDes Thesis   Taro Narahara

Advisors   Martin Bechthold

Kostas Terzidis, Takehiko Nagakura

Renewed interest in the problem of patterning within architecture in the last decade has been facilitated by new methods of digital production. However, given the complexity of and knowledge necessary for computational pattern generation, this shift has been limited to relatively few computer-savvy designers. The introduction of visual scripting tools has helped to expand the user base of pattern generation tools to some extent, but more can be done to make digitally assisted intuitive pattern-making accessible to a larger number of designers, as well as introduce real-world constraints into pattern definitions. This project is seen as a statement towards the integration of systems thinking and creative sketching within architecture, and it suggests an interactive software framework for accomplishing this goal.

Most of the research for this project was accomplished through the creation of an experimental patterning tool as a plugin for Revit. The main goal of the patterning tool was to provide an interface for sketch-like pattern generation within an associative modeling environment. A key challenge for the plugin was the difficulty of combining topological variation, and the inherent problem of temporal destructibility of its elements (vertices, edges, faces), with a resilient stack of geometric pattern modifiers. In other words, it is difficult to make modifications to specific vertices, edges, or faces and ensure that these modifications remain after the pattern changes, because those specific elements may no longer exist. Because explicit references between pattern elements and modifier controls would not have the desired persistent quality, it was necessary to make non-explicit associations. To accomplish this, the topological data-structure was disassociated from the modification structure. Two discrete systems were introduced, one to discretize the pattern into topological elements, and another to modify those elements. The discretization of the pattern uses the half-edge data structure to define its topological elements, and modification of elements is defined by a secondary grid structure in the form of a bitmap image that influences all topological elements based on proximity. The rules for how elements are influenced vary by modifier. The plugin was successful in achieving fast, easy, and interactive generation of topologically variable patterns by novice users; integration of contextual building data into the pattern generation; integration of construction and fabrication constraints into the pattern generation; and a robust patterning tool for Revit, which is currently very restricted in this area.

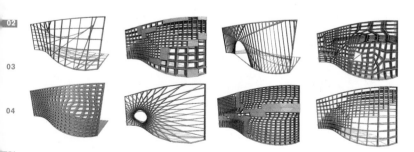

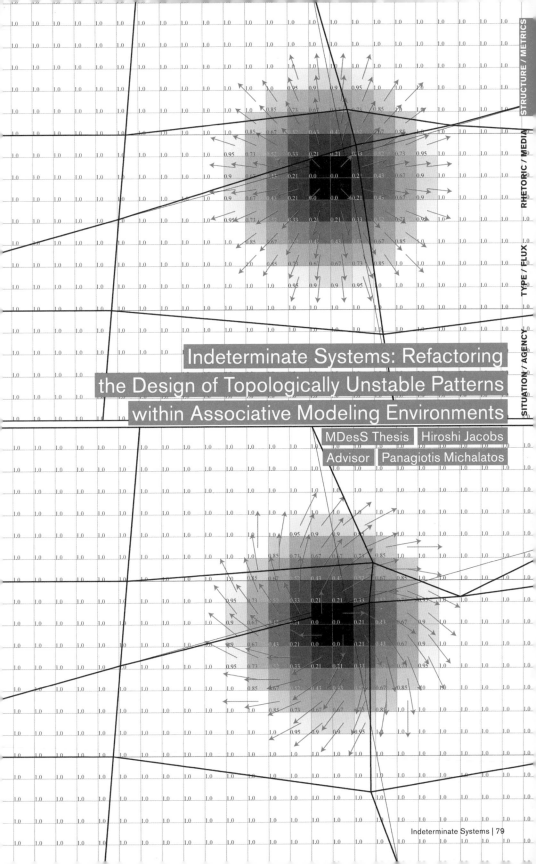

Indeterminate Systems: Refactoring the Design of Topologically Unstable Patterns within Associative Modeling Environments

MDesS Thesis | Hiroshi Jacobs

Advisor | Panagiotis Michalatos

STRUCTURE / METRICS

RHETORIC / MEDIA

TYPE / FLUX

SITUATION / AGENCY

"The creation of new energy landscapes and the abandonment of traditional sites are two sides of the same process, an insatiable drive toward the end of the earth that has seen the extractive frontier constantly redefined."
—Gavin Bridge, *The Hole World: Scales and Spaces of Extraction*

Landscapes of extraction are experiencing a monumental and unsettling shift. What were once vessels of production and fruitful resources are now sites of exhaustion, depleting surrounding ecologies and economies. In the realm of extractive landscapes, coal mining towns and their corresponding abandoned "minescapes" have been some of the hardest hit. A century of industrial processes has forever changed the landscapes of these towns, leaving behind literal holes below ground and heaps above ground, as well as factory structures that embody the hard labor of previous generations.

What is the next chapter for extractive landscapes? To avoid the continuance of these landscapes as sites being transitory, liminal, and forgotten, it is worth considering the plausibility of renewable forms of energy and alternative means of stimulating economies. Layers of geological morphing coincide with layers of coal mining history, and the rising and falling of industrial economies. The future of these landscapes will depend on their success in redefining themselves as providers once again, while minimizing degradation and destruction and providing a variety of site uses for their adjacent communities. The ability for design to transgress regions as well as be implemented at a local scale allows for new ways of affecting the next wave of energetic landscapes.

This thesis project studies the adaptive reuse of a former mine site and its ability to be reused for biomass and geothermal energy types. The proposal involves Huber Breaker, the last standing coal colliery of its kind, which resides on the site and is structurally sound, allowing for its buildings to be repurposed as biomass storage and manufacturing facilities. The proposal for the main Huber Breaker building would be as an industrial heritage center heated by geothermal pumps that are derived from water that fills underground mines. Additionally, the proposal involves an adjacent open pit mine site, which is transitioning between states of remediation. This 75 acre site would have a wetland treatment area for acid mine drainage, several biomass growing zones, phytoremediation growing zones, a biomass waste area, an All-Terrain Vehicle (ATV) park, and a Research and Development Center for researching energy prototypes on site. The intent is for the site to be tested so that facets of the proposal could be implemented at a regional scale, thus allowing for alternative uses to mine sites beyond remediation alone.

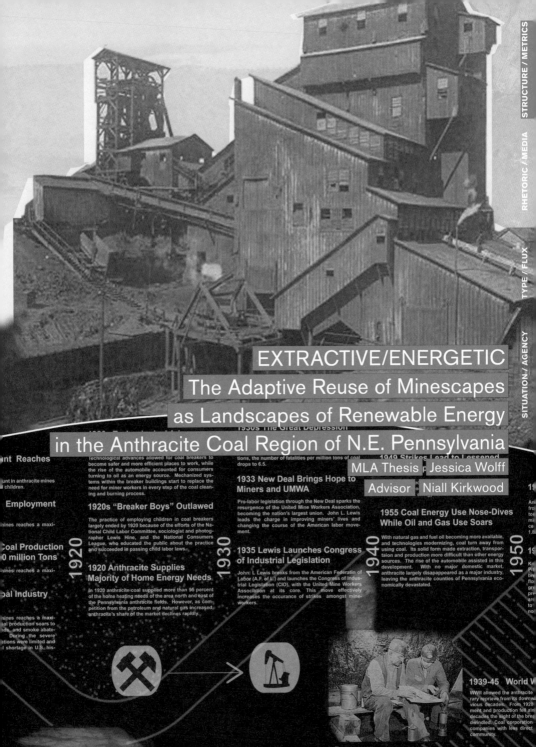

EXTRACTIVE/ENERGETIC
The Adaptive Reuse of Minescapes
as Landscapes of Renewable Energy
in the Anthracite Coal Region of N.E. Pennsylvania

MLA Thesis | **Jessica Wolff**

Advisor | **Niall Kirkwood**

1930s The Great Depression

int Reaches

unt in anthracite mines
children.

Employment

ines reaches a maxi-

**Coal Production
0 million Tons**

ines reaches a maxi-

al Industry

ines reaches a maxi-
al production soars to
ds, and smoke abate-
During the severe
ations were limited and
l shortage in U.S. his-

Technological advances allowed for coal breakers to
become safer and more efficient places to work, while
the rise of the automobile accounted for consumers
turning to oil as an energy source. Mechanized systems within the breaker buildings start to replace the
need for miner workers in every step of the coal clean-
ing and burning process.

1920s "Breaker Boys" Outlawed

The practice of employing children in coal breakers
largely ended by 1920 because of the efforts of the National Child Labor Committee, sociologist and photog-
rapher Lewis Hine, and the National Consumers
League, who educated the public about the practice
and succeeded in passing child labor laws.

1920 Anthracite Supplies
Majority of Home Energy Needs

In 1920 anthracite coal supplied more than 95 percent
of the home heating needs of the area north and east of
the Pennsylvania anthracite fields. However, as competition from the petroleum and natural gas increased,
anthracite's share of the market declines rapidly.

tions, the number of fatalities per million tons of coal
drops to 6.5.

1933 New Deal Brings Hope to
Miners and UMWA

Pro-labor legislation through the New Deal sparks the
resurgence of the United Mine Workers Association,
becoming the nation's largest union. John L. Lewis
leads the charge in improving miners' lives and
changing the course of the American labor movement.

1935 Lewis Launches Congress
of Industrial Legislation

John. L. Lewis breaks from the American Federatin of
Labor (A.F. of L.) and launches the Congress of Industrial Legislation (CIO), with the United Mine Workers
Association at its core. This move effectively
increases the occurance of strikes amongst mine-
workers.

1949 Strikes Lead to Lessened

Ar
fro
to
mi
1.8

1955 Coal Energy Use Nose-Dives
While Oil and Gas Use Soars

With natural gas and fuel oil becoming more available,
and technologies modernizing, coal turn away from
using coal. Its solid form made extraction, transpor-
taion and production more difficult than other energy
sources. The rise of the automobile assisted in this
development. With no major domestic market,
anthracite largely disappeared as a major industry,
leaving the anthracite counties of Pennsylvania economically devastated.

Kin
Pio
bre
floo
ope
pre
ate
no

1920 **1930** **1940** **1950**

1939-45 World W

WWII allowed the anthracite
rary reprieve from its downw
vious decades. From 1920
ment and production fell alm
decades the sight of the bre
dwindled. Coal corporation
companies with less direct
community.

Pre-1930s Employment in
Underground Mines

Until the 1930s mining provided the primary basis of
employment in scores of settlements that had been
built around a deep mine. Yet this changed drastically with the periods of lessened production, such
as when employment dropped from 139, 431 to 121,
243 from 1931-1932.

Patch Town Adjacencies

Anthracite Coal Mining Region of
Northeastern Pennsylvania

Abandoned Mines in Northern Anthracite Coal Fields

Susquehanna River

Regional Underground Mine Network

Acid Mine Drainage Stream

Surface Mining Site

"Patch Town"
Ashley, Pennsylvania
Population: 2,900

Reclaimed Mine Site

Agricultural Land

09

10

11

12

01

02

03

04

05

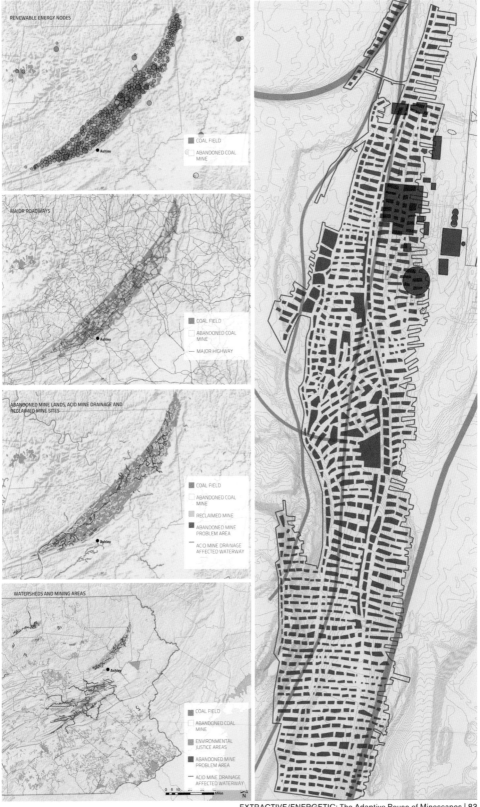

RENEWABLE ENERGY NODES

COAL FIELD
ABANDONED COAL MINE

MAJOR ROADWAYS

COAL FIELD
ABANDONED COAL MINE
MAJOR HIGHWAY

ABANDONED MINE LANDS, ACID MINE DRAINAGE AND RECLAIMED MINE SITES

COAL FIELD
ABANDONED COAL MINE
RECLAIMED MINE
ABANDONED MINE PROBLEM AREA
ACID MINE DRAINAGE AFFECTED WATERWAY

WATERSHEDS AND MINING AREAS

COAL FIELD
ABANDONED COAL MINE
ENVIRONMENTAL JUSTICE AREAS
ABANDONED MINE PROBLEM AREA
ACID MINE DRAINAGE AFFECTED WATERWAY

EXTRACTIVE/ENERGETIC: The Adaptive Reuse of Minescapes | 83

Eduardo Rico: Well, cities go up at an amazingly fast speed, and not only they go up, no, I think it was Dubai that at some point in time was told, we were told that one, every fifth crane in the world was there in Dubai building up houses, which are all empty now. And but somehow like planners and the people that work with the city they are, I mean they are totally hopeless in the attempt to critique in the attempt to control, or in the attempt to actually do something about those rates of urbanization, and actually trying to engage with the processes, and actually the decisions that shape and create our cities.

One of the critiques that we like most to decide is that of David Harvey, which actually explain how the utopianisms that we have been inheriting this, whether it is the real planning, whether it is the more infrastructural sort of modernism or the more engagement of the infrastructures, how just because they were thought as fixed space and form they actually never managed to materialize in, and I would say real or realizable utopias, now that there was somehow this, I mean like planners and architects they have this group of people that actually forgot about process, and just fixed with form while the rest of the professionals that deal with the city were dealing with processes themselves, by whether it's planners, they cannot want as planners, but economists and developers. They think about processes and relations because while the planners didn't do so. What we are trying to see is how this new and emergent field of operations which is linking relational geometry software to these kinds of cities can bring new light about the way in which we operate in cities.

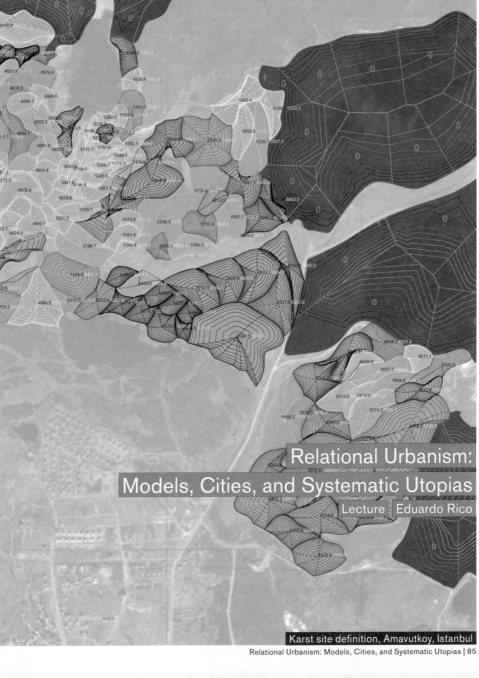

Relational Urbanism:

Models, Cities, and Systematic Utopias

Lecture | Eduardo Rico

Karst site definition, Amavutkoy, Istanbul

Photo: Justin Knight

Photo: Shanshan Qi

Photo: Jacob Belcher

Photo: Stephanie Lin

Students tour Fogg Museum Construction Site
Photo: Aaron Orenstein

Photo: Bradley Crane

Photo: Shanshan Qi

In the age of spam and spin, of unsolicited commercial speech and persuasive political speech, both what and how we communicate are essential to design practices where aspects of RHETORIC and MEDIA are leveraged to exploit the possibilities of new formats and interfaces.

The popular revolutions known as the Arab Spring, at the beginning of 2011 demonstrated the power of **MEDIA** to organize people into a political force capable of toppling established regimes. Despite state attempts at censorship, the spread of demonstrations across the region, facilitated by social media systems, attests to the resiliency of informal communications networks.

Information technologies and **MEDIA** shape every aspect of modern life, from how we work and communicate, to how we define our identities. As such, media has become a legitimate area of design exploration and ambition. As designers, we use new tools to manage information, new techniques to enhance implementation, and new means of material integration to embed information in designed artifacts. Using media as material has expanded the disciplinary tools for designing material space and atmospheric environments. Additionally, the design of representation disseminated through global media gains increasing importance within the domain of Architects, Landscape Architects, and Urban Planners.

As attention shifts to how design as media communicates, the question of **RHETORIC** emerges as a critical issue. Rhetoric is the art of persuasion; the building of an argument. Within the discourses of Architecture, Landscape Architecture, and Urban Planning, rhetorical attitudes are employed to build arguments and establish conceptual context. The design process, like a legal case, is assembled and presented as a highly rhetorical activity.

In the age of spam and spin, of unsolicited commercial speech and persuasive political speech, both what and how we communicate are essential to design practices where aspects of **RHETORIC** and **MEDIA** are leveraged to exploit the possibilities of new formats and interfaces. Gregory Tran's thesis project, *Mediating Mediums: The Digital 3D*, looked at new graphic interfaces as both techniques for, and objects of design. The *Architecture Core II* studio coordinated by Ingeborg Rocker positioned design work within architectural discourse by making explicit design methodologies vis a vis canonical texts. Neil Denari's option studio, *Formagraphics*, investigated the potential of techniques from graphic and industrial design to inform the creation of new urban artifacts.

Rhetoric /
Media

Kaz Yoneda: We were wondering why do you think contemporary Japanese architecture has this tendency to evoke a sense of innocence, naiveté, or childlike playfulness, at least from outsiders' perspective? If so, is there a difference in cultural value system that is contributing to the difference in how we perceive architecture?

Sou Fujimoto: I think for me the kind of innocence or childlike playing things is a kind of a rethinking about the architecture. To really start to think about architecture from the beginning is my attitude. So going back to the beginning and to think about architecture, just depending on the relationship between the human body and space. So that is a very, very fundamental thing and then really starts to construct or really starts to make architecture again. That means for me it's really, really innocent attitude, but at the same time a really fundamental attitude.

KY: So you would say that what Europeans or Westerners might call innocent or childlike from a Japanese point of view would be, let's say fundamental, or going back to some idea of Essentialism?

SF: Yeah, yeah, yeah. So I think we can share—not only for Japanese people, but European people, American people—we can share a kind of fundamental starting point again, especially in this twenty-first century.

KY: Now that the lecture is organized under the theme of New Innocence—I think you partially defined this, but would you critique it or would you embrace that idea of New Innocence?

SF: Yeah. When I heard about the New Innocence from Mohsen, I was really surprised because it's very, very new, unexpected words, but it fits so much for my primitive thinking of architecture. So I think, yeah, I understood what I had been doing is a kind of a New Innocence, we can say. It's giving sentence to New Innocence. I now understand what I am doing more deeply, but, of course, innocence means positive things, I think. It's really, really fitting to my theme of primitive things and I sometimes like to behave as if I don't know anything about architecture and I like to start from this kind of point of view. So, if possible, I like to rethink about every element, every kind of thing about architecture.

KY: So you're not interested in convention? You're questioning convention?

SF: Yeah. But at the same time, we have to think about history too. So I understand history as a nice example of how people understood the relationship between a human body and a space, so that is a nice example and the layers of the history are really important, of course. Sometimes I try to understand the history itself or I really misunderstand the history itself. But that is another attitude of innocence for the history.

Kenzo Nakakoji: Would you characterize that as kind of a form of critical thinking? Do you see it as criticizing to some extent the existing architectural status quo in order to reach that stage?

SF: Yes. I think some of—yes [laughter] part of creating something is containing criticism about something, but not just criticizing, but creating and criticizing and taking some new point of view from existing architecture, existing history.

A New Innocence:
Emerging Trends in Japanese Architecture

Lectures	Sou Fujimoto - "Primitive Future"
	Junya Ishigami - "Recent Work"
SANAA - "Architecture is Environment"	
Toyo Ito - "Contemplating Architecture to Come"	

Junya Ishigami & Associates

Sou Fujimoto

Junya Ishigami

Kazuyo Sejima and Ryue Nishizawa of SANAA

Toyo Ito

A New Innocence: Emerging Trends in Japanese Architecture | 97

What the private house was to architecture in the first half of the twentieth century, the temporary installation is today. Transient constructions, such as pavilions and exhibition designs, arguably represent the premier site for innovation and experimentation in our time.

To UNStudio, these specific temporal typologies are like design models brought to life. They share the characteristics of the visionary, the unknown, and the unexpected with the prototypical disembodied design model, but elaborate a physical materiality. Short-lived forms of architecture provide an excellent opportunity to demonstrate how the design process operates. There is a strong relationship between design and building research carried out in a pavilion and subsequent generations of projects. The pavilion as a prototype is situated somewhere between technological research and artistic production.

The pavilion can also be seen as a next step in the evolution from the diagram to the design model and now to this form of architectural expression. That means that to us the pavilion is intrinsically experimental. It provides an opportunity to "switch off" the utilitarian mindset, and "switch on" the imagination.

A theme that has been explored time and again is that of Mobility in Matter. In various installations the effects of perspective, light, color, space, and material on viewer perception are tested. Within those transitional spaces, optical illusions such as moiré and trompe l'oeil effects are brought to contemporary public places with the aim of engaging the visitor and generating an experience that stands out within a mundane place.

These temporary installations are so significant to architecture because they show up in sites that manifest the most salient questions of our time. The private house in the early twentieth century addressed fundamental changes in the social unit of the family; today's issues, reflected in our new laboratories, pertain to how we live with new media, in the urbanized world, at greater speed, with our leisure time, and with a new sense of both individuality and collectivity.

UNStudio has been experimenting with the typology of the temporary installation for some time, resulting in a series. The serialization itself is an important aspect of this type of work, as this exhibition shows.

MOTION

Ben van Berkel

Motion Matters
Exhibition   UNStudio

Back into the Future: Postscript to Modern Architecture

The second architecture core semester focused on the debates and production of architecture in the past, present, and future. It was a highly speculative approach that allowed students to critically assess and position themselves towards the disciplinary legacy inherited from their predecessors. Students developed two projects—a "modern project" and an "after-modern project"—each with its own set of references and spatial/material logics that correspond with two different temporal contexts. Each project highlighted how discursive, material, sociopolitical, and technological considerations inform architecture.

The first project revisited concepts of the early twentieth century, a period when industrialization significantly impacted the building industry and radically new construction materials became available. This was paralleled by a new social demand on architecture, as millions of workers moved into the cities to reside in proximity to newly erected industries, requiring a new attitude towards architecture and necessitating new amenities in the public realm. Architects tried to respond to the changes they encountered in the urban and social constructions of society by suggesting a modern, often industrially produced architecture.

Students critically positioned themselves towards the works of Loos, van der Rohe, and Le Corbusier, and developed a conceptual model, an architectural hypothesis, that used architecture as a vehicle for debate, as a vehicle to engage in the social-political as much as in material-technological concerns.

Back into the Future: Postscript to "After-Modern" Architecture

The second project revisited concepts of the later twentieth and early twenty-first century, a period when discussions of "Complexity and Contradiction" (Venturi, Wigley and Johnson) and "Complexity and Continuity" (Lynn, Kipnis, Schumacher) unfolded as postscripts to modern architecture. Both approaches were grounded in the discourse of architecture, yet also related to developments external to the discipline: the social political reformation of society in late 1968, paralleled by a radical change from mechanical to digital logics of production. Computation and information exchanges significantly impacted the modes of everyday life. The logics of industrial and architectural production had to be rethought. Newly emerging theories, particularly information theory (Shannon) and Cybernetics (Wiener), became directly associated with computation, suggesting not only new technological possibilities but also new models for comprehending human perception and interaction. Subjects and objects alike seemed to quickly dissolve into feedback circuits, in which signals and signs began to constitute "being," and perception turned into pattern recognition.

If we presume today, in 2011, that computation is in command, what are the effects of post-Taylorism and post-Fordism, and the effects of the computation of everyday life? To what extent do/will new materials, altered production processes, and new sociopolitical challenges call for an alternative architecture and urbanism?

Architecture II

Core Studio | Ingeborg Rocker, Angus Eade
Danielle Etzler, Elizabeth Whittaker, Cameron Wu

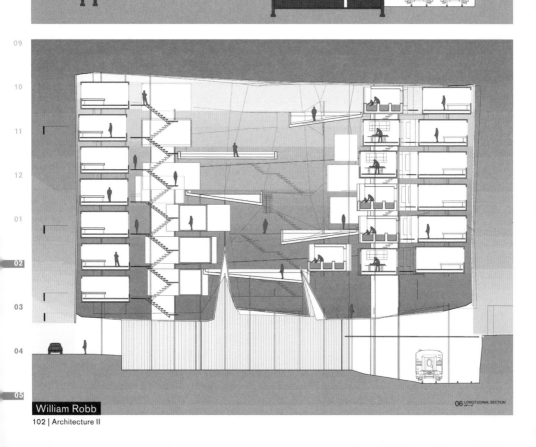

06 LONGITUDINAL SECTION

ELEVATOR/STAIRS

SUN DECK

SWIMMING POOL

SUITES

PRIVATE ROOMS

BAR/CAFÉ

WELLNESS CENTER

SHOWERS ON FACADE

DANCE/EVENT SPACE
OPEN PLAN GYM

FLOWER BATH
OYSTER BAR
HAIRCUT
MASSAGE
OUTDOOR BATH 36°C

BAR/CAFÉ

THEATER

URINALS ON FACADE
LOCKERS

SIGN-IN PORTAL

BANK

STREET

COLD BATH

MASSAGE BATH

STEAM BATH

TRAIN

Lauren Bordes

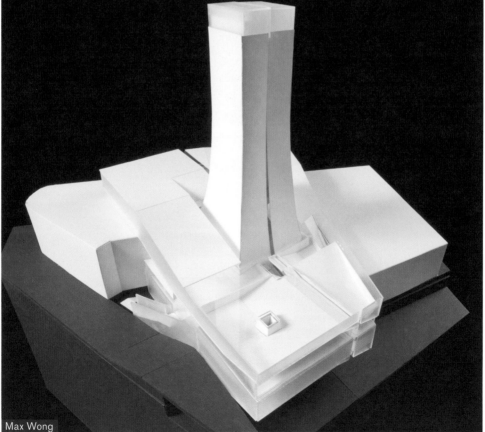

Max Wong

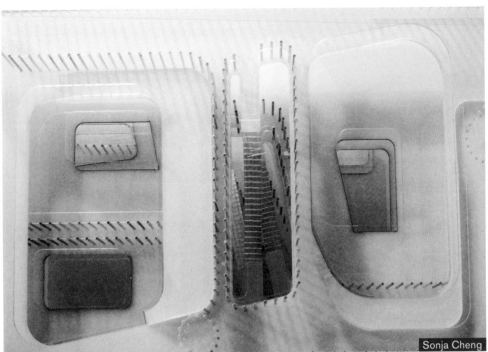

Sonja Cheng

Lulu Li

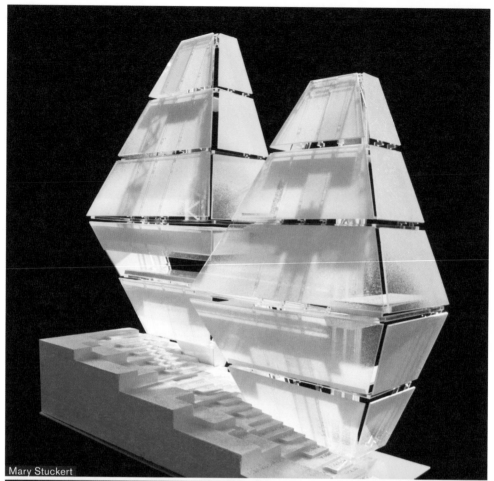

Mary Stuckert

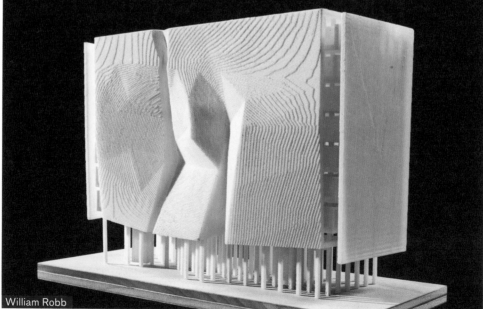

William Robb

09

10

11

12

01

02

03

04

05

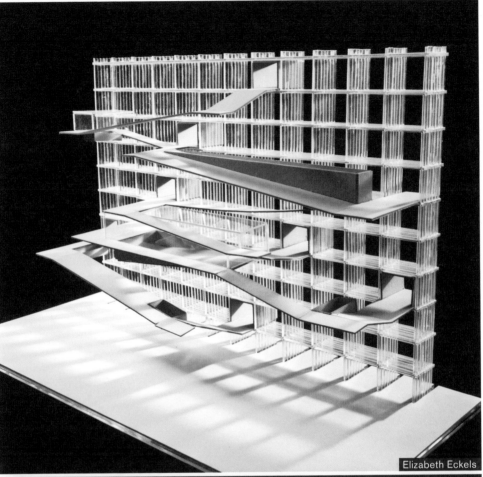

Elizabeth Eckels

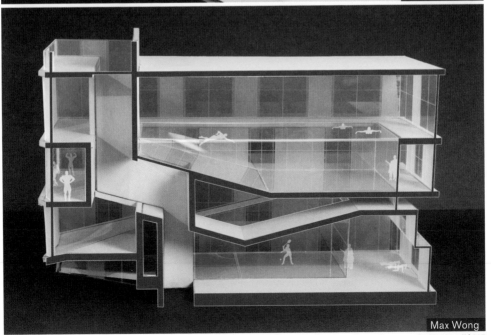

Max Wong

Sara Tavakoli

Lulu Li

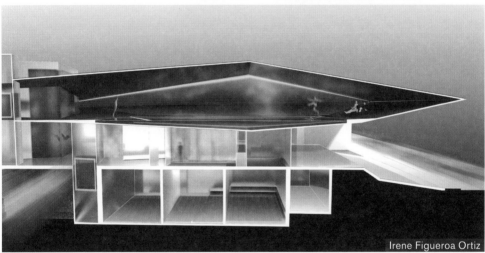

Irene Figueroa Ortiz

Sara Tavakoli

This studio course introduced students to the fundamental elements of landscape architectural design at the scale of the public garden in an urban context. As the first of a four-term sequence of design studios, the course aimed to help students develop spatial literacy, critical design thinking, and skills in the representation of landscape architecture. The studio introduced and explored various issues of perennial concern to landscape design through a typological reading of and intervention in canonical projects from the history of the urban public landscape. Topics included the examination of promenade and path, permeability and pavement, ground cover and texture, spatial enclosure and bound, threshold and limit, topographic complexity and sectional variation, horizontal envelopment and canopy, prospect and refuge, among others.

Using a range of two- and three-dimensional media, both analog and digital, members of the studio worked with orthographic, axonometric, and perspective projection drawings as well as physical modelling. Throughout the semester, students were exposed to and expected to develop an iterative work process, an understanding of the stages of the landscape design process, a critical engagement with contemporary landscape architecture practice, an awareness of the complex ecological and social forces that constitute and affect urban landscapes, the ability to translate ideas into spatial form, visual and verbal presentation skills, and a culture of peer review. The studio examined the imponderable gaps between site, representation, and built work, in the context of landscape design. Emphasis was placed on the status and role of representation and the studio as a performative venue for the production of landscape design.

09
10
11
12
01
02
03
04
05

Landscape Architecture I

Core Studio | Jane Hutton, Charles Waldheim
Andrea Hansen, Paula Meijerink, Michael Van Valkenburgh

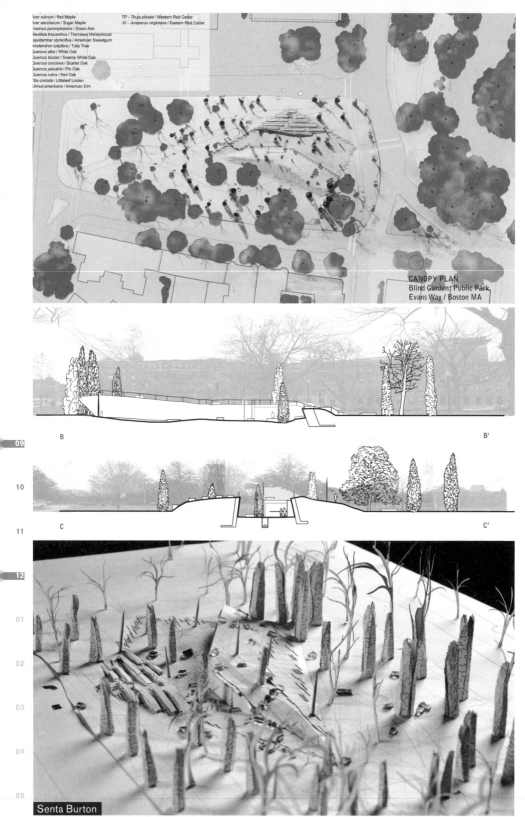

Acer rubrum / Red Maple
Acer saccharum / Sugar Maple
Fraxinus pennsylvanica / Green Ash
Gleditsia triacanthos / Thornless Honeylocust
Liquidambar styraciflua / American Sweetgum
Liriodendron tulipifera / Tulip Tree
Quercus alba / White Oak
Quercus bicolor / Swamp White Oak
Quercus coccinea / Scarlet Oak
Quercus palustris / Pin Oak
Quercus rubra / Red Oak
Tilia cordata / Littleleaf Linden
Ulmus americana / American Elm

TP - Thuja plicata / Western Red Cedar
JV - Juniperus virginiana / Eastern Red Cedar

CANOPY PLAN
Blind Garden; Public Park
Evans Way / Boston MA

B   B'

C   C'

E

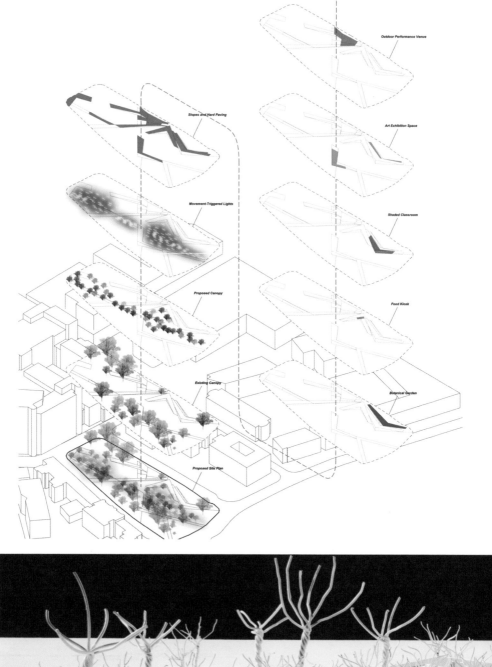

Outdoor Performance Venue

Slopes and Hard Paving

Art Exhibition Space

Movement-Triggered Lights

Shaded Classroom

Proposed Canopy

Food Kiosk

Existing Canopy

Botanical Garden

Proposed Site Plan

09

10

11

12

01

02

03

04

05

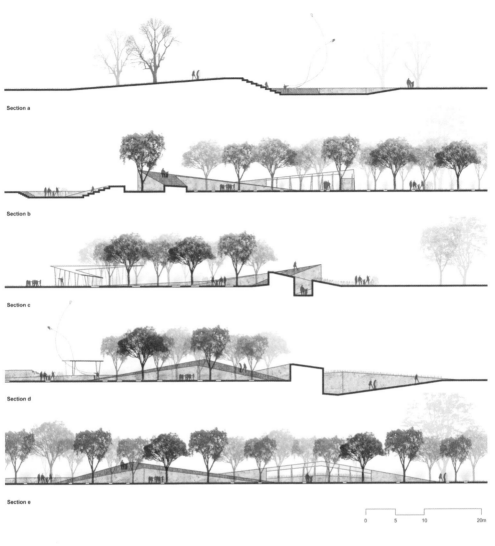

Section a

Section b

Section c

Section d

Section e

0   5   10   20m

Yizhou Xu

Preston Scott Cohen: I have a problem here. For one thing, this could not possibly just be the result of the convergence of forces and multiple wills. It's not an inevitability in any way. This is a diagram, by the way, which corresponds to a character, a Chinese character. It means "people." Now, you discovered this. And you embraced it. But the reason you embraced it is a very important thing that I wanted you to also talk about. But is this the survival of the fittest? Maybe it's the survival of the fittest in your office. But is that the survival of the fittest—does it stand, is it on a par with the goo, with the gray goo of Denmark? How do you characterize it that way?

Bjarke Ingels: I think it's important to understand also the mechanism of Darwinian evolution because the whole analogy of evolution, which I think is a very accurate description of almost all creative processes, is not that it dumbs everything down to the strictly utilitarian because a major element in natural selection is, of course, you have the predator-prey arms race. Big predator teeth sort of favors thick skin. The turtle is too slow to run away, so it has to have a thick skin so you can't eat it. But then another very important aspect is sexual selection, or more specifically a female mating preference. The peacock is the ultimate example. There's nothing more inefficient than dragging this giant tail around, but the girls like it.

PSC: So that's how you see this. But wait a minute. The fittest that survives, by the way, is you. See, this is what I find odd here. On the one hand, you impart this survival to architecture. On the other hand, this seems more to me like it's about the survival of the architect, not the architecture. This project made its way into the world because it found its connection to this business, this developer's reading to this sign. Now, you had to take it out of Sweden, where no one would take it because it didn't mean anything and because it was too impositional and overwhelming in a certain way, not gray enough or gooey enough. And you bring it to

Photo Credit: Iwan Baan

Discussions in Architecture:
Bjarke Ingels with Preston Scott Cohen

Lecture | Bjarke Ingels with Preston Scott Cohen

China, where power is so centralized that the author, the single architect, is affirmed in the old heroic model. This is the old model of the architect, China. Building like this, I know it. Listen, what do you think I'm doing there? You're there, too, for the same reason. You can't pretend that you aren't engaging in the production of heroic and gigantic sculptural shapes that are—and that by virtue of the shape that it happened to have, it made you the survival of the fittest. Some other architect didn't get to build it. I mean, come on.

BI: But actually, I think it's again because you're trying to fit it in to the old dichotomy between doing something that's like expressive or experimental or whatever and trying to make everybody happy. Somehow you see it like either you're a sell-out that's like a service-oriented architect, or you're like some kind of crazy radical that says—

PSC: Okay, but this is something else. This has to do with the survival of the fittest, surviving because he gave a shape to somebody that they liked.

BI: One of the other main aspects of evolution is migration, essentially that something that has evolved in one context, like the fish, it evolves some big flippers at some point. And at some point it goes on land, and suddenly the flippers work as legs. And in this case, the image at the bottom is actually the image when we did the project for the waterfront of Umeå in the north of Sweden, where it was really responding to the context of allowing the street to pass down to the water, opening up the promenade to pass between the lakes, placing the hotel right where it was supposed to be and then merging with the conference center and the pool. But it looked too [wack] in a Swedish context. And I think when we finally discovered this potential meeting, it felt much more at home even though it evolved in Sweden. When migrating to China it was—

PSC: You did say you were troubled by the literalness of it being a letter, a character. But then you embraced it because you realized that it would bring about the realization of the project. It became circumstantial, in a way, political. That is, when it enabled you to build, it became part of what you call the process of the production of architecture that has a kind of inevitability built into it. In other words, this moment of opportunism is explained as circumstantial to the project. And therefore, it's acceptable that it enters into this kind of trivial symbolism. And you don't mind it anymore. You embrace it. It's just part of that whole process. Is that right? Are you reluctant about the shape?

BI: I think it's too simple to reject symbols.

PSC: I'm not rejecting. I'm just asking you.

BI: But I think that meaning and symbols, sometimes, are powerful elements that need to be reckoned with. I must say, when we discovered that the people—the whole idea of the People's Building that would create this vast public square in the shade of this gateway. It somehow seemed to have found its true potential, which was somehow—it was always an awkward alien in Sweden, even though it grew from that context.

Image Copyright: BIG

Landscape as Digital Media was a seminar aimed at fostering both conceptual and technical approaches to the introduction of digital design and fabrication techniques in landscape design and construction processes. Students dedicated the semester to develop a project that took advantage of a number of emerging and established digital techniques and processes in order to develop prototypes for new landscape systems that reshape and reorganize surface and topographical ground conditions.

This focused project was the means through which a wide range of skills and approaches towards the utilization of digital design and fabrication techniques were introduced and developed to inform and enrich the process from design conception to the development of various application scenarios, and finally prototype fabrication of landscape construction and material systems. Students followed a process from initial concept design to physical fabrication of scaled prototypes and models. The course developed digital design skills in 3D modeling, parametric tools, and digital fabrication.

Existing precedents of construction and material systems were studied and considered during the course in order to inform and inspire the development of the projects. Novel expression as well as performance (topographical, hydrological, modalities of mixing hard and soft landscapes, etc.) was encouraged.

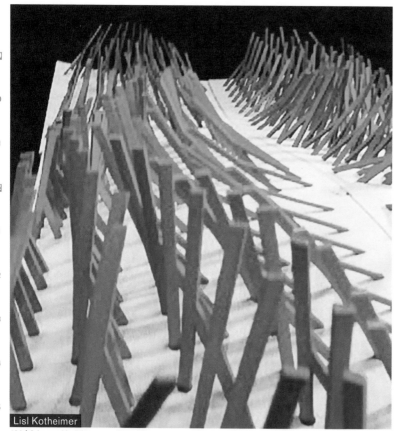

Lisl Kotheimer

120 | Advanced Landscape as Digital Media: Fabricating Grounds

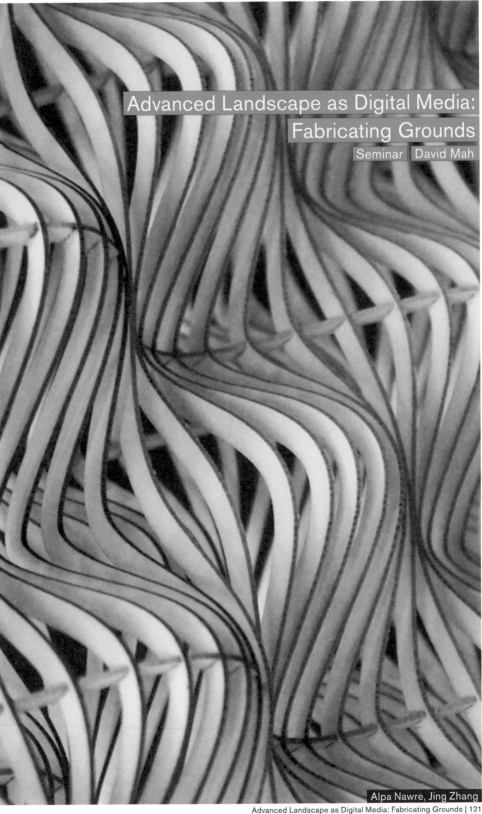

Advanced Landscape as Digital Media:
Fabricating Grounds

Seminar | David Mah

Alpa Nawre, Jing Zhang

This elective seminar studied the work of artist Joshua Mosley, in particular his methods of representing landscape through sequential photographic animation. In conjunction with four workshops delivered by Mosley, weekly lectures and technical exercises advanced a workflow of sequential drawing and photography to computer graphics (Maya) to editing and compositing (After Effects). Assignments responded to topics in landscape architecture, explored through the lens of animation, cinematography, and change over time.

The ambition of the course was to incorporate these digital techniques into the design process and work towards developing a more expressive model of representation for the interstitial stages of landscape design. Work produced in the seminar in counterpoint to screenings of animation in film and contemporary art formulated a basis for assessing design methods that unfold in time.

Vera Shur

Landscape as Animation

Seminar   Joshua Mosley
Darina Zlateva

Andrew Zientek

This studio looked at London, a city where design ingenuity has been nurtured by the unpromising parameters of layered historic regulation, international trade, and extraordinarily high land values.

London was a starting point for testing the more general proposition that design intelligence and wit should be better utilized to accommodate ideas of need and raise ambitions to the point where commerce values delight.

A visit to London engaged the studio in conversations with the actual producers (commissioners) and directors (designers) currently remaking large urban tracts, and encouraged students to consider how their visions are informed by different understandings of the city's past, present, and future potentials.

The site was Shoreditch, a dynamic district located on the edge of the financial City of London yet creatively engaged with the entrepreneurial City of Westminster, where the twenty-first century opportunity is not to clear away, but to recycle, renew, and overlay.

Here the studio researched the "city sandwich," a project of the immediate future that responds to the programmatic, financial, and civic need for a new urban architecture, one that reorganizes the essential requirements for working, living, and playing and consequently rethinks the structure of the urban theatre.

The proposition was that a better understanding of the tension between site, opportunity, and market helps describe critical design processes that rethink and reinvent architectural models and types. The challenge was to think and act as both producer and director. The project was the exploration of what these reconstructed models and types might be.

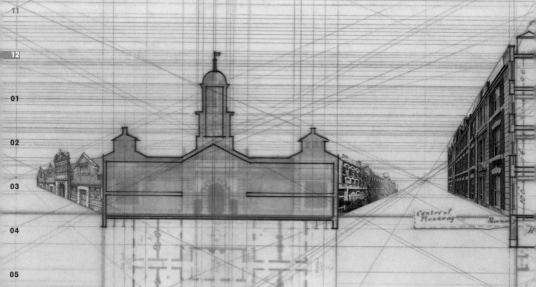

London: A Particular Proposition

Option Studio | Simon Allford

Hallie Chen, Jessica Knobloch

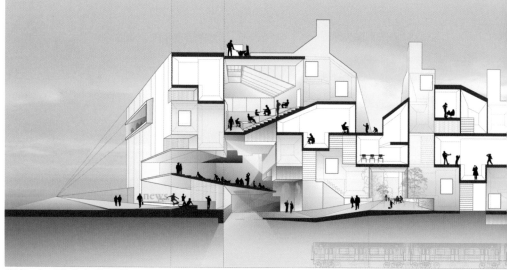

Hallie Chen, Jessica Knobloch

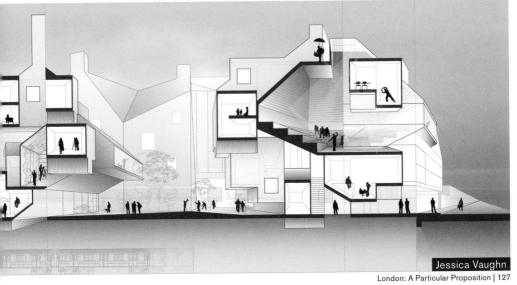

Jessica Vaughn

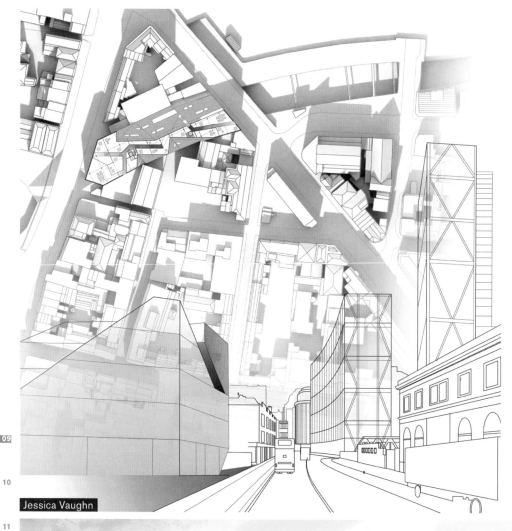

09
10

Jessica Vaughn

11
12
01
02
03
04
05

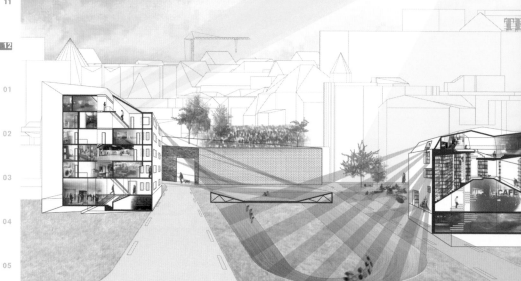

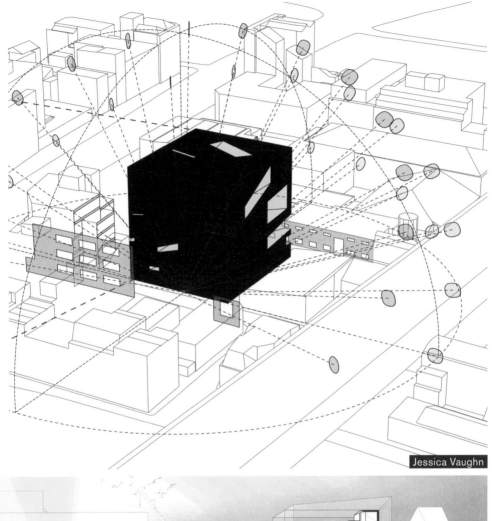

Jessica Vaughn

Natalya Egon

One thing architecture has always seemed to resist is the concept of immediacy, of consumption. In the world of advertising and graphic design, legibility is perhaps one of the most axiomatic conditions of successful design. On the other hand, when buildings appear to be (too) diagrammatic or too simple, they seem boring or undeveloped, unable to hold our imaginations. But unlike typography, architectural language is not a written language, and therefore it does not bear the burden to be read in any literal way. More like a logo, buildings take on signform qualities regardless of how abstract they may be, as ALL objects, according to Roland Barthes, cannot escape signification of one form or another. In this, architecture is deeply related to the larger systems of objects in our world and by extension, it is related to the compressed surface of graphic figures and objects. Here architecture is thought of as being connected to a kind of immediacy or a sense of recognition that might typically be accorded the spectacle or one-of-a-kind building.

Despite this logic, a more cynical view has cropped up recently about architecture's apparent ambition toward the spectacular. Somehow blamed on exotic form, excessive scale, or material extravagance, this anti-design view presumes that architecture is now ordered up to perform like dancing elephants, large objects hoping to defy gravity in an effort to entertain.

It could be argued that architecture has given up nothing and has in fact added a sense of immediacy rather than spectacle to its performance criteria, a sense that architecture could be absorbed (understood) in the context of other media without losing its inherent complexity. In this studio, the ambition was to find the ultimate merger between the cultural performance of the graphic, spatial, and technical performance of form: Formagraphics.

For 2010, the Formagraphics studio focused on the excavation and projection of architecture out of 2D material. The work launched from conditions that architecture shares with many other media, in particular that of graphic design with its dependence on color, flatness, profile, pattern, contrast, and field composition. The program called for a 1,600 square meter building located in Shibuya, Tokyo. The Sori Yanagi Center for Design consists of permanent and flexible exhibition rooms, offices, café, store, and educational support spaces.

Formagraphics

Option Studio | Neil Denari

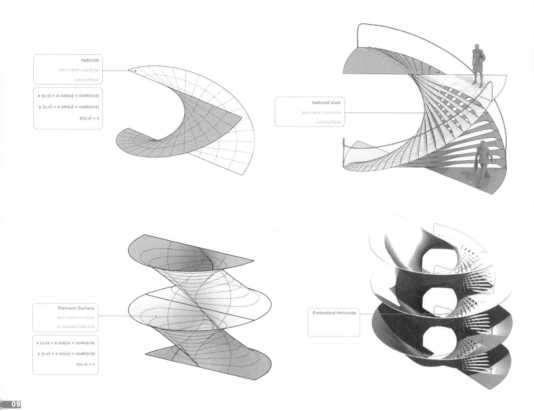

helicoid
zero mean curvature
ruled surface

$x(u,v) = a \cos(u) = \cosh(v/a)$
$y(u,v) = a \sin(u) = \cosh(v/a)$
$z(u,v) = v$

helicoid stair
zero mean curvature
ruled surface

Riemann Surface
zero mean curvature
embedded helicoids

$x(u,v) = a \cos(u) = \cosh(v/a)$
$y(u,v) = a \sin(u) = \cosh(v/a)$
$z(u,v) = v$

Embedded Helicoids

09

10

11

12

01

02

03

04

05

Jonathan Scelsa

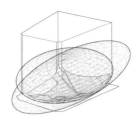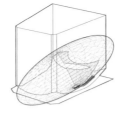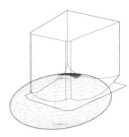

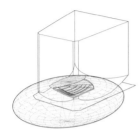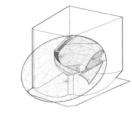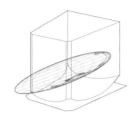

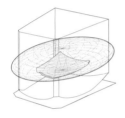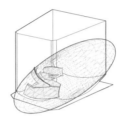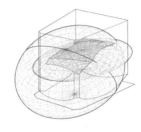

James Leng

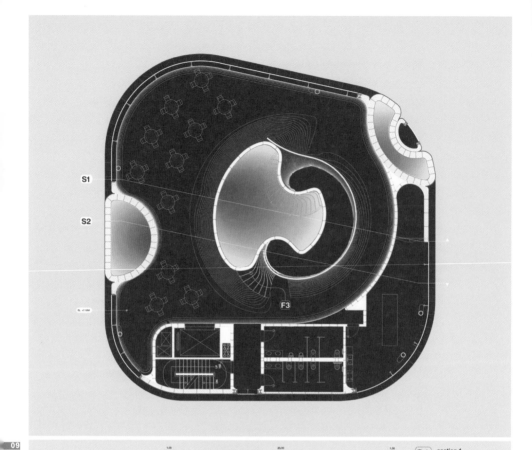

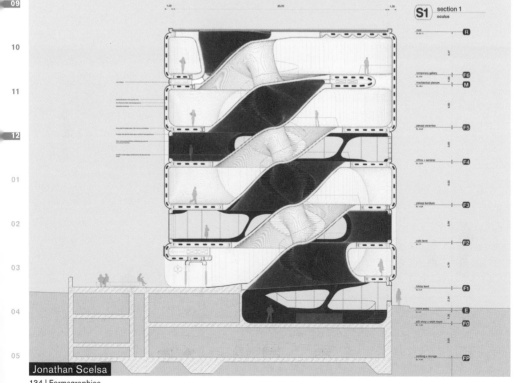

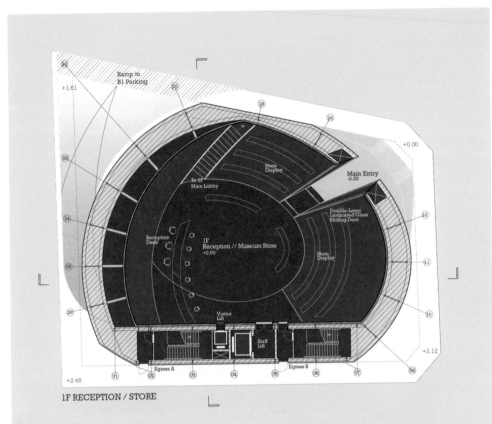

+1.61

Ramp to
B1 Parking

+0.00

Store
Display

Main Entry
-0.60

To 2f
Main Lobby

Double-Layer
Laminated Glass
Sliding Door

Reception
Desk

1F
Reception // Museum Store
+0.00

Store
Display

Visitor
Lift

Staff Lift

+2.12

+2.46

Egress A

Egress B

+2.12

1F RECEPTION / STORE

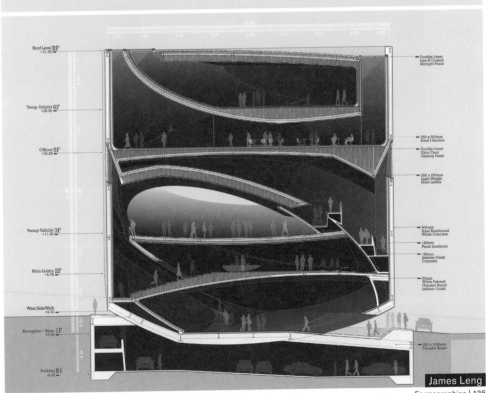

Roof Level RF
+31.50

Double-Layer
Low-E Coated
Skylight Panel

Temp. Exhibit 6F
+25.00

250 x 900mm
Steel I-Section

Offices 5F
+20.25

Double-Layer
Ultra Clear
Glazing Panel

250 x 250mm
Light Weight
Steel Lattice

Yanagi Exhibit 3F
+11.35

800mm
Steel Reinforced
White Concrete

160mm
Panel Insulation

150mm
Interior Finish
Concrete

Main Lobby 2F
+6.75

50mm
White Painted
Gypsum Board
Interior Finish

West SideWalk
+2.50

Reception / Store 1F
+0.00

250 x 1000mm
Transfer Beam

Parking B1
-4.50

James Leng

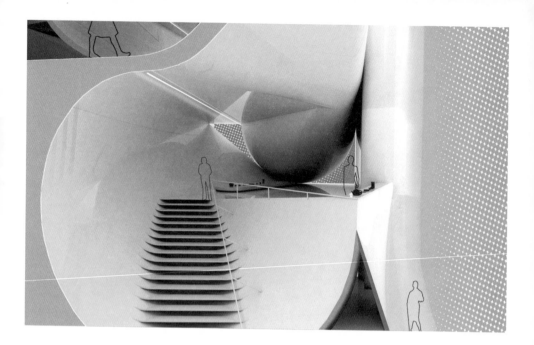

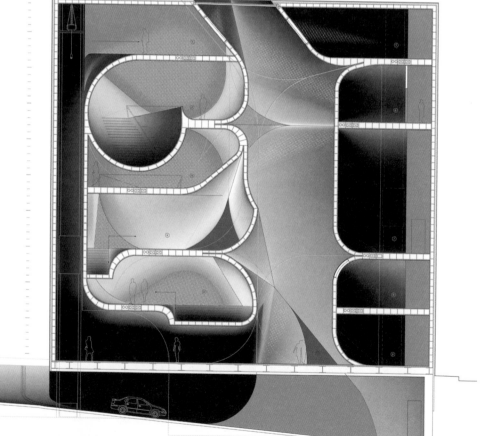

Carl D'Apolito-Dworkin

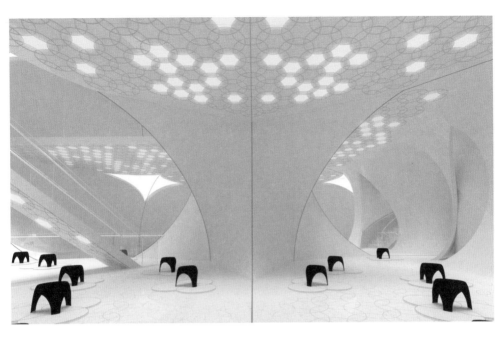

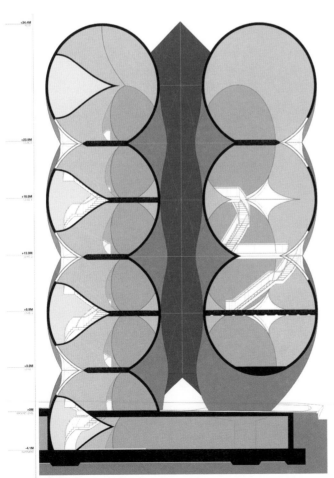

Allison Austin
Formagraphics | 137

The city of Madrid is undergoing today one of its most important urban and infrastructural challenges; the burying of the M-30 ring highway has recovered the river Manzanares for the city and has created a linear park 7 kilometers long, connecting the historic center, where the Royal Palace, the Cathedral and the Opera House are located, with the west developments of the city integrating urban, landscape, and infrastructural environments. The park is now under construction and needs to be complemented with facilities located at specific sites that will activate the area in different ways. Students worked in this energizing context developing an Institute for Innovation in Infrastructure at the riverbank. Concrete was the base material to build with. Students developed an understanding of its essence to manipulate it freely, from its liquid informal condition to its formalization into final prefabricated products. Clear structural systems were designed working with these two opposite natures: from dense structures to stressed structures.

Students developed their projects in this real situation with freedom while also trying to attach to this manifesto:

1. Work with your hands, experience. Control the process better than the result.

2. Look for the origin of the processes, the raw materials, try to know the essence of the elements and construction systems. And this scientific understanding will enable an extreme freedom to operate outside the preconceived processes. Use industry at the service of architecture but not vice versa.

3. Conceive the space, design the construction accurately, play with the scale of the building elements to affect the scale of space; and the final form will be simply the result of following a clear strategy.

4. Move easily in the contradiction. And do not trust appearances. Heavy elements can build light and transparent spaces.

5. Do not ignore history, study and reread it. But use current technology and face actual problems in a contemporary way.

6. Structure is architecture, which is not only entrusted with the important task of dealing with gravity, but also traces the space, frames the landscape, orders the program, expresses; and so, defines architecture. Without dressings or disguise, with constructive honesty.

7. And above all, do. And if you make mistakes, learn. The perseverance in doing will keep you alive.

Dense Structure / Stressed Structures

Option Studio | Anton Garcia-Abril

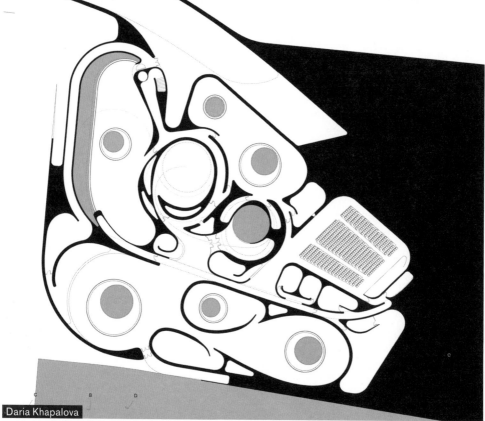

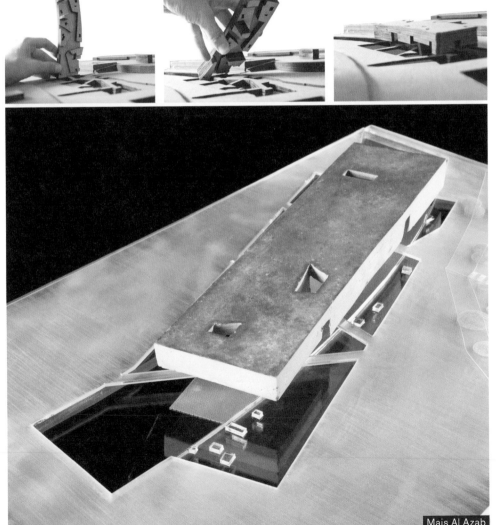

Mais Al Azab

Jarrad Morgan

Virtually all of what we do as humans takes place within the space of architecture. The design of space is the defining claim of the architect. This claim is an illusive demand and distinguishing privilege; it is what most sustains the discipline. This personal search for the character and consequence of the spatial experience is what most sustains the virtuous architect.

Arguably, at a moment when architects have become more and more dependent on technology as the generative resource for the form and calibration of architectural space, it is a good time to take a fresh look at how we design spaces, give them relevant meaning, and make them places of beauty.

One premise of this studio was that the design of architectural space is first necessitated by personal instinct, will, and imagination, and then facilitated through the use of present-day technologies.

The studio involved three exercises:

1. The first (re-memory) established a site. A place of memory, where at an early age something was learned about architecture—a spatial experience.

2. The second (De(i)con) defined a program through a close encounter with an object of close encounters—a chair.

3. The third [consolidate and (de)corate], made whole and embellished the re-memory and the De(i)con.

Among the requirements of each exercise (along with the prerequisite of personal instinct, will and imagination) were soul-searching, great leaps of faith, research, analysis, physical and digital modeling, computation, photography, welding, video and/or film production, revelations of taste and other acts of justifiable radical behavior.

09

10

11

12

01

02

03

04

05

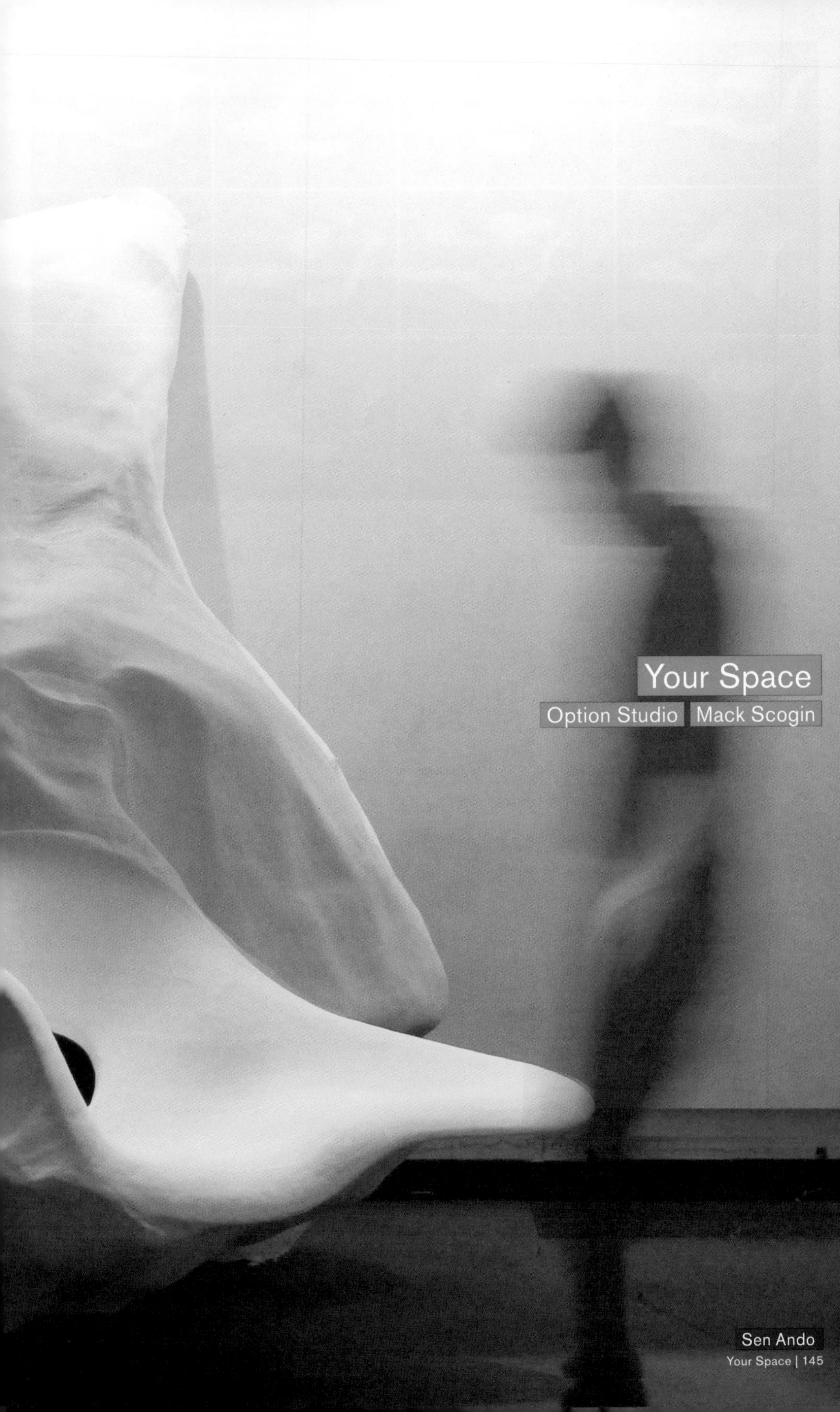

Your Space

Option Studio | Mack Scogin

Sen Ando

Natalya Egon

Preston Scott Cohen: Which one is more like your work, if I had to take three things here? Is it the plane inside the Guggenheim, and somehow this dialectic, whether or not it evokes a crash, imminent flight, or the filmic still shot, all of those things? Or do you identify more so with Frank Lloyd Wright's Guggenheim, with the way it sequences and dynamizes a certain experience for the museum? Or is the airplane, is the fuselage the graphic encasement of this machine? Which one is most like your work, or any of these?

Neil Denari: I think it's, in a kind of autobiographical way, it's also an endgame to a certain reading of the work. Because before we were able to build where the idea of occupying space became really the primacy of it all, the obsession with the object and all of the heavy reference that machine modernism had. This is basically a Russian doll effect, which is there's a big volume; there's a void inside that volume, then there's another solid. And inside that solid, there's another void inside the airplane. And so for me, it's a sort of relational situation between void and object that is going on in the work now. You can't attribute one quality or another to what we're working on now.

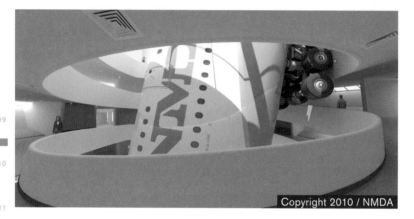

Copyright 2010 / NMDA

PSC: But right now, if everybody were to say, "What's the big moment of Neil?" It's presently the building in New York. Isn't it, really? Right now everyone is seeing it. It just finished its HL23, High Line 23, which I believe most of you know about. And I would say it's more like the plane than it's like the Guggenheim. It's more like the plane without the Guggenheim.

ND: I would agree that it is. And partly it's because the program, being so repetitive and also private, not a public project and also a project that's, in terms of its space, it's dominated by real estate, not by the demands or the whims of the architect in a way. So—

PSC: Yeah. And you've argued that there's a performative principal behind it, that the idea of trying to gain airspace over the High Line, the cantilever, motivated this structure. So you're kind of evoking Corbusier here on the right side of the argument he would be making about the automobile more so than, let's say, what he talks about when he's looking at the Parthenon.

STRUCTURAL FRAME
SECTION - SOUTH

STRUCTURAL FRAME
SECTION - NORTH

Discussions in Architecture:
Neil Denari with Preston Scott Cohen
Lecture   Neil Denari with Preston Scott Cohen

"Three States of Hors d'Oeuvres" was characterized by distinct cloud opacities, lighting conditions, and the smells of food-cloud. The exhibit consisted of four chambers filled with different clouds of vaporized food; the four unique cloud flavors were lemon-cardamom, barbeque, bonito fish, and vanilla-maple. Upon arrival, visitors were handed a tray with four different solid and liquid food samples, which they consumed while moving through and breathing in the chambers' food clouds. These food samples were picked in collaboration with local gastronomists (from an epicurean market called Savenor's) in order to produce interesting combinations with the food clouds. Thus the smell and taste of the food cloud in which visitors stood mixed and/or contrasted with the smell and taste of the solid and liquid samples. This resulted in a spatial form of food consumption, whereby the space in which visitors stood mingled and interacted with their eating and drinking experience.

The work was a collaboration with the Lab at Harvard, a new university-wide testing ground for ideas that defy the typical dichotomy of art and science. "Three States of Hors d'Oeuvres," a one-night exhibition-event, held on October 7, 2010, kicked off the annual opening ceremony for the Lab and attracted over 700 guests.

Project on Spatial Sciences was founded in 2009 by students from the Harvard Graduate School of Design. The group believes that space should no longer be thought of as an empty, lifeless void. In truth, space is always full and always in flux. Many spatial properties, such as sound, temperature, humidity, electromagnetic waves, and smell should not be seen as accidental by-products of building practices, or as unrelated supplements to architectural space, but could instead be thought of as integral to architecture. Space could therefore be purposefully calibrated to actively engage the lives and practices of its inhabitants.

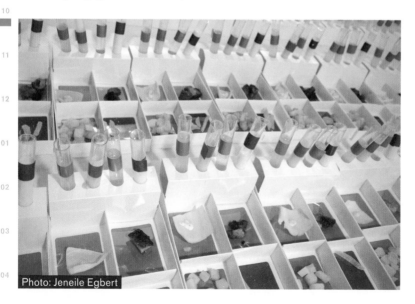

Photo: Jeneile Egbert

Three States of Hors d'Oeuvres

Project on Spatial Sciences | Mariela Alvarez, Day Jimenez
Etien Santiago, Zenovia Toloudi, Andrew Zientek

Photo: Jeneile Egbert

The visual and material arts work within the realm of a few defined categories...in a conventional sense, the first objects ever created by humans fall into the first, which is the material 3D. These are things like tools, weapons, eventually sculpture and architecture. At some point writing and cave paintings were invented and began to form the second category of the material 2D and things like photography and the moving image engendered the digital 2D. People assume we have digital 3D already but that doesn't seem to be the case. When you rotate your model on a screen or watch a Pixar animation it's actually just a digital 2D representation of material 3D. What people are calling 3D TV and 3D Movies are just a form of shallow depth or Bas Relief.

As it escapes the screen to become digital 3D it enters into the realm of architecture and ceases to function merely as representation. This concept expands on and encompasses "augmented reality," and describes visual and operative conditions that can function spatially within a site-specific context.

The visual category allows for things like material overlay, perceptual barriers, building transparencies, and the creation of artificial spatial depth. These can be viewed by one or more groups, depending on the designer's intent. The operative condition allows invisible spatial barriers to turn functionalities on and off and also have awareness of your spatial location, identity, and preferences. A wireless network is a perfect example of this type of barrier, and if we turn that weak boundary into a more spatial one, it can be tied to material walls and work as a part of the building itself. The operative can also act as a social organizer and affect the physical space through user efficiencies based on time and occupancy.

The ideal condition is an architecture that is designed simultaneously with the digital; projects that consider both material and digital realities from conception to finish and allow architects continued effect and commission throughout the lifespan of a building. With this new agency, architects are able to update and maintain the digital and can reauthenticate digital spatial paradigms as the audience changes. The digital 3D has the potential to alter perception and action, but it is fundamentally unable to replicate material effects like shelter, texture, touch, and heightened privacy. The new medium, it is not meant to supersede material architecture and would be unable to if it tried. The tools simply provide new potentials for architects and create a site-specific condition that can empower and give agency to the profession at-large.

4th floor balcony

RhinoD3d

Mediating Medi
The Digita

MArch Thesis | Greg

Advisor | Mack

James Templeton Kelle

Mediating Mediums: The Digit

spatial expansion

remote connectivity

09

10

11

12

01

02

03

04

05

My work challenges the accepted notion of the disembodied observer as precursor to the modern subject. Using studies of perception emerging in late nineteenth century psychology, I examine the modern observer as experimental subject and ask how this changed traditionally held paradigms of representation, imitation, abstraction, and illusion in art. The exchange between aesthetics and science of new knowledge produced by instruments and empirical methodologies of calibrating psychological responses to visual and sensual stimuli leads to an ontological shift in the concept of representation. This physiological aesthetics not only provided the terms for new formalist languages of art and criticism, it also instigated a reconsideration of the limitation of the classical definition of representation in art. The emergence of early modernism depends on the new psychologism not only to explain the effects of a work of art and the new role of the observer, but also suggests that a new mechanics of thought is necessary to rationalize the reality of modernism through representation. This project contributes not only to the way in which we characterize the modern subject and perception, but offers art historians, aesthetic theorists, and media scholars a way to critique current work in neuroaesthetics, studies of perception in psychology, and the relation between perception and representation.

09
10
11
12
01
02
03
04
05

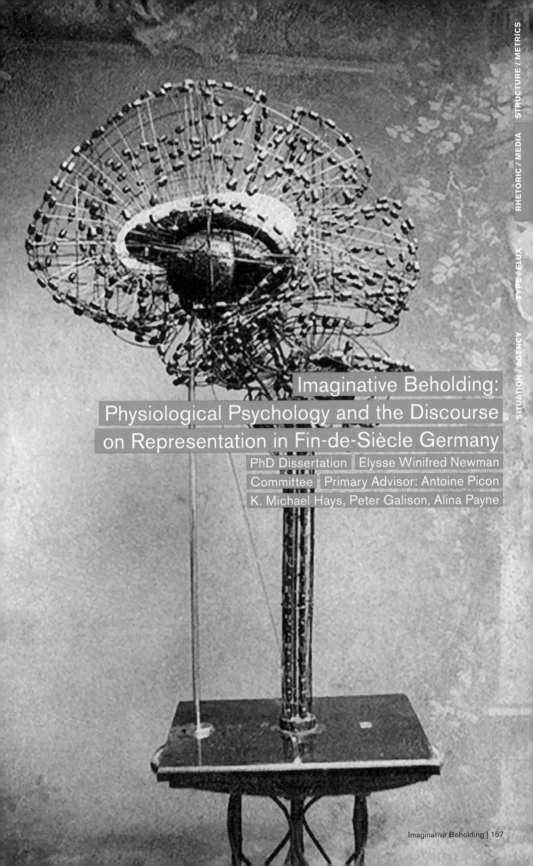

Imaginative Beholding:
Physiological Psychology and the Discourse
on Representation in Fin-de-Siècle Germany

PhD Dissertation | Elysse Winifred Newman
Committee | Primary Advisor: Antoine Picon
K. Michael Hays, Peter Galison, Alina Payne

"Sharpen your organs as you would sharpen a blade."

This statement, originally from Deleuze, is both a call to action, a plea, and an explanation.

Developments in the fields of cognitive science, neuroscience, and biology require us to question the Cartesian legacy that splits mind from life in the world. We can no longer understand ourselves to be isolated bodies controlled by a mind that is separate from and judges an independent environment. The mind, body, and environment form an inseparable and recursive entity.

There is no thinking that is independent of the feedback mechanism linking sensory input, body chemistry, the body map, and neural activity. The experience of our environment is mediated by our brain-body chemistry (body states) at the same time that our environment influences our nervous system. Environment and experience co-produce each other. What if landscape architecture could consciously embody, employ, and reveal this recursive condition?

This project, Nervous Landscapes, is primarily interested in the mechanics of experience and the subjectivity of perception. The world is not given to us objectively and fully formed—we actively construct it. We construct it by valuing certain things over others in our perceptive system. We notice some things and not others.

In this sense, perception is the foundation of ecology. What we place a value on we let into our lives and care for. Think of the desert and the language describing the desert. Barren. Desolate. Empty. This language was written by early pioneers who were homesick for wet landscapes, and this language came back and wrote policy and structured cultural values, all based on a subjective way of seeing.

Gilles Clement speaks of the third landscape—neither wilderness nor designed space. He says it is here that our future, our biodiversity, our imagination lies. My neighbor calls it a vacant lot but it is far from vacant. Think of all the different plant species and insects. Think of the discarded objects—beer bottles, broken toys, old coke cans. Robert Rauschenberg once said he felt sorry for people who thought discarded coke cans were ugly. And that's the great thing about our perceptive ecology being subjective—we can change it. We can adopt new ways of being in the world. New ways of seeing the terrain we occupy in our daily lives.

We are evolutionarily constructed on the scaffolds of the rhythms and changes in our environment. We survived by being able to predict and detect change. Our culture is becoming more and more divorced from these rhythms and defined by rapid change, and we are losing our ability to occupy these other, longer, slower landscape temporalities. But we can learn, we can train ourselves, to become sensitive to these more subtle gradients.

Nervous Landscapes is an immersive environment based on the historical model of a hortus conclusus, and seeks to highlight the delicate interplay of mind, body, and environment by compressing and revealing the exchanges and rhythms that exist in human-landscape relationships. It is in a sense a machine for viewing—an observatory for what goes on over time. The project is not interested in a kind of broad utopic theory or approach. It is, rather, focused on pursuing a kind of individual utopia—a potential inherent in each individual's relation to the surrounding world.

Nervous Landscapes

| MLA Thesis | Andrew Zientek |
| Advisor | Sanford Kwinter |

Norman T. Newton Prize

This thesis examines the apex and subsequent dismantling of the theory emblematized by the Bridge on the Basento, which was conceived in 1967 by the Italian architect and engineer Sergio Musmeci (1926–1981). Trained under the auspices of Pier Luigi Nervi and Riccardo Morandi, Musmeci developed an iconoclastic approach to structural design that revolved around his idea of "minimum structure." This notion aimed to reduce as much as possible the amount of matter from which an edifice was built, in order to approach the limit that he mathematically proved, in his book *La Statica e le Strutture* (1971), to be the absolute minimum necessary for a given structure to exist. In the thesis, I reveal how this ambition was embedded in a broader cosmology of structure. Musmeci had developed a sweeping new way of thinking about the structure of edifices, for which *La Statica e le Strutture* served as the theoretical handbook while the Bridge on the Basento comprised its quintessential example. He took apart the conventions of structural design in order to rebuild them on new mathematical, philosophical, and lyrical bases. Most importantly, his approach towards structure resonated strongly with the precepts of structuralism, an intellectual movement born in the early twentieth century linguistics of Ferdinand de Saussure and which, during Musmeci's time, came to permeate many realms of cultural study.

Saussure's structuralist linguistics proposed that language gained meaning not through the positive aggregation of its individual units, each of which allegedly referred to a world beyond themselves and contained a definite, culturally and historically ascribed value, but rather through the prismatic and malleable relationships internal to the system of communication itself. Musmeci's theory presented an analogous approach in that it rejected the notion that successful structural designs should be derived from the positive properties of actual building materials, whose strength grew as their quantity and depth increased. Instead, he proposed that structure comprised its own source of coherency: one defined negatively by relationships through space. In the same way that Saussure developed a synchronic method of study to investigate the inner workings of language independently of history, content, and context, Musmeci placed a strong emphasis on a static conceptualization of physics that removed the elements under consideration from time, matter, and external influences. He refused the idea that structural design consisted of a struggle against outside forces, and rather saw his task as that of purging structure of all superfluous concerns such that it emerge freely from its internal laws. It is for this reason that Musmeci was so intent on minimizing the amount of material in his projects. He did not necessarily wish for his designs to appear light, but rather desired to conceptually and methodologically liberate their structure from all other concerns, leaving behind only its absolute rules: structure qua structure. The Bridge on the Basento vividly expresses this radical logic of purging; its twisted, contorted forms evoke both the fleetingness of spatial relations as well as the weighty voids of a seemingly missing solid structure. As its complex curves attest, Musmeci's isolation of structure from time, outside factors, and physical matter enabled him to accentuate the role of spatial geometries in making assemblies stand up. This emphasis on synchronic

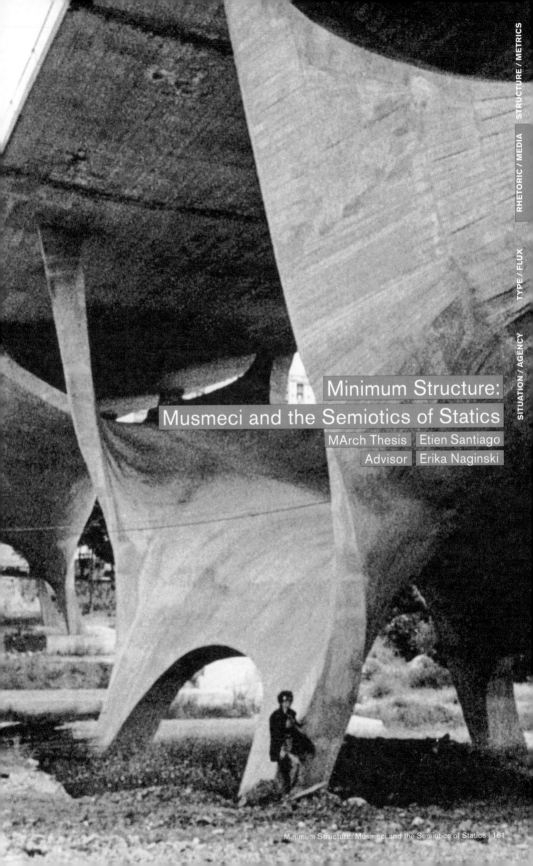

Minimum Structure:
Musmeci and the Semiotics of Statics

MArch Thesis | Etien Santiago
Advisor | Erika Naginski

patterns of organization closely echoes the geometrization and spatialization of language and signs that was typical of structuralist thought. In Musmeci's theory as in structuralism, structure was understood to consist of insubstantial relationships rather than substantial bodies.

Musmeci's take on structural design classified structure as something fundamentally missing from the actual world, or detached from real objects: something that gained its coherency and usefulness precisely through this removal. Just as structuralist writers searched for systems of order that were valid independently of specifics and could be transposed from one set of elements to another, Musmeci also saw structure more as a general organizing principle than a concrete fact. This view allowed him to develop a strong theory independent of its resulting objects—a theory which, much like the definition of structure that it outlined, was meant to permeate the world as an invisible yet all-powerful ghostly presence. Particulars could vary, but the theory remained the same; an infinite exfoliation of new iterations bloomed under its regime. Along comparable lines, the structuralist

reading of myth undertaken by Claude Lévi-Strauss in the 1960s argued that the meaning of myths resided not in their stories, but in the timeless arrangements of their mythical components. Around the same time that Lévi-Strauss was extracting the core of myth from the particularities of its variants and the unique societies from which they originated, Musmeci was envisioning structural design as the task of disengaging structure from all other concerns: to make it into its own impetus, to isolate the root of structure and lay it bare.

The second section of the thesis turns to Musmeci's work following the 1976 Friuli earthquake, which arguably prompted him to unravel his theory and rethink the rapport between his ideas and creations. Here, I uncover the impact of this catastrophic event on his science of statics, as well as the implications of Jacques Derrida and Umberto Eco's post-structuralism for Musmeci's understanding of structure. After Musmeci's experience of the ravages caused by the quake and his involvement in the reconstruction effort, both the literal and philosophical limitations of his search for minimum structure must have become glaringly clear. His theory conceptually endangered

the assurance of structure not only because it worked to purge the amount of structure down to a terrifyingly small volume, but also because it perilously attempted to excavate the roots of structure itself: to expose the absent structure of structure. In Musmeci's work, as in the contemporaneous writings of Derrida and Eco, the impossibility of locating an ultimate, stable base upon which even the concept of structure could rely eventually prompted questions of form and spatial organization to give way to questions of force and non-grounding. Time and outside influences came rushing back in the door; the non-hierarchical and ever-delayed essence of structurality become more evident than before. In literal terms, the seism drove home the fundamental lack of a stable ground condition upon which built structures could rely; in figurative terms, the seism underlined the grave consequences of Musmeci's paradoxical search for structure outside a metaphysics of presence. While his projects after 1976 continued to explore his longstanding interest in the idea of absence playing a key role in structure, they also emanated a new uncertainty and intricacy. He wrestled with how to adapt his theory of minimum structure

precisely as it was proving increasingly untenable, and in doing so produced a series of works that both echo and significantly undermine it. The story of Musmeci's last projects helps us to better clarify his evolving matrix of ideas regarding minimum structure, and paradoxically compounds its richness by revealing its limits.

In order to illustrate how the complex evolution of ideas broached by Musmeci's work can have consequences for architectural thinking, I conclude with a short design exercise that develops three-dimensional iterations of an elevation he drew for a hypothetical bridge over the Natisone River. The resulting designs demonstrate how the problem of conceptualizing solid and void, mass and surface, inside and outside, hierarchy, absence, directionality, and inversion can propel design explorations. Although this thesis undoubtedly revisits a closed chapter in the history of cultural and intellectual production, I have also tried to demonstrate how the network of questions raised during this period can enable and inspire vital new terrains of inquiry that are likewise equally relevant to problems in the sciences, humanities, and design.

This course went back to what are considered to be crucial years for architectural history in the second half of the XXth Century. The class followed an unusual format–that of a dialogue between two architects who have witnessed the scene they are talking about: the decades of the 1950s through the 1980s. The fact that these two architects have known many of the protagonists of this narrative gave these lectures the value of becoming a first hand oral history. The course connected architecture and ideological attitudes throughout the various decades, paying attention to both the works and the theoretical texts believed to still be alive in many ways in today's architectural horizon.

The lecture course was a conversation with a double frame of reference–Europe and America–that in spite of the differences are bound by a common origin. To recognize the continuous interaction between America and Europe is very necessary in order to understand how history evolved. Peter Eisenman took the lead in presenting the American scene, while Rafael Moneo did the same with the European field.

Peter Eisenman: You could argue that the notion of project comes into thinking in the U.S. brought by the Italian word "to project–projection," in other words, instead, they teach in their schools at the time, and I imagine to this day, project as opposed to design. And I would argue that just for the sake of provoking Rafael or Jorge or anyone in the audience that Rossi had a project, a conceptual intellectual ideological project, and Stirling did not. Stirling was an architect, he had an architectural practice, but he did not have a project. That doesn't mean good or bad, it means to distinguish something that was in fact becoming energizing to the United States. I would argue that the same thing could be said for the two German architects, Ungers and Kleihues, where Matthias Ungers could be said to have a project, Kleihues could be said to have a practice. That struggle would play itself out in the IBA exhibition of 1982 in Berlin, where both of them–Kleihues and Ungers–were vying for the running of this project. Had Ungers done this project, I would argue the results would have been very different because they where more ideological and political in a certain way, moreso than what Kleihues was doing.

Rafael Moneo: I would say that if I am sharing with you my feelings or my taste, I like better the Ungers that we saw in the 1960s or late 1950s than the Ungers we are seeing now (in the 1980s). Ungers was an extremely articulated person.

PE: You prefer the Rossi of Modena to the Rossi of Berlin?

RM: Of course I do.

PE: We should make clear that the late Rossi and the late Ungers are problematic when you see them against their early works.

RM: This raises the difficulty between Ungers and Rossi. Rossi committed himself more to theoretical approaches. In the case of Ungers, I come back to your observation yesterday between having a project, or having a practice. In the case of Ungers, practice and project go together. In the case of Rossi, you could say he had a project but not a practice. Ungers can be seen on different terms. Curiously, in the days to come, the critical future of Ungers is probably going to be related to Koolhaas. To have nurtured, helped, and contributed so determinately to Koolhaas's education is somehow going to be the glory of Ungers.

Conversations on Architecture of the Second Half of the XXth Century

Seminar Rafael Moneo
with invited guest Peter Eisenman

The project of Olafur Eliasson has been to subject spatial and aesthetic practice to the rigors of both knowledge and invention, and at one and the same time. But if the spirit of the laboratory and of the counting house seems cold and out of place within an art practice, it is notable that every work of Eliasson figures at once as experiment or "reality test" and as a confident affirmation of the mysteries and enchantments of nature.

Eliasson's importance has been to frame artistic action to make it rigorously historical, concrete, and specific to a "here and now" and hence to detach it from all metaphysical propositions about art and experience. This approach also detaches it from the incessant flow of trivial images that characterizes not only our economic, work, and entertainment worlds but our artistic ones alike. If the work remains difficult to situate, it is because it insists on exploring the foundations of artistic expression and reception simultaneously; its aim is to submit these together to philosophical scrutiny as well as to empirical experimentation, evidence, and proof.

Photo: Ken Yip

For Eliasson, art is both the place where human "experience" in its purest form is invented and where it is to be ideally interrogated. There is no certain, or relevant, world outside of experience, and there is no experience without time. Hence the secrets of how we inhabit our world are to be found nowhere else but in the ways we employ our nervous systems to sample it, compile it, capture it, and transform it in and through movement. Eliasson's essential discovery, consonant with that of neuroscientists in the last two decades, is that "the world" is not found but made, and made by our active and enduring encounters with it. Perceiver and perceived are indissociable—to alter one, without exception, is to alter the other. Among his essential accomplishments has been to dissociate seeing from knowing, to reconceive cognition and perception as themselves productive acts and hence to turn most of the pieties of

The Divine Comedy:
Exhibition & Artists' Talk

Exhibition | Olafur Eliasson

Lecture | Olafur Eliasson and Tomas Saraceno with Sanford Kwinter

Photo: Lauren Kim

art reception, and our beliefs about how we inhabit our environments, on their heads. If, as he shows, we are exiled from fact, and if indeterminacy presides over most of our relationships to the realities of our world, we are therefore bound to one another in collectivities in entirely new ways through the same noble if desperate need to cobble a workable fiction from nothing but the particulars of sensation.

It may be said that Eliasson, like Duchamp, does not produce works of art. Rather, he organizes and transforms conditions of experience. The widely known Weather Project at the Tate Modern in London in 2003 is a primary example. Every Eliasson work entails the production of a machine that activates other machines—in particular, the sensation-producing body-machines of the viewers themselves. In the exhibition presented here are displayed 54 experiment-machines (they could also be called "perceiving machines") that each explore an aspect of how the human body and nervous system orients itself in space and time by tapping clues implicitly or explicitly from its environment, from which it innovates its own irreducibly unique "life in space."

—Sanford Kwinter

Photo: Iwan Baan

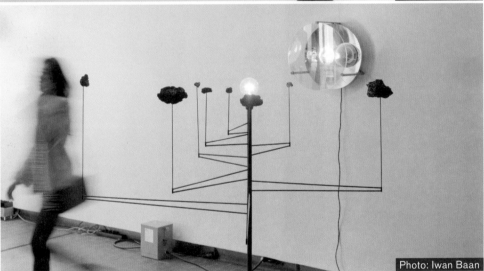

Photo: Iwan Baan

Ai Weiwei's absence

Extreme Jenga: MIT and GSD
Photo: Lian Chang

Belinda Tato

Rafael Moneo

Charles Waldheim

Guy Nordenson

Michael Hays

Preston Scott Cohen

Achim Menges

Neil Denari

Shirin Neshat

Ben Van Berkel

Rahul Mehrotra

Edward Norton

TYPE and FLUX embody two seemingly opposed contemporary forces where the tension between disciplinary continuity and dynamic cultural and environmental situations create opportunities for innovation and invention.

The impact of the 2011 Sendai tsunami forcefully underscores the power and volatility of dynamic natural forces. Increasingly, designers are working with models of nature that are not static or idealized, but rather in **FLUX**. Instead of crafting singular proposals and fixed master plans, contemporary work must conceptualize temporality, phasing, and evolving implementation strategies. Contingencies plan for unknowns while variables plug into parametric models allowing for greater complexity, flexibility, and control in the design process.

Despite the dynamic nature of site and situation, questions of **TYPE** and typology focus on continuities and constants within architecture, landscape, and urban form. Historically, buildings were divided into types based on their program (housing, office, theater, church, etc.) or organization (axial, long span, mat, etc.) Recent investigations have questioned the stability of program, its assumptions of spatial demand, and its implied organizational structures.

TYPE and **FLUX** embody two seemingly opposed contemporary forces where the tension between disciplinary continuity and dynamic cultural and environmental situations create opportunities for innovation and invention. Preston Scott Cohen's *Type and Topography* option studio grappled with new degrees of variation within existing building typologies enabled by parametric models. Chris Reed's Landscape Core IV studio, entitled *Flux*, explored the dynamic forces at work within urban landscapes of the East River estuary in Queens, NY. Jonathan Scelsa's MAUD thesis, *Morphing Manhattanism*, takes the bridge as an urban type and proposes a number of programmatic and typological hybrids. These projects engage issues of variability and continuity as active agents for design.

Type /
Flux

What has happened to architectural beauty? It used to be the fundamental value of architectural theory and practice, the touchstone of every conceivable achievement for a discipline that considered itself primarily as an art. Today, the word is seldom pronounced by theorists and professionals, at least in public. Even critics and historians tend to avoid the loaded term.

What has happened to architectural beauty? Its eclipse is all the more surprising given that architectural aesthetics is everywhere. The architectural star-system is to a large extent based on signature forms that herald the originality of their authors. The so-called "Guggenheim effect" has fundamentally to do with the visual seduction exerted by Frank Gehry's project on a large public, from connoisseurs to simple passers-by. It has paved the way for all sorts of prestigious architectural commissions, often linked to the cultural sector, museums, libraries, opera houses, requiring visually striking answers that can be appreciated by a broad audience.

Usually entrusted to a relatively small cohort of elite architects, these commissions nevertheless contribute to define the tone of contemporary architectural debate. Even if the term beauty is rarely invoked to characterize their power of seduction, the aesthetic dimension plays a determining role.

09

10

11

12

01

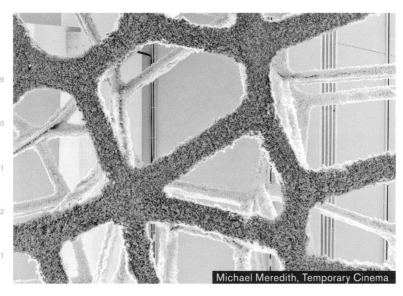

Michael Meredith, Temporary Cinema

02

The rise of digital culture and the new perspectives opened by parametric design are likewise raising all sorts of questions regarding the visual principles applicable to a production that no longer follows modernist aesthetic principles. Almost every architect was able to judge the visual value of a project using a formal vocabulary inspired by the works of Mies van der Rohe or Le Corbusier. However, the smooth surfaces produced with the help of the computer defy the aesthetic canon that we have inherited from modernity. More generally, the question of new visual codes that should sooner or later supersede the modernist legacy is opened. A theoretical vocabulary is emerging in relation to the various

03

04

05

The Eclipse of Beauty

Symposia | Co-convened by Preston Scott Cohen and Antoine Picon

Speakers include Mario Carpo, Michael Meredith, Ingeborg Rocker

Evan Douglis, Georges Teyssot, Timothy Hyde

Catherine Ingraham, Mack Scogin

attempts made to clarify this issue without being willing to deal frontally with beauty. The success of notions such as elegance or affect must be interpreted in this light.

Formal and aesthetic considerations are everywhere, while beauty remains officially absent. The same paradox characterizes other crucial aspects of contemporary architectural debate and practice. As Rem Koolhaas argued forcefully at the turn of the 1990s, architecture is confronted with the challenge of massive urbanization processes that are without equivalent in the past.

Their character seems to call for a new aesthetics that Koolhaas himself began to sketch through widely advertised publications such as *S,M,L,XL*, *Mutations*, or the Harvard Design School *Project on the City*. The influence of these publications stemmed as much from a new two aesthetic reading of the contemporary urbanization processes they suggested as from their analyses of these processes proper and their advocacy of architectural realism and effectiveness.

Among the conditions of contemporary architectural practice related to massive urbanization, one finds a profound transformation of the relation between architecture and infrastructure, which results in the frequent blurring of the distinction between the two domains. In such a context, is it still possible to distinguish between the aesthetics of the engineer and that of the architect? The ambiguities that have arisen may well explain the success of propositions like the "non-Cartesian" structural engineering advocated by Cecil Balmond in his essay *Informal*. From a renewed interest in materials to the research of innovative tectonic principles, contemporary engineers and architects share a number of common preoccupations, even if significant differences remain between
09 their approaches. Whereas architects used to talk more readily about the aesthetic dimension of his practice, they are now equally reluctant to invoke beauty as a fundamental aspect of their work.
10

Has beauty become the architectural unspeakable in the manner of an obsession that should never be officially acknowledged? And if such is the
11 case, what are the reasons for this Freudian-like repression? Finally, what are its consequences for the theory and practice of architecture, and what would happen if beauty were to make an official comeback?
12

01

02

03

04

05

Evan Douglis, Helioscope

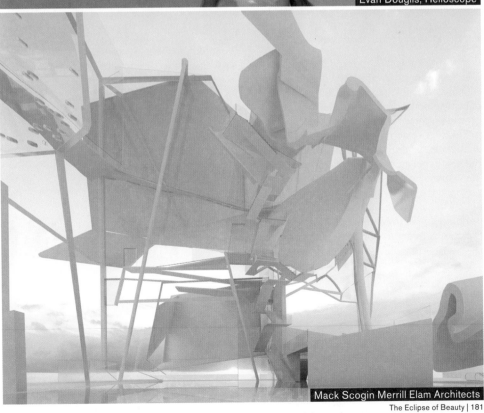

Mack Scogin Merrill Elam Architects

"Performing Arts" is the rubric we use to differentiate the arts that occur in real time and depend on an audience from those that are synchronic. But the concept of "performance" as an umbrella for grouping music, dance and drama is wholly inadequate as a description of what they share. "Performance" is to art as "facility" is to architecture—a literal mechanical description of what is a much broader and deeper cultural phenomenon.

All of these artistic acts are present to each other and intermingled with one another; all relate to literature and rely on the simultaneity of the visual and the aural. However, the experiential phenomenon that most clearly differentiates these events from the "normal" experience of fact and necessity is the seemingly paradoxical immersion of the self in a totally inner world of imagination and desire, while at the same time one is being present to community in the most public and exposed of places.

Indeed, somehow through the vehicle of community assembly, the inner self is actualized and comes to be known in ways that are otherwise concealed. The persona or publicly constructed self comes to meet the anima or the true interior being.

In the simplest terms, we weep in public. The theater or concert hall is therefore very much a set for the staging of our own public/personal drama. Like the ancients processing from the city along the Attic coast to Eleusis, we come as spectators of one another, in full civic regalia, ready to refresh our emotional intimacy with ourselves through the witnessing of a communal mystery—in our case the poetry of art in the moment. To satisfy this demand for community based performance activity, this studio—the third in the core sequence—engaged in the creation

of a New Boston Center for Music, Dance and Drama on the North End waterfront. The new center would be administered by a non-profit organization co-coordinating a wide spectrum of both community and specialty professional organizations that now have limited access to the larger and costlier venues in Boston. Two major halls were to be provided—a 1,200 seat concert hall/dance pavilion and a 600 seat studio theater (formerly known as "black box").

The sloped floor concert hall was to have acoustics and amenities equivalent to Symphony Hall, serving as an extended instrument for the projection of serious music—classical, contemporary, and concert jazz. It would also accommodate the staging of both traditional and non-traditional dance troupe performances.

The level floor studio theater would allow for a variety of dramatic presentation types including proscenium, theater in the round, and thrust stage formats. It was meant as a community house that could accommodate both experimental workshops and formal performances.

Key to the community aspect of the New Center was the inclusion of education functions such as rehearsal, practice, and classroom spaces that would enliven the building and its relationship to the surrounding community.

Architecture III

Core Studio | Jonathan Levi, Danielle Etzler, Eric Howeler

Mariana Ibanez, Florian Idenburg, Maryann Thompson

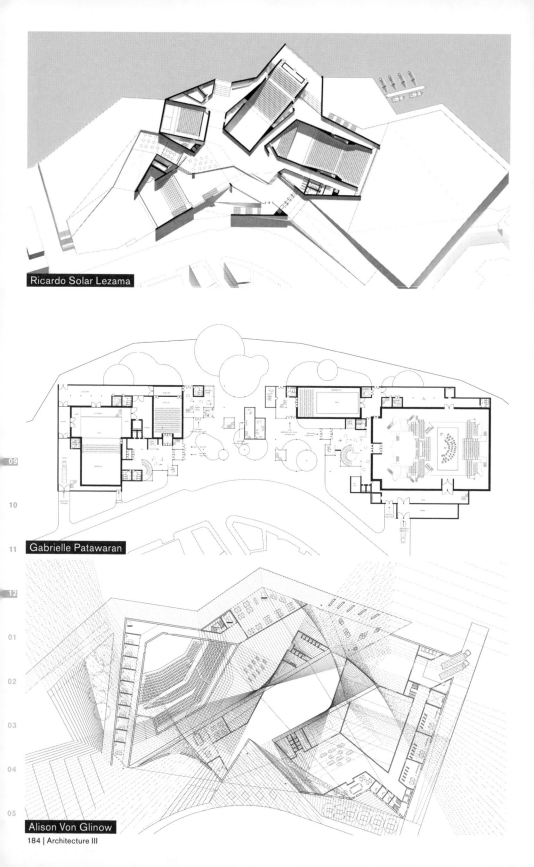

Ricardo Solar Lezama

Gabrielle Patawaran

Alison Von Glinow

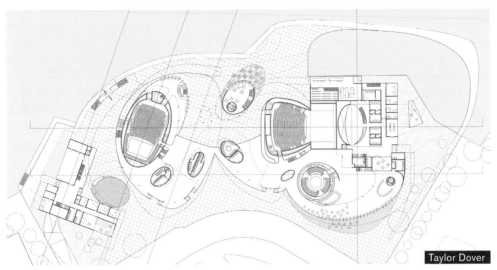

Taylor Dover

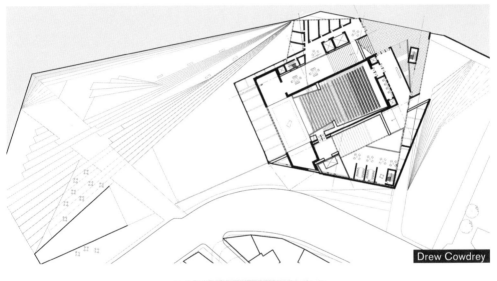

Drew Cowdrey

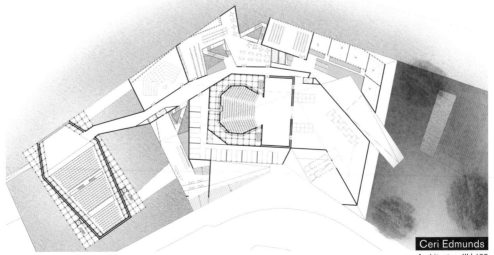

Ceri Edmunds

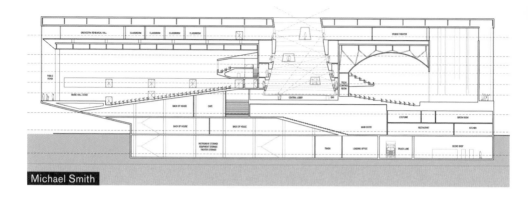

Michael Smith

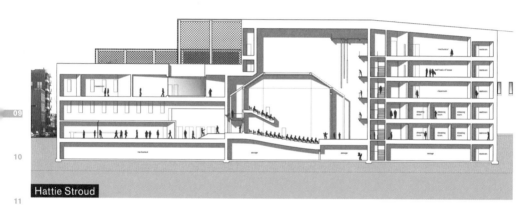

Hattie Stroud

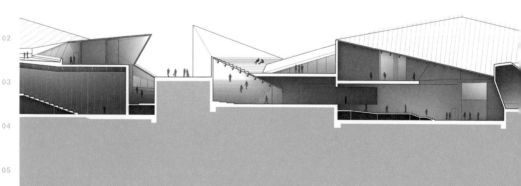

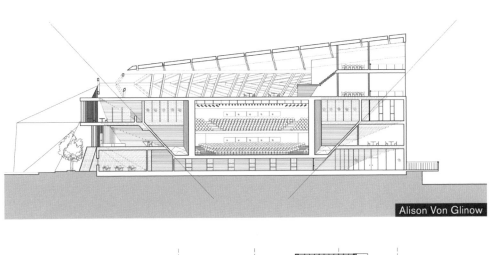

Alison Von Glinow

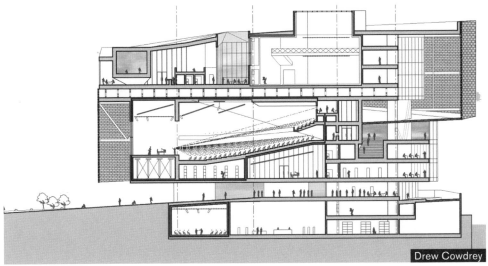

Drew Cowdrey

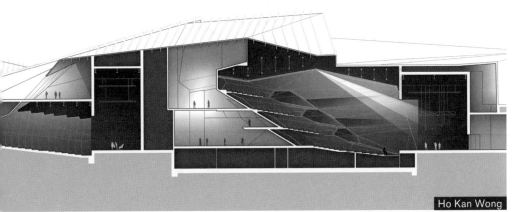

Ho Kan Wong

Alison Von Glinow

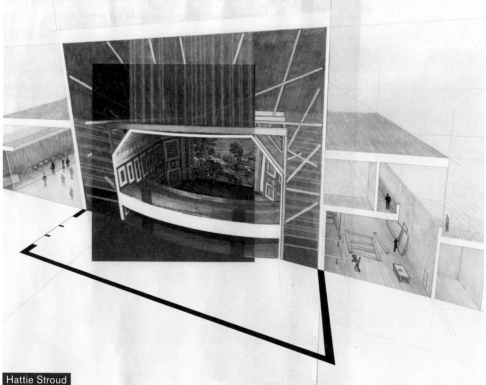

Hattie Stroud

Drew Cowdrey

Michael Smith

James Martin

Michael Smith

Alison Von Glinow

This studio focused on the development of urban form as driven by ecology and environmental dynamics—a landscape-based urbanism. It introduced methods and representational techniques for describing urban form and the dynamic underlying and adapted ecologies that might be invoked to shape urban infrastructure and the urban fabric.

Representational strategies began with mapping and diagramming larger ecological processes and dynamics on an urban brownfield site, then focused on the description of local and regional infrastructures, building form and fabric, and the various dynamic relationships between the city and its reconstituted riverine setting.

Students developed fully rounded landscape urbanist strategies, conceived in relation to the broader ecological, environmental, infrastructural, and social-cultural processes and systems that constitute them. While the proposals developed for the urban fabric were specific and concrete, they relied on principles that are flexible, dynamic, and adaptive—able to accommodate and respond to varying inputs over time. The studio supported this agenda with targeted research and urban design studies at multiple scales and in multiple formats, which accumulated over the semester and were calibrated with one another. Most broadly, the studio addressed fundamental questions of what it means to be urban, actively engaged within an environmental context.

Most traditional Western cities are founded on principles of stability and permanence: where change or uncertainty are present— often in the form of rich and complex landscape systems—they are typically erased, filled, leveled, denuded, marginalized, and/or stabilized.

This studio took a different approach to city making—or, in this case, to urban renovation: we assumed change is the norm. In doing so, this studio built on ecologists' reconceptualization of their field over the past quarter-century, in which ecology has moved from a classical Newtonian concern with stability, certainty, and order, to more contemporary understandings of dynamic, systemic change. With this reconceptualization comes the related phenomena of adaptability, resilience, and flexibility—phenomena applicable not only to ecological systems (whether native or adapted), but also applicable to city-system, infrastructure, and city-building writ large. In this sense, then, the studio moved away from traditions of master planning, which value the comprehensive and fixed vision in favor of more dynamic and responsive frameworks for small- and large-scale civic change. Students also explored multiple development scenarios (deployments) over time, rather than a singular and totalizing plan. These scenarios operated according to set rules or parameters, but were programmed to respond to a range of differing inputs over time. In this way, the proposals aspired to a level of resilience with regard to long-term environmental, social, political, and economic shifts, and therefore were made truly sustainable over the long term.

CITY FIELD +

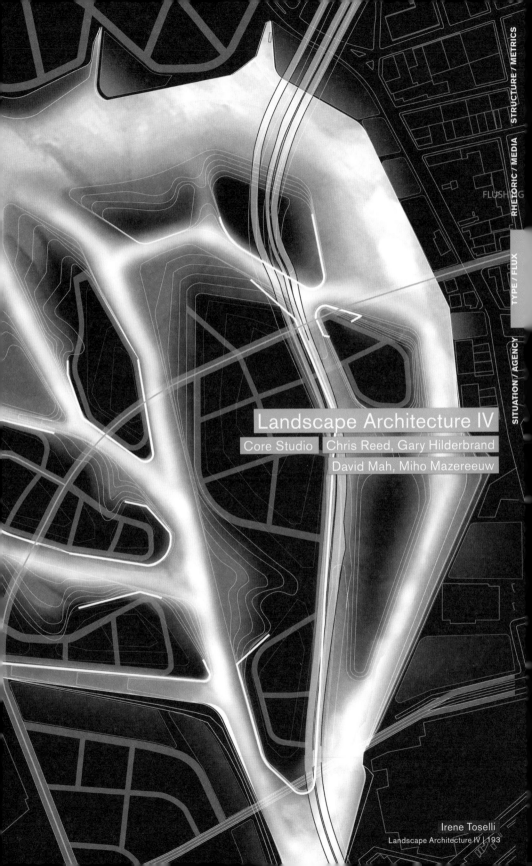

FLUSHING

Landscape Architecture IV

Core Studio   Chris Reed, Gary Hilderbrand

David Mah, Miho Mazereeuw

Aisling O'Carroll

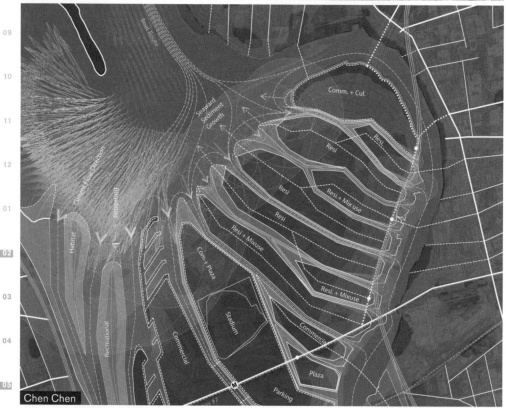

Chen Chen

Melissa How

Flushing Meadow park
(Flood release channel destination)

BH - 2
Inland Residential
(High Density)

DM - 1
Connection Block
(Mid Density)

Flushing Creek

BL - 1
Inland Residential
(Low Density)

AM - 1
Waterfront
Residential
(Low - mid Density)

Road
Connecting
every other
island
to mainland

Tidal Channel
Type 1 - Dynamic
(Temporary Waterline)
Dynamic + Reclaimation

09
10
11
12
01
02
03
04
05

Patchara Wongboonsin

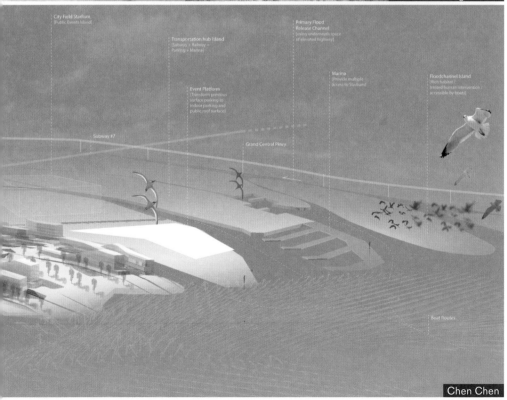

City Field Stadium
[Public, Events Island]

Transportation hub Island
[Subway + Railway +
Parking + Marina]

Primary Flood
Release Channel
[using underneath space
of elevated highway]

Event Platform
[Transform previous
surface parking to
indoor parking and
public roof surface]

Marina
[Provide multiple
access to Stadium]

Floodchannel Island
[Rich habitat /
limited human intervention /
accessible by boat]

Subway #7

Grand Central Pkwy

Boat Routes

Chen Chen

Xinpeng Yu

Elements of Urban Design is an advanced core studio for the post-professional programs in urban design. The course focuses on the American city in order to introduce critical concepts, strategies, and technical skills associated with current thinking on urbanism, and speculates on the designer's role in analyzing and shaping complex metropolitan systems.

As emergent models of urban development in the North American urbanized geographies continue to depart from the more time-honored envelope of the traditional compact city, the canvas of action for designers necessarily expands and diversifies. The customary twentieth century divide between the cultivated city and its peripheries has, in the past decades, been partially supplanted by newer morphologies fueled by urbanization pressures at the scale of the mega-region. Fast paced forms of metropolitan development, paired with new "geo-political annexation" procedures, have transformed the urban/suburban dyad into a much more complex system of loosely associated spreads and densities, fundamentally altering the original kit of parts of the post World War II suburb, and its social, economic, and spatial dynamics.

The course engages five main pedagogic objectives:

1. To establish constructive forms of exchange between analytical research and design through diverse conceptual frameworks and projective representational techniques;
2. To explore the wide range of scenarios currently at play within urbanized landscapes, and the diverse design procedures that can inform their transformation at multiple scales;
3. To rethink the role of landscape and infrastructure as significant building blocks in the creation of new urban systems, and in the reconfiguration of existing systems;
4. To establish an open dialogue between

09
10
11
12
01
02
03
04
05

larger design motivations and actions, and how they might be tested and explored through specific design hypotheses; and
5. To critically explore and appropriate environmental and ecological factors at the urban scale.

Using two specific sites within Queens (NYC)–Willets Point and Sunnyside Yards– as an open laboratory, the Elements of Urban Design studio served as a research/design platform from which to investigate current physical and social systems that are shaping the American metropolis. Throughout the course of the semester students developed sound hypotheses regarding the scope and ambition of the urban project within the emergent scenarios of a twenty-first century urban terrain.

Elements of Urban Design

Core Studio   Felipe Correa, Anita Berrizbeitia, Rafael Segal

Monica Earl, Carlos Garciavelez Alfaro

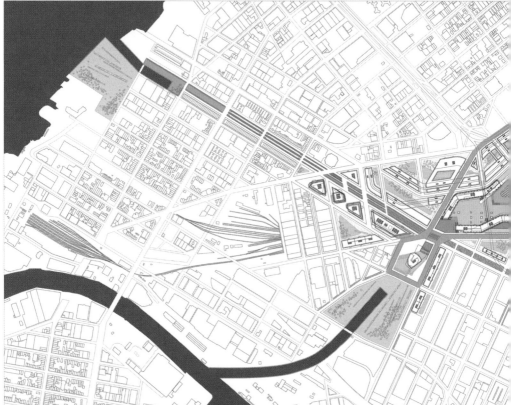

Nicholas Croft, Adam Greene

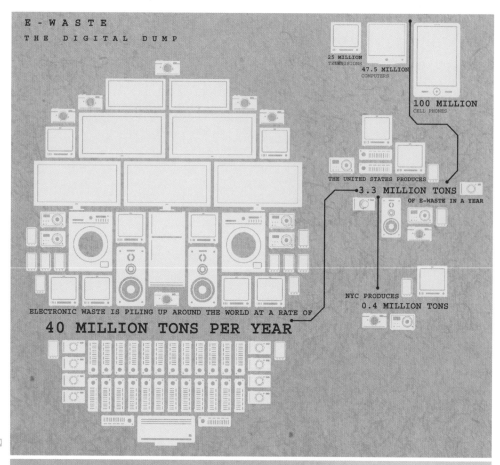

E - W A S T E
T H E   D I G I T A L   D U M P

25 MILLION
TELEVISIONS

47.5 MILLION
COMPUTERS

100 MILLION
CELL PHONES

THE UNITED STATES PRODUCES
3.3 MILLION TONS
OF E-WASTE IN A YEAR

NYC PRODUCES
0.4 MILLION TONS

ELECTRONIC WASTE IS PILING UP AROUND THE WORLD AT A RATE OF

40 MILLION TONS PER YEAR

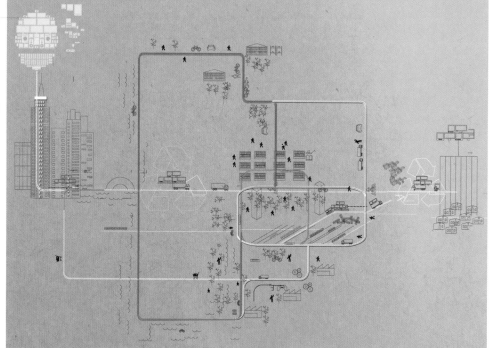

Hana Disch, Clementina Vinals

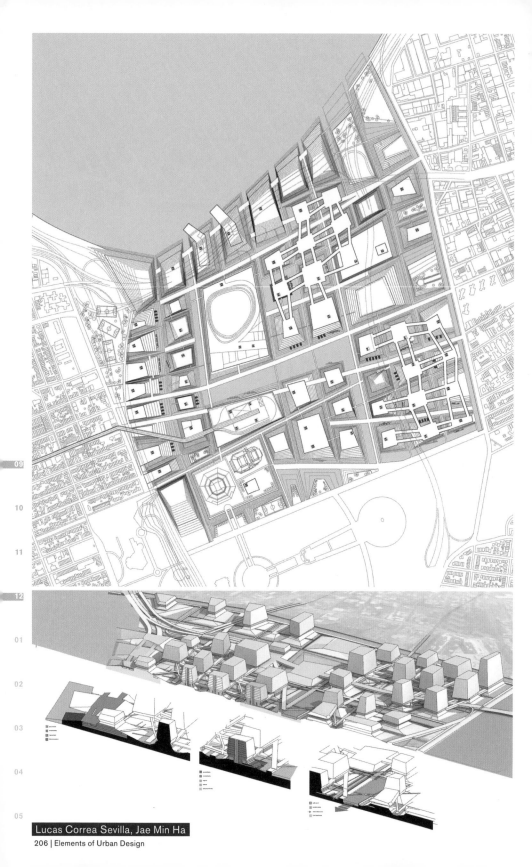

Mariusz Klemens, Eric Schuchardt

What is a VERTICALSCAPE? A hybrid entity that, due to inertia, we momentarily continue to call vertical construction or "architecture." This vertical "entity" is an amalgam, a material at once natural and artificial, which seeks to construct a similar experience to what our modern masters called public space, modernizing its sinusoidal connection to this end. By so doing, generally folded around itself, it not only generates a different spatial modality that can be manipulated to construct hybrid architecture programmes for culture, leisure and production, it also generates self-sufficient entities, energy parks that use wind, water, light or the earth as active materials in construction, capable of generating and storing energy, and at the same time serving as public and economic resources. In the urban context, the verticalscape aims to be a catalyst that renders the historic or modern fabric contemporary, in both the formal and the social or cultural realms.

The studio focused on Chicago as a site of reference. The city is home to one of the first modern skyscrapers—giving rise to a new city model that succeeded worldwide in the twentieth century metropolis.

This studio explored the urgency of a new way of understanding the high rise and its impact in the public realm, a "prototypology" that we call verticalscapes, applied to the current American metropolis and the urban landscape, as defined by definite multiracial human clusters that require new scenarios for public life and new links between the world of objects and nature.

The project addressed a new proto-typological field that is seeing the crystallization of a series of ideas and technologies now emerging in our world, which have not yet been adequately problematized. Students investigated new proto-typological strategies based on an up-to-the-moment technological conception and consideration of emerging societal values in the contemporary city.

Through the course of the studio, projects explored the contribution today's technical culture could make to high rise building and public space in a city like Chicago.

Verticalscapes / Chicago

Option Studio   Iñaki Ábalos

Carlos Garciavelez Alfaro, Clementina Vinals

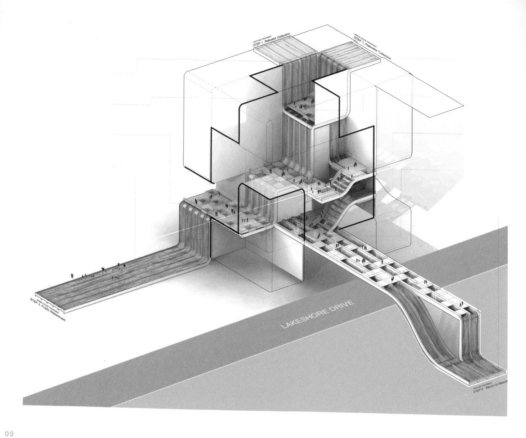

LAKESHORE DRIVE

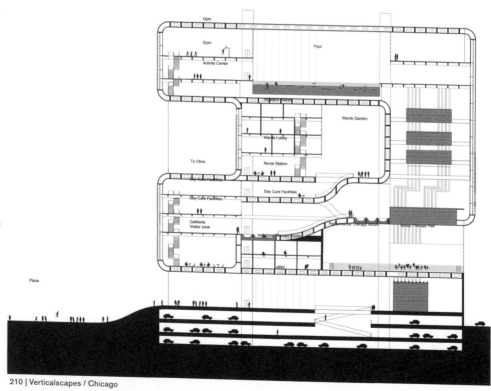

Xi Chen, Wanjing Ji

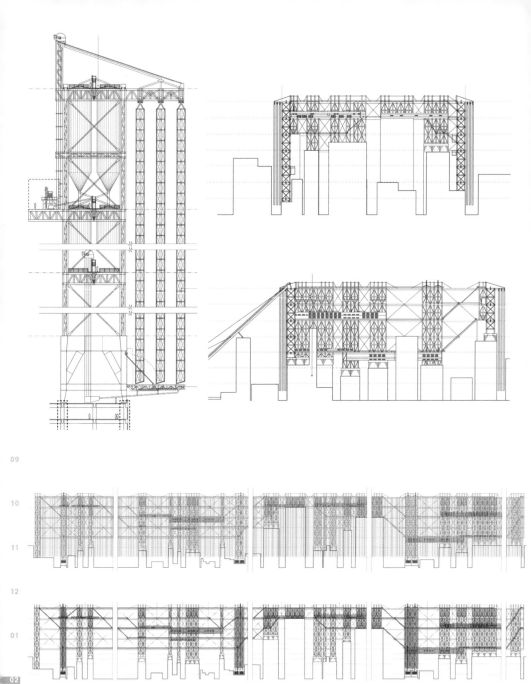

09

10

11

12

01

02

03

04

05

Drying Purification

Steep Tanks & Germ Seperation   Grinding

Gravity Table Electric Eyes &Test Pop & Voluem Test

Washing Screens & Centrifugal Seperators

Hydrolysis & Enzyme Additive & Column Enzyme

Packaging

Grinding   Protein & Soybean Added

Monica Earl, Yu Ta Lin

This studio was the third in a series that explored the mutual determinacy of architectural and urban form. The aim was to explore new models of interdependency in which architectural typologies are intrinsically destabilized by an external cause: infrastructure, plotting, and topography in conflict with one another. The studio accounted for two contemporary trends in architectural culture: the desire to be liberated from the tired and futile formal devices of design in the face of the larger collective power embodied by the city, and the relationship of internal typology and external envelopes, i.e. the relationship between interior and exterior scales of spatial articulation. Numerous strategies of architectural production were explored with the aim of producing new forms of complexity that were analogous to urban forms. Architectural composition was substituted with other processes of design, including computational techniques, that elude authorial control. The two tendencies, to merge architecture with the city and to conceive its forms by means that thwart conscious design, were made all the more acute by the case study city, Chongqing, China, where the large buildings and wide roads of Soviet-era planning are utterly incommensurate with the topography of the setting. Difficult urban circumstances were used to spur the architectural development of two programs: the theater and the hotel. In both cases, the program and its form were parameterized to permute on differently shaped sites of varying topography. A trip to China included visits to several important contemporary architectural case studies in selected cities, exploration of sites in Chongqing, and a tour of one of the leading manufacturers of building envelopes in China.

09

10

11

12

01

02

03

04

05

Type and Topography

Option Studio | Preston Scott Cohen

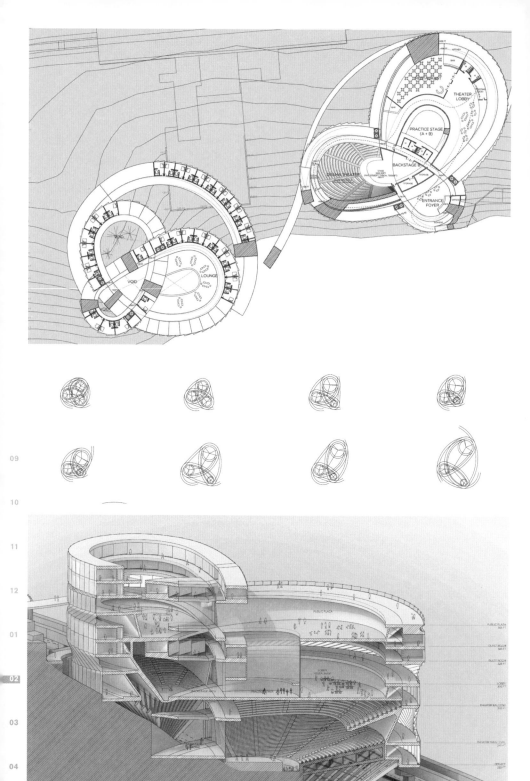

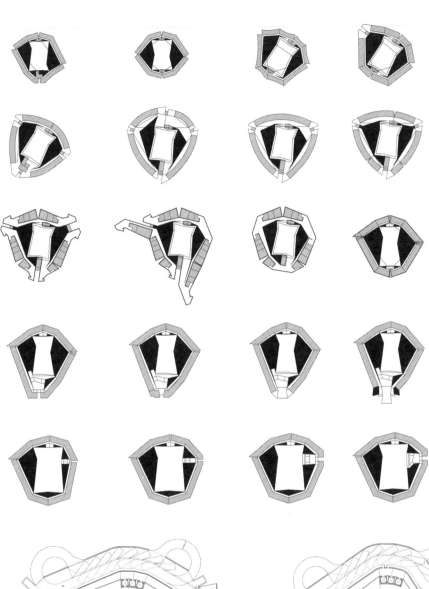

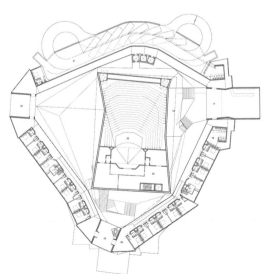

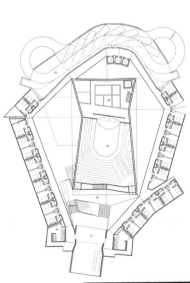

Carl D'Apolito-Dworkin

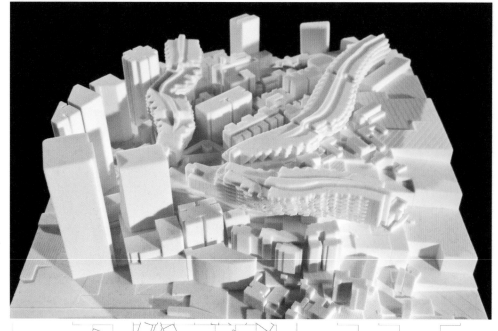

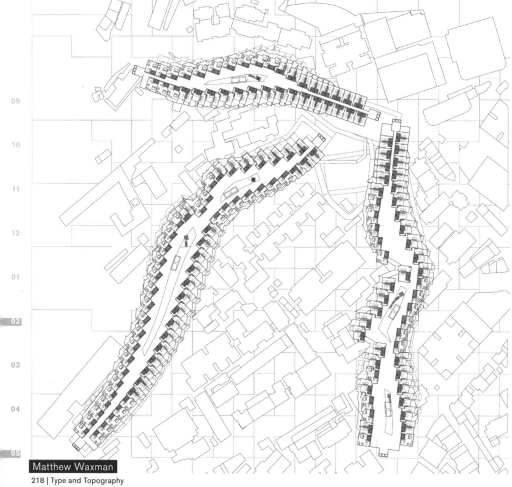

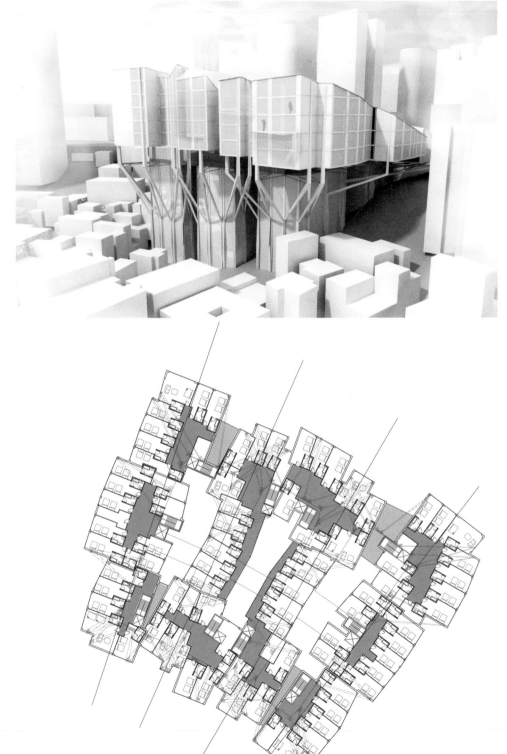

Robin Bankert
Type and Topography | 219

This studio focused on the transformation of a former airfield into a metropolitan park over a 10-year period with landscape as a medium between infrastructure and urban planning. The studio approached landscape design through topographic systems that register a more ecological urbanism in relation to existing and proposed infrastructures. The goal was to redefine the notion of the fixed master plan towards a more elaborate and flexible design process. Three-dimensional topographic maneuvers unfolded operational strategies in terms of hydrology, planting, circulation, and public events. Working with CNC technology offered an interesting analogy to landscape architecture.

Milling is a subtractive process where material is taken away from a uniform foam block. This is similar to the way landscape is modified and sculpted; earth is also subtracted or displaced. The CNC proceeds from a rough to a fine surface as bulldozers do in digging, terracing, and leveling the earth. The output of the studio included: Foam models made with the 3 axis mill, videos, axonometric, phasing diagrams, plan, sections, etc. The site was Toulouse, France.

Landscape Morphology
Option Studio | Philippe Coignet

Lisl Kotheimer

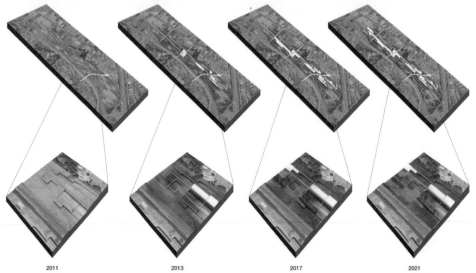

2011   2013   2017   2021

Lisl Kotheimer

Conor O'Shea

Yarinda Bunnag

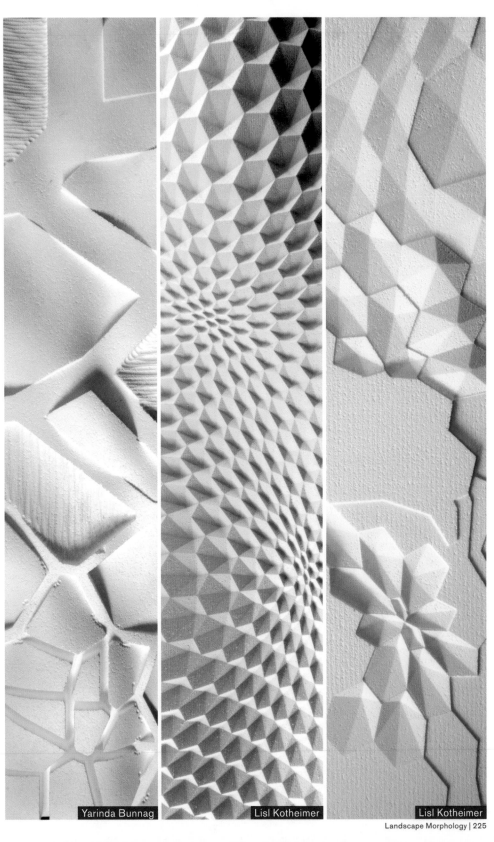

Yarinda Bunnag

Lisl Kotheimer

Lisl Kotheimer

In the context of today's debates on sustainable approaches for high-density cities, contemporary architectural practice increasingly seeks new possibilities for integrating green spaces in projects, including extensive sky terraces, living facades, vertical parks etc. Combinations of these, mixed with residential typologies, hotels, and offices, conjoin at times to produce vertical cities in which the building section becomes what the horizontal plane has entailed up to now.

In Dense+Green, students investigated these issues in the context of Singapore's Tanjong Pagar Waterfront, an approximately 150 hectare site that is currently part of one of the world's busiest ports. The area has been indentified to become Singapore's next waterfront city with a wide range of programs and uses. Being located between the old and the new city, and in close proximity to several universities, a large island resort, and the CBD area, it is meant to be packaged with large structures to deliver a plethora of spectacular buildings. The role of this studio was both to question and reason through the transformative pressure that is exerted on this particular site, and to find innovative ways of approaching the debates surrounding dense and green building typologies, taking into account their effect beyond their immediate architectural scale and interpreting them as a new collective entity.

The architectural approach explored in Dense+Green investigated ways in which the design of smaller elements such as sky gardens, as well as housing, office, and retail units can constitute the "DNA" for a large building by packing these within a three-dimensional cohesive whole. Instead of determining a priori a legible final building configuration, or deploying specific semantic preoccupations, form in Dense+Green emerged from the composition of organizational logics of the project and its programs.

09
10
11
12
01
02
03
04
05

Dense+Green

Option Studio | Thomas Schroepfer

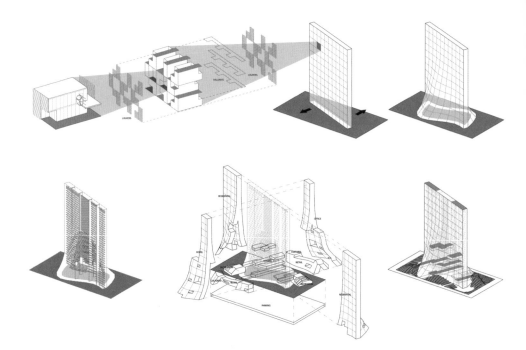

Giorgi Khmaladze

Sen Ando

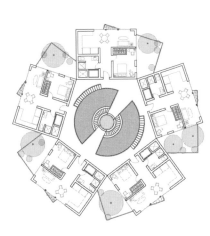
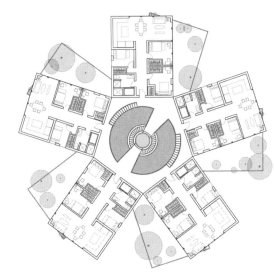

Ben Brady

The conceptual launch pad for this studio was the far-reaching question of what constitutes a knowledge space, and moreover, how such a space further facilitates the generation and dissemination of knowledge. Students explored new programs emerging within education, with projects that responded to the attendant changes implied.

The interest of the studio was simultaneously about how we can approach design, and how we can twist this approach so that we can surprise ourselves with the outcomes. The studio, hence, began with the design of a prototype to focus in on the single social interactions of a small group. The studio considered the opportunity to learn from each prototype and transition their study through a multiplication in scale, with the anticipation for repetition, proliferation, and systems thinking. Inspired by the potential interactions that each prototype generated, the studio was asked to work with an emerging knowledge institute to translate qualities from their design model throughout the building.

Education, and how we design for education, figured prominently in the remainder of the studio. How will architecture design relate to a varying field of knowledge-based typologies? Schools, community centers, universities, private research campuses, libraries, and virtual social systems formed the backdrop of our design explorations. With the acquisition of knowledge taking precedence in the twenty-first century, the concept of "collaboration" or network was interrogated to produce an expanded notion of learning spaces. The studio explored the ongoing history of education, and posited how social behaviors can be affected by the built environment, and ultimately, how knowledge spaces might be rethought.

09

10

11

12

01

02

03

04

05

Islands in Time
Option Studio | Ben Van Berkel

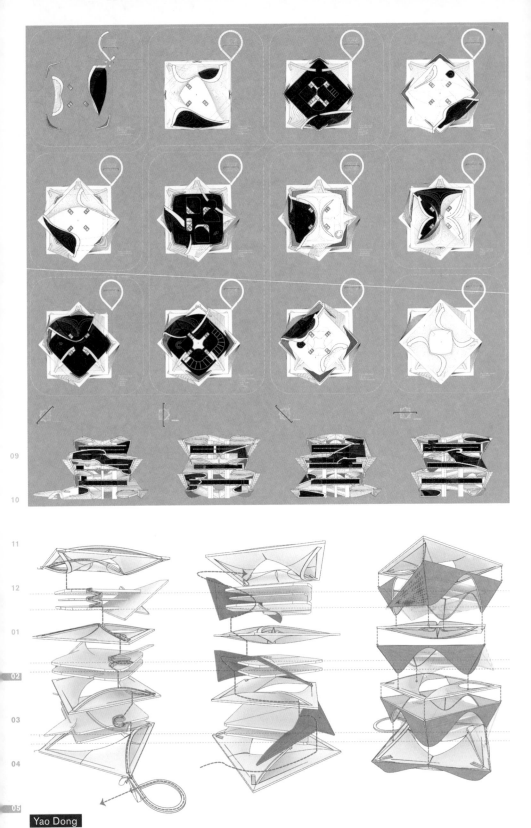

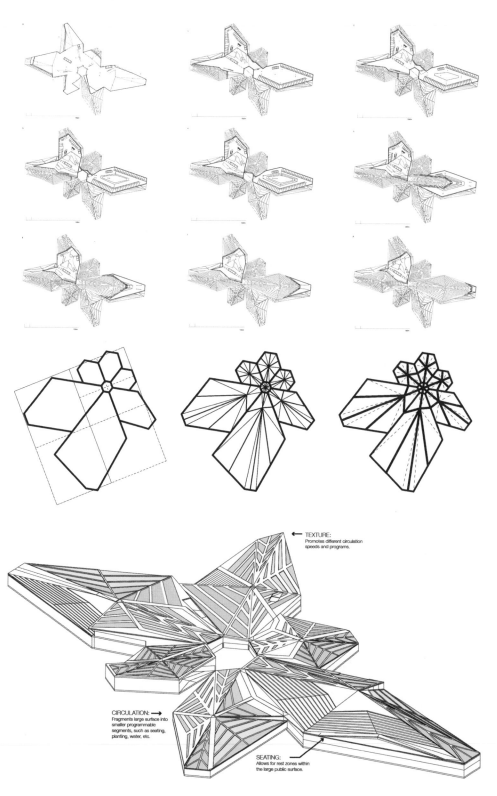

TEXTURE:
Promotes different circulation speeds and programs.

CIRCULATION: →
Fragments large surface into smaller programmable segments, such as seating, planting, water, etc.

SEATING:
Allows for rest zones within the large public surface.

The effects of climate change necessitate a radical rethinking of the role of ecology and infrastructure within the city. While the full magnitude of the problem is still unfolding, it is urgent to envision new systems for managing rising sea levels, increased storm surge, and increased population. This studio explored the development of an urban plan for an overlooked segment of lower Manhattan located between the Brooklyn and Manhattan bridges. Students were to consider that any such plan must weave disparate neighboring conditions while uniquely expressing a new strategy for the integration of adaptive soft infrastructure systems into the city. The participants were multidisciplinary teams of landscape architects, architects, and urban designers working to develop a speculative proposal for the future of the city.

The studio site was the 165 acre swath of lower Manhattan between the bridges, along the East River. This area is characterized by layers of urban planning and design histories that were evaluated and analyzed by the students in relation to future planning. In particular the studio considered the urban condition in relation to infrastructure, jurisdictions, economics, ecological considerations, and the physical qualities of the site. This work occurred across scales from the geographic to the architectural in order to engage critical thresholds in the city. The students received input and presented their work to agency leaders from the New York City Departments of Environmental Planning, Transportation, Parks and Recreation, City Planning, and the Mayors Office of Long Term Planning and Sustainability.

The New York City Commissioners Plan of 1811 was radical in its rethinking of the nature of the city: it was designed to maximize efficiency in economic and traditional urban terms. This studio was looking for an equivalent rethinking of the nature of the city in the age of climate change. The studio drew upon research developed for the Latrobe Foundation and the Rising Currents exhibition at MoMA.

Between the Bridges

Option Studio | Stephen Cassell, Susannah Drake

09
10
11

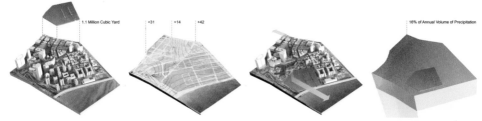

1.1 Million Cubic Yard   +31 +14 +42   16% of Annual Volume of Precipitation

12
01
02
03
04
05

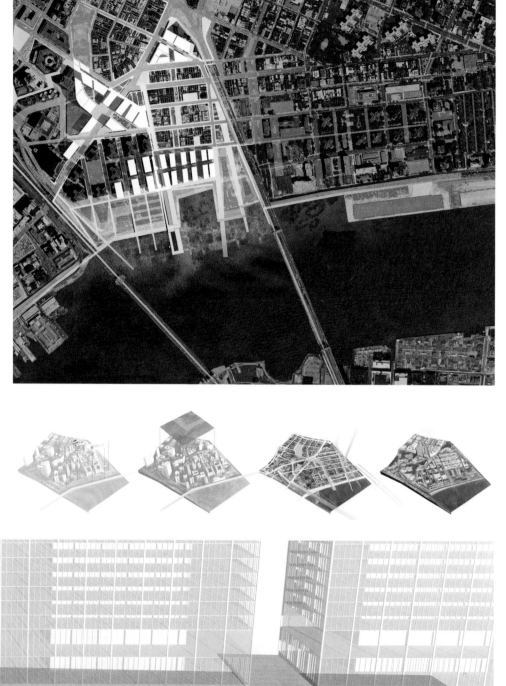

Chon Supawongse

Somkiet Chokvijitkul

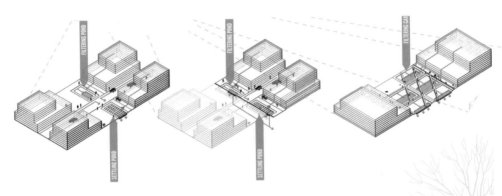

Anna Cawrse, Nina Chase

The project for this studio was a Spa Resort located in Wadi Rum, one of the most important natural history sites in Jordan. Wadi Rum is large valley cut into the sandstone and granite rock of the southern desert region. The valley covers acres of unspoiled landscape consisting of red sand dunes, rock formations, and mountains that reach up to 1,800 meters above sea level. The zone is a protected national park and is one of Jordan's most prominent tourist destinations.

The site for the project was located on the periphery of the park with an area of two square kilometers. It affords spectacular views of the surrounding mountains and the characteristics of the site itself are an extension to that of the park. The program was a twenty-room resort built around Spa facilities.

The site presents many challenges in terms of its climatic geologic and topographic properties. Its seismic activity, extreme temperature changes, sand movement, and rugged terrain make it an extremely difficult environment to navigate and inhabit. The visual character of the site is powerful and at times hostile, however, it is a delicate and fragile landscape that could be easily disturbed. It could be described as a complete and closed visual structure, which outlines and singles out any foreign element present within it. Any human intervention in that zone appears to be radically more apparent and visible than other contexts.

This studio focused on defining alternative design strategies drawn from both the extreme nature of the site itself and the substandard or harsh conditions of architectural practices in the region in general. The strands of work that outlined these strategies were based on the premise that the norms by which buildings, use, and habitation are understood and conceived cannot apply unaltered or untailored to address that particular context. In fact, a re-evaluation of certain standards, whether functional, technical and/or typological was necessary in order to devise architectural approaches that were place and culture specific. Landscape, in this sense, played an instrumental role in altering the conventions of technique as well as form and space making.

The studio also examined the idea of human adaptability to space such as landscape, shelter, interior, etc., while redefining the parameters and standards of comfort and pleasure. Program or function consequently underwent parallel mutations. Such investigations entailed a broader study of the potentials of architectural practice and production in developing countries with the strict borders and boundaries that define their culture of building. The intent was to expand such limits by accepting and adopting the parameters of building techniques, budget, craftsmanship, availability of materials and local technology. It constituted an approach that subverts from within, and that proposes change by an economy of means and by precise transformations to the constituents of building processes. The change, though not necessarily radical, opens a field of possibilities or forms experimental platforms by which the evolution of architecture in a given place may be manipulated and directed.

The studio articulated and defined design driven strategies by internalizing the particular conditions of place, context, and culture into an architectural discourse that aims to transform from within.

Architecture, in Extremes:
A Spa in Wadi Rum, Jordan
Option Studio / Sahel Al Hiyari

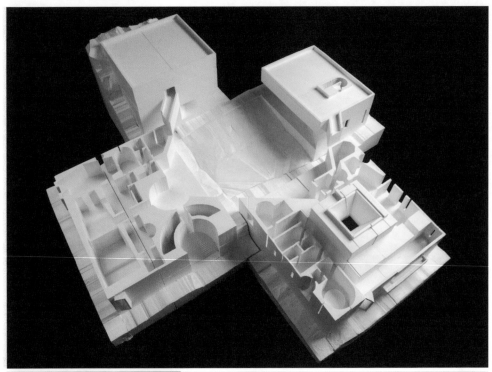

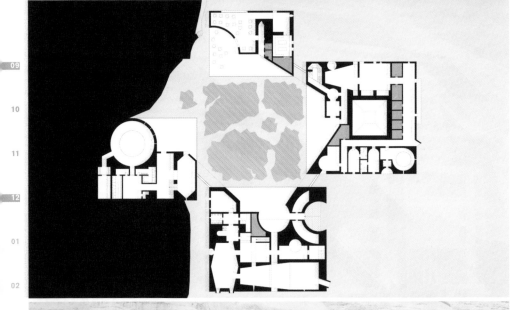

Andre Passos

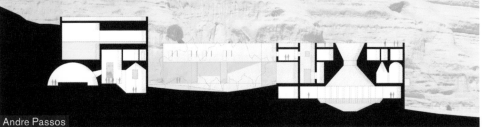

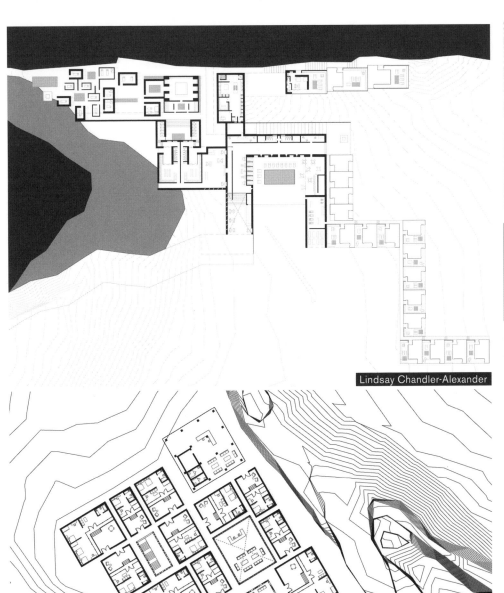

Lindsay Chandler-Alexander

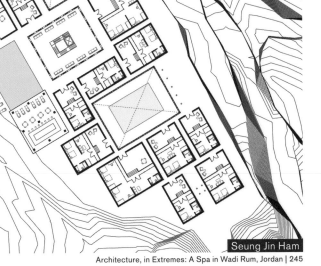

Seung Jin Ham

Sebastien Marot: Sub-urbanism is a word that I started to use when looking at the work of landscape architects in the early 90s in France and Europe. This is how I summarize, for me, what they were doing, what they were bringing to the field of urbanism. I would say that they carried with them a kind of subversion of traditional urbanism that would go from site to program. Instead of being in composition, looking for an equilibrium between the given of the site and the given of the program, they would go from site to program, that they dreamt of a way of engendering the program from the site itself, a kind of poetic or [inaudible] of design that I thought was very interesting. Of course, I was and I am aware that another subversion of urbanism coming from one of the most creative vanguards of architecture at that time did exactly the reverse, engendering the site from the program, using the program as a way to produce, literally, a programmatic carpet or tapestry. I like both, actually. I'm interested in both.

09

But I think that super-urbanism, as I call it, has an undeserved advantage on sub-urbanism. And that undeserved advantage is that it has a hero, 10 a fantastic poet whose name is Rem Koolhaas, who provided super-urbanism not only with a fantastic project, but also with a manifesto, *Delirious New York*, which I consider as the undisputed manifesto for 11 super-urbanism, for that way of designing. And Koolhaas transported the field of landscape architecture itself, that super-urbanist way of designing with his famous project for La Villette. La Villette, a place where today we 12 have what I consider one of the masterpieces of sub-urbanism, meaning the bamboo garden dug into the depth of this industrial ground here.

01 So I thought the two things are so symmetrically opposed that it would be good to do a relative manifesto for sub-urbanism, relative for two reasons. Relative because I do not intend to advocate sub-urbanism absolutely in 02 every circumstance, but relatively. And relative also because it would be relative to that of Rem Koolhaas by turning his manifesto upside down, if possible, so I could use his to shape this little manifesto. But he has 03 Manhattan as a site for his manifesto, a fantastic site, what a powerful site. And I didn't find any powerful site where I could do that demonstration with the same—I thought I had found one when—I remarked to myself, I 04 noted that several people, several figures that I was interested in, at some point had been in the little city of Ithaca in upstate New York.

05

Palimpsestuous Ithaca:
A Relative Manifesto for Sub-Urbanism

Frederick Law Olmsted Lecture   Sebastien Marot

Sebastien Marot

This thesis is an exploration of the space of social discourse between the academy and the public domain. The academy has surely earned its reputation as the ivory tower since its policies of exclusion are not relegated only to their admissions processes but also to their physical campuses which are frequently surrounded by walls and gates and comprise buildings which are set off from their contexts; deferring to the normative horizontal-vertical plane relationships.

As progeny of the agora, the academy has enjoyed a historically divergent relationship with the public square, which has evolved into its own horizontal and barren form. Harvard square, with its history of academia and commons, and strict adherence to the normative boundary conditions that have come to define and reinforce them typologically is the site of this intervention.

Internally, this exploration is a reinvention of traditional academic program by locating diverse disciplines in the same space, and creating individual academic territories for depth of expertise, and collective academic territories for broad-spectrum, problem-based collaboration and exploration across those disciplines. Externally, public commons amenities, already in place on the site in the form of retail, transportation, points of historical interest and places of assembly, are impressed on the envelope of the building creating an involution of the normative boundary condition.

The first spatial strategy is the creation of a smooth condition to dissolve a discreetly defined horizontal and vertical as part of site circulation and create a continuity between the spaces of public transportation, street-level pedestrian circulation and the vertically organized spaces of academic production. Circulation moves vertically and obliquely in a closed looping spiral, broken only to allow access. Staccato movements of the former site circulation yield to the legato openness of the public commons.

The second strategy is performing operations of exceptional differentiation in the friction zones where the public program encounters the collective spaces of the academic program which are enhanced though distillation. These "organs" overlay functionality as disruption, horizontal with the oblique, and respite within instability. The shearing of the form into a klein bottle condition yields hierarchy and when experienced as a whole create an experience of programmatic ambivalence, which defy the normal relationships of these programs.

As an urban object, this ambiguity is further accentuated as the building is deferential to its contextual massing, appearing similar in its solidity from a distance, but also highly porous, cradling the bright center of its creative energy as public commons.

09
10
11
12
01
02
03
04
05

Innovation Commons

MArch Thesis | Daniel Sullivan

Advisor | Eric Howeler

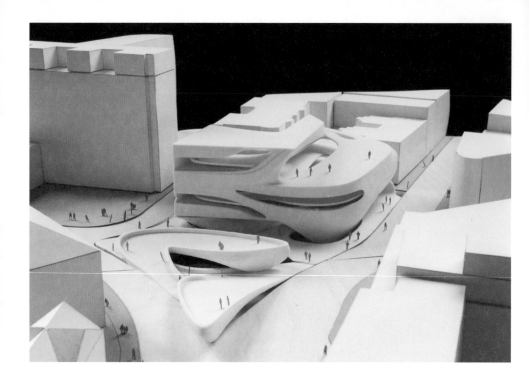

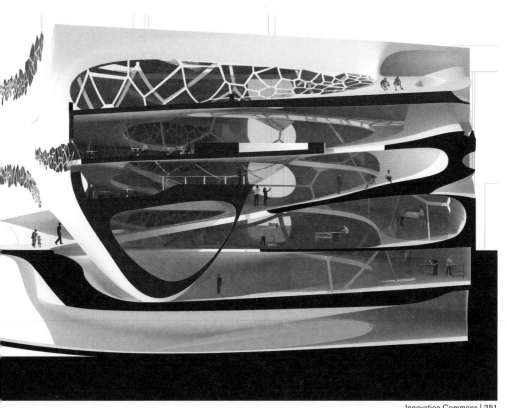

The rapid shrinking of Lake Chad—by over 90% in the past 40 years—is emblematic of increasing global water insecurity. The Food and Agriculture Organization calls the shrinking an "ecological catastrophe" and warns of an impending humanitarian disaster without a radical change in water management practices.

With or Without Water does not try to "save" Lake Chad, but instead considers how technologies used to prevent desertification and sustain livelihoods in the Lake Chad Basin can be designed to succeed where they have previously failed. Shelterbelt plantings are paired with transportation infrastructure and incrementally deployed as Lake Chad's shoreline recedes. The system provides a resilient scaffold for future rural development—with or without water.

This Thesis works at three different scales—the lake, the town, and the linear system. Three scenarios are identified for water resources in the Lake Chad basin: (1) with water (2) status quo and (3) without water. Whichever scenario occurs, the basin is expected to experience increasing desertification, in turn resulting in increasing food insecurity.

The primary technology currently employed to prevent desertification across the Sahel region of Africa is shelterbelts. Shelterbelts decrease evapotranspiration and wind erosion to improve crop yields by up to 140%. In the past a series of physical design and program flaws contributed to project failure; after studying these, I developed a new methodology for planting shelterbelts in the Lake Chad Basin. In addition to basic orientation and spacing lessons learned, one of the most successful shelterbelt projects paired planting with road infrastructure to develop both simultaneously. My approach responds to two needs on the lake—the need for better transportation infrastructure and increased crop production.

A series of infrastructure typologies respond to the range of conditions encountered throughout the lake area. When combined, these typologies act as a long linear system, with the transportation network as the backbone for shelterbelt construction.

To deploy this joint shelterbelt and transportation system, I focused on the shifting edge of the lake moving in response to changing climatic conditions. This edge consists of a gradient of moisture regimes supporting different livelihoods ranging from farming to fishing. Baga, a town on the northern Nigeria on the lake's edge, served as a case study for the deployment of the shelterbelt system. The town has moved several times to follow the lake's changing shoreline. Shelterbelts are concentrated in two areas: along linear roads extending from the lake's edge and around villages with arable land. Though the community may no longer have access to water based resources, preventing future desertification before it can begin will build the resilience of local populations to the unpredictable climate of Lake Chad.

The resulting shelterbelt road systems across the basin will provide a solid backbone for development, providing 250,000+ ha of arable land and access to local and regional markets, healthcare, and education. Instead of wasting the growing drive of both local and international communities to "save the lake" on a large-scale water infrastructure project, this work proposes an adaptive infrastructural scaffold to build the resilience of ecosystems and populations to water scarcity and desertification.

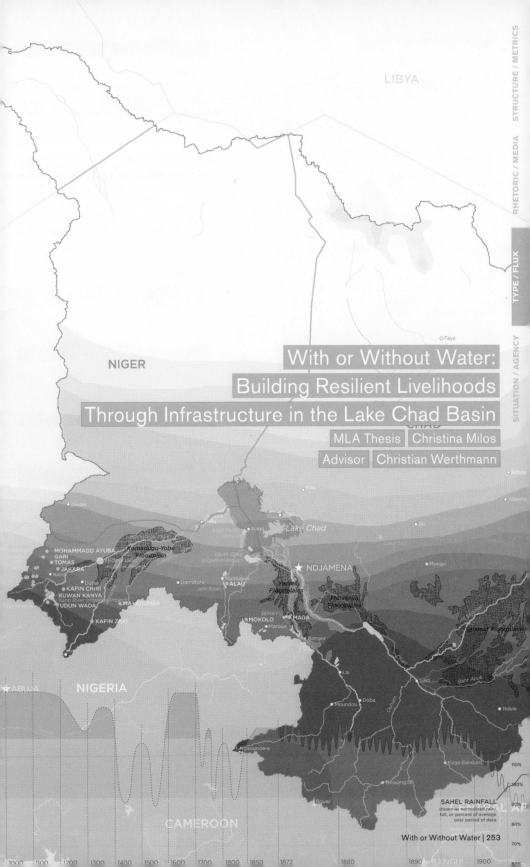

With or Without Water:
Building Resilient Livelihoods
Through Infrastructure in the Lake Chad Basin

MLA Thesis | Christina Milos
Advisor | Christian Werthmann

SAHEL RAINFALL
shown as normalized rain-
fall, or percent of average
over period of data

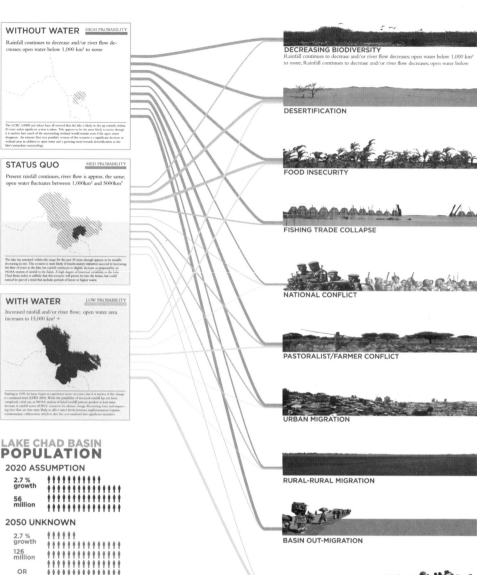

WITHOUT WATER
HIGH PROBABILITY

Rainfall continues to decrease and/or river flow decreases; open water below 1,000 km² to none

STATUS QUO
MED PROBABILITY

Present rainfall continues, river flow is approx. the same; open water fluctuates between 1,000km² and 5000km²

WITH WATER
LOW PROBABILITY

Increased rainfall and/or river flow; open water area increases to 15,000 km² +

DECREASING BIODIVERSITY
Rainfall continues to decrease and/or river flow decreases; open water below 1,000 km² to none, Rainfall continues to decrease and/or river flow decreases; open water below

DESERTIFICATION

FOOD INSECURITY

FISHING TRADE COLLAPSE

NATIONAL CONFLICT

PASTORALIST/FARMER CONFLICT

URBAN MIGRATION

RURAL-RURAL MIGRATION

BASIN OUT-MIGRATION

BASIN IN-MIGRATION

LAKE CHAD BASIN
POPULATION

2020 ASSUMPTION

2.7 %
growth

56
million

2050 UNKNOWN

2.7 %
growth

126
million

OR

? %
growth

?
million

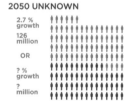

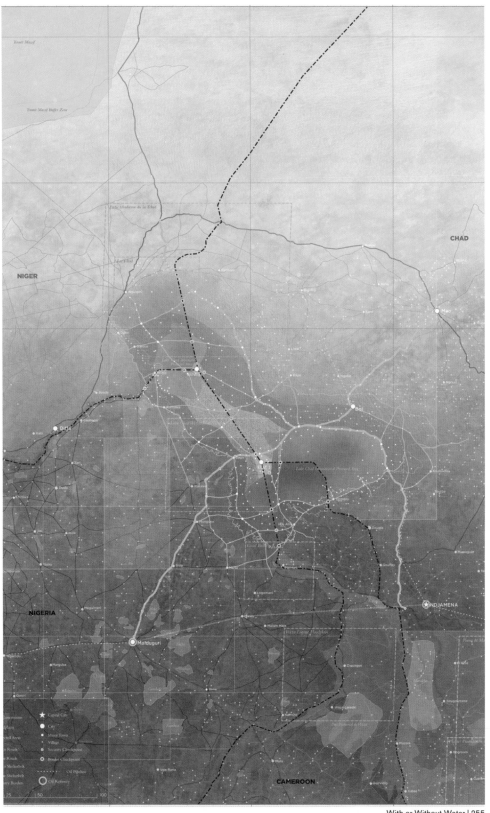

CHAD

NIGER

NIGERIA

CAMEROON

Maiduguri

N'DJAMENA

Mao

Diffa

★ Capital City
● City
● Major Town
● Village
◉ Security Checkpoint
◎ Border Checkpoint
Oil Pipeline
Oil Refinery

25   50   100

Richmond, Virginia is a place of conflict and of paradox. Over it a history of both oppression and achievement hangs, overshadowing the present in a way that defines it. It is a city of firsts and of lasts; it is a city of ruins and of monuments. It is in this context that we encounter the unknown object. It is both on the margins and at the center. It is on the highest hill, straddling the lowest valley. It is found embedded on its forgotten and shabby site between a trio of emblems to the varied stages of the city's history: an early plantation home now converted to a convent, the church in which Patrick Henry gave the speech that enflamed the fledgling colonies of the American South to revolution, and a spare concrete radio tower designed by Philip Johnson at the height of the modern age. Amongst these icons, the Public Boarding School establishes a firm and yet porous boundary with its plinth. Rising above this strongly horizontal datum, the quizzical expression of the unknowable monument ripples and distends out and across the site. It is the tower above the plinth. It is a blank object that both captures and defines the essence of a city in need of an anachronistic and dynamic departure from itself. In its extremity it is reaching to push beyond its formal and programmatic typological expectations in order to attain a distinct and enigmatic other.

It is through the extremity and inordinate grandeur of this monumental urban gesture that the paradoxical relationship between the subject and object becomes apparent. The school is organized in such a way that all members of the junior year high school classes of the metropolitan districts of Richmond have the option of living in this environment for a single semester. This finite time period is spent exploring and understanding the unknowable environment of the school that is at once exuberant and restrained. Its place of prominence over the city privileges the individuals, while its public nature denies exceptionalism. The Public Boarding School is introduced into the lives of the city's students in a brief and ephemeral way, leaving a lasting impact. The students elope into an experience not unlike summer camp, given the opportunity to shed preconceptions and pursue an educational mission uniquely personal to them. Through this personal improvisation, the individual is invited to engage with peers in an open and vast yet intimate environment.

Each level of the tower carries housing sandwiched between communally shared elements such that no single living unit is situated at the true top or bottom of the building. All units are related to one another as much horizontally as vertically, and organized on floor plates contiguous with other programs. Frequently punctuated by open volumes and multiply redundant circulation methods, the tower is a vertically suspended maze where no one path coincides experientially with the next. Alternately, the podium carries all classroom and support spaces, and is organized with a playful relationship to an artificially and relentlessly fragmented ground plane. In this setting, the constantly shifting route of progress through a given day gives way to discovery on the personal as well as social scale.

Public Boarding School

MArch Thesis | Kevin Hirth

Advisor | Mack Scogin

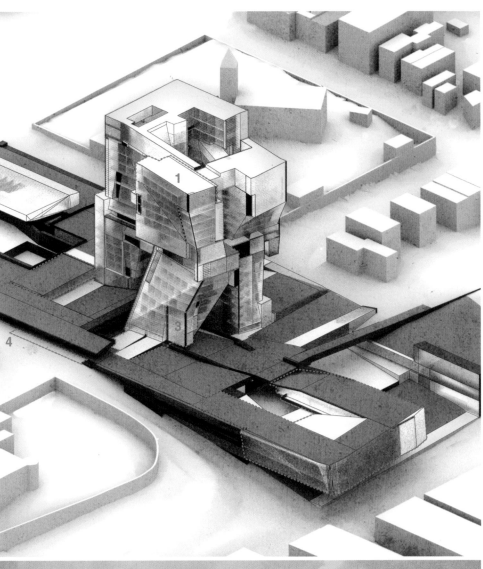

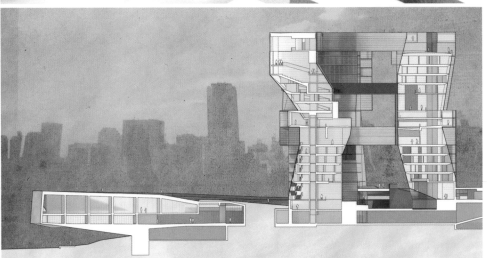

The objective of this thesis is an attempt to argue for the use of the bridge as an organizing device in urbanism through the way it can systematically construct the visuality of the city and break down our perception of geography. This study is conducted through an analysis of bridge types of the city, and ways that the use of larger mobility infrastructure can systematically compress geography into visual consumption using the panorama. Further, the Urban Bridge was constructed in a time when bridges needed to vault over existing waterfront harbors, activate the z-axis, and register dramatic obliques into the depths of the grid of the city that maintain themselves as a part of the fabric, while also preserving their own discrete worlds within the region. This urbanistic duality of being discrete and meshed parts of the city, is a project that has been sought within various architectural proposals of the past ten years, and posits for the proposal of an infrastructural urban architecture beyond the liminal functionality of infrastructure into an elevation of the idea of formal worldliness.

The thesis is manifested as a test within the island of Manhattan as the ultimate conceptual realization of the dense center to rural periphery exemplified under the twentieth century model of urbanism known as Manhattanism. Manhattanism has run its course in the history of urbanism; the eponymous city within which it was founded is ready to breed a new paradigm. This new "Morphed Manhattanism" promotes an inter-regionalism whereas Manhattanism promoted isolationism. It subverts the center-periphery relationship established in that old order in light of a dispersed model. As Manhattanism reaches its grave, so too does its verticalized architecture; new archetypes are spawned on a regional order based in infrastructural connectivity and large-scale agendas. The transfiguration of the city pulls the worlds from the captivity of the grid and creates a new understanding of worldliness in architecture, bridging between continental divide while simultaneously maintaining the old interiority. The island is broken—its shores have been breached.

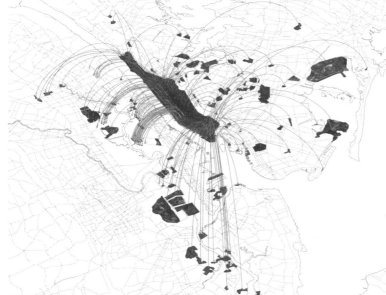

Morphing Manhattanism

MAUD Thesis | Jonathan Scelsa

Advisor | Hashim Sarkis

2011 Urban Planning and Design Thesis Prize

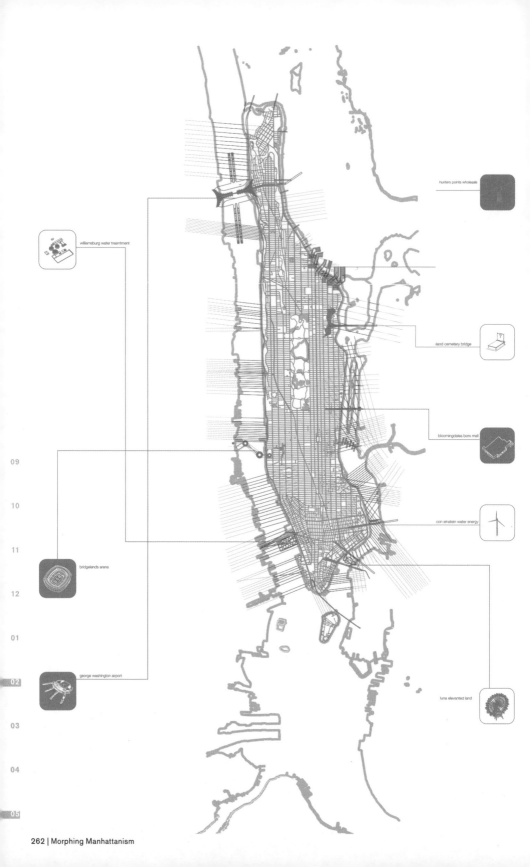

hunters points wholesale

williemsburg water treatment

land cemetery bridge

bloomingdales boro mall

09

10

con einstein water energy

11

12

bridgelands arena

01

02

george washington airport

03

luna elevanted land

04

05

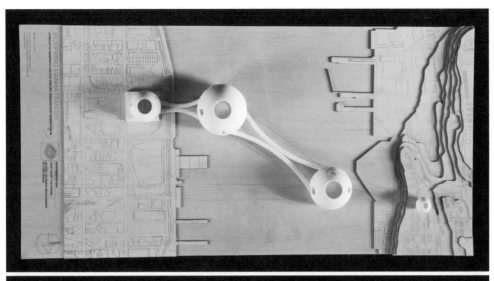

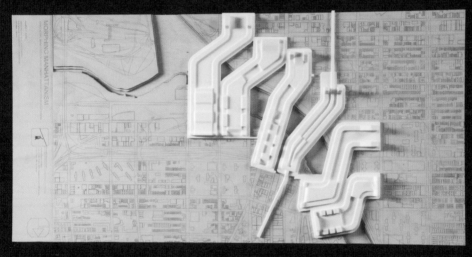

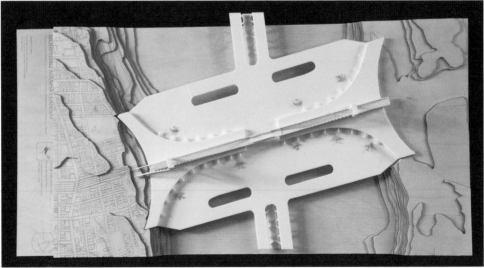

Mohsen Mostafavi: I think many of you know that over the past couple of years we've been trying to do more and more things of course on a range of topics both in dealing with urban issues, landscape issues, and architecture. But I think it's also clear that today it's really critical for us as a school to be engaged with issues related to the evolution and development of our urban environments. What kind of urban environments are we to live in? What is our responsibility? How are we to design these places and how are we to think about them? And I think if we are to think about these places, we of course need to not only think about the design of them, but we really need to think about the circumstances, the conditions that go into the imagination, the imagining of future urban environments in a way. In anticipation of some of these ideas of course we did, for example, the year before last and then the publication that followed on *Ecological Urbanism* and many other discussions.

These were focusing more specifically on issues of sustainability and its relationship to processes of urbanization. I think the emphasis now is for us to find other venues, if ecological urbanism was only one way, is really to develop multiple discourses that relate to processes of urbanization. So we want now, with your help, with your support, to really put on the table other ways of dealing with this urban issue, with this urban question.

It also seems that when we are dealing with the question of design, one of the things that I think is more and more common is the issue of scenarios, of alternative scenarios for design. And I think today's presentation and tomorrow's, in some ways without us being too explicit, have tried to create the right kinds of circumstances and framework for developing that concept of scenario, or scenario planning if you like, in relation to urban environments.

It's a colloquium that is by definition a sort of collaborative colloquium because we have people who are coming from their background in design but also people who come from literature, from social sciences. And this dimension of people from multiple disciplines working together is not just about being cross-disciplinary but it's actually one of the things that makes it absolutely necessary if we are going to construct, if you like, an alternative framework for imagining cities of the future, that we need that help. We need to think together for that sort of alternative way of thinking.

Beirut

264 | In the Life of Cities: Parallel Narratives of the Urban

In the Life of Cities:
Parallel Narratives of the Urban
Conference | Various Speakers

Preston Scott Cohen in Chongqing, China
Photo: Stephanie Lin

Rahul Mehrotra in Mumbai, India
Photo: Ken Yip

Ben Van Berkel & Imola Berczi in Amsterdam, Netherlands
Photo: Carl Koepcke

Sahel Al Hiyari in Wadi Rum, Jordan
Photo: Ricardo Munoz

Sahel Al Hiyari in Wadi Rum, Jordan
Photo: Ricardo Munoz

Jorge Silvetti in Rio de Janeiro, Brazil
Photo: James Leng

Anton Garcia-Abril in Madrid, Spain
Photo: Shanshan Qi

SITUATION and AGENCY highlight design work located strategically within explicit mechanisms of power, supported by expanded concepts of context and temporality.

As part of the Divine Comedy exhibition at Harvard three artists, Tomás Saraceno, Olafur Eliasson, and Ai Weiwei, were brought together by curator Sanford Kwinter. However, during the moderated discussion panel on April 8, 2011, Ai Weiwei was conspicuously absent. The Chinese conceptual artist and outspoken critic was arrested five days earlier by Chinese police and held at an undisclosed location for almost three months.

Ai Weiwei's absence during the GSD event highlighted the inherent risks of political activism as well as the political dimension of design practice. It also emphasized the current need for political engagement and **AGENCY** in design. Decisions related to organization, material, and energy have an inherent political dimension and therefore, power. By strategically locating the scope and target of design, contemporary practices work effectively within and upon the built environment, impacting the way we live, work, consume, and govern.

Simultaneously, we are increasingly conscious of the "nowness" of design. The concepts of site and **SITUATION** are expanded to include temporal, political, cultural, and disciplinary contexts. This contemporaneity of design becomes highly self-conscious by leveraging the non-physical particularities of its own context. The temporality of phased implementation, the duration of an installation, and the afterlife of materials reinforce an understanding of design as an interconnected, contemporary activity.

SITUATION and **AGENCY** highlight design work located strategically within explicit mechanisms of power, supported by expanded concepts of context and situation. The Architecture Core IV studio, coordinated by Timothy Hyde, looked at codes and computation as means of designing urban architecture through formal and informal constraints and conventions. Rahul Mehrotra's *Extreme Urbanism* option studio brought together interdisciplinary and interdepartmental teams to address issues of informal urbanism within Mumbai's rapidly evolving center. Kathryn Soven's MArch thesis project, *The Liminal Space of Emplacement*, takes the UNHCR's manual for refugee housing as its object of inquiry. The thesis seeks to address the system from within, improving the living conditions of refugees through redesign of the regulations themselves. These examples demonstrate agile design work that attempts to be impactful by strategically engaging the forces and temporalities through which design happens.

Situation /
Agency

Much of the literature about urban development today presents cosmopolis as the inevitable outcome of globalization with which we have to contend. World migration patterns towards the urban, collective ecological risks, and the global economy are generating intense but ultimately undesirable cities. We have benefited enormously from two decades of rigorous documentation and analysis of this condition, but this literature persists in describing these phenomena within the confines of nation states, through gradients of density and centrality such as urban-suburban-rural and with conventional land-use categories that overlook many of the radically different morphologies and typologies that are emerging. Ultimately, many of these methodologies compromise the originality and potentials of emerging forms of settlement.

Increasingly, designers are being compelled to address and transform larger contexts and to give these contexts more legible and expressive form. Problems that had been confined to the domains of engineering, ecology, or regional planning are now looking for articulation through design. This situation has opened up a range of technical and formal possibilities that had been previously out of reach for designers. The need to address these "geographic" aspects has also encouraged designers to re-examine their tools and develop means to link together attributes that had been understood as either separate from or external to their disciplines.

Yet engaging the geographic does not only mean a shift in scale. This has also come to affect the formal repertoire of architecture, even at a smaller scale, with more architects becoming interested in forms that reflect the geographic connectedness of architecture, by its ability to bridge between the very large and the very small or to provide forms that embody geographic references.

Curiously, while most of the research around these different attributes has tended to be quite intense, the parallel tracks of inquiry have remained disconnected. For example, the discussion about continuous surfaces in architecture ignores the importance of continuity of ground in landscape ecology. This seminar did not propose that a common cause is driving these different geographic tendencies but it did insist that a synthesis is possible, even necessary, in order to expand on the formal possibilities of architecture and its social role.

We are seeing an increasing number of new interdisciplinary positions that try to adequately respond to the complexity of the problem, like landscape-now-ecological urbanism or post-metropolitan studies, but these positions are ultimately too preoccupied with the nature of their inter-disciplinarity and not focused enough on the formal consequences of their undertaking.

The course proposed that we cast the question of human settlements at the scale of the world, that we can identify new spatial patterns that transcend the limitations of cosmopolis and help us imagine a better city-world. The course focused on the emerging geographies of urban regions, infrastructures, new urban conglomerations, mega-forms, and on the emergence of new geo-aesthetics. The city-world is not the opposite of the world-city or the global city or of cosmopolis. The city-world is the possibility of imagining the spatial parameters, geometries, land-uses, infrastructures that connect the world and make us actively take part in its description and construction as a totality.

New Geographies:
Imagining a City-World Beyond Cosmopolis

Seminar | Hashim Sarkis

P Merrill, T Wolcott, A Garlock, J Doran, J Leng, L Sun, S Ellmam, C Garunay, M Ha

T Renwick, A Dharwadker, M Verges,N Croft, W Quattlebaum, C Vinals, Y Lin, M Klemens, E MacWillie

G Kroeber, R Madson, J Crisman, R Maliszewski, D Cho, B Kellogg, B Cranston, Y Cheng, H Disch

G Kroeber, R Madson, J Crisman, R Maliszewski, D Cho, B Kellogg, B Cranston, Y Cheng, H Disch

C O'Shea, J Linkus, D Ibanez, R Miguel, S Lee, Y Bunnag, M Kameni, F Masoud, A Passos

P Merrill, T Wolcott, A Garlock, J Doran, J Leng, L Sun, S Ellmam, C Garunay, M Ha

C O'Shea, J Linkus, D Ibanez, R Miguel, S Lee, Y Bunnag, M Kameni, F Masoud, A Passos

Architecture acts in and upon the city through mediums of code—building codes, zoning codes, civil codes, social codes, environmental codes, representational codes. The design of architecture in the city is less the design of objects than it is the configuration of multiple and differentiated codes into new sequences and relations.

A code is a systematic arrangement of relationships that specifies the legitimate and illegitimate functions of the objects, images, behaviors, or processes that are contained within its purview. Codes may be statutory or customary; preventative or exhortatory; formal or informal; artificial or biological. Codes may be expressed textually or graphically or with gestures, colors, or sounds. The contemporary city is a dense mesh of codes, overlapping one another in complementary and contradictory ways. To undertake an act of design in the city is to enter into this frantic dialogue of codes. For whether that act of design begins from the perspective of economics and finance, or politics and communities, or forms and images, the codes exist in advance, as property rights, real estate pro forma, mass transit capacities, closing times, marriage laws, traffic signals, or historic overlay districts. In addition, even as it becomes the corollary of these external codes, architecture carries along its own embedded codes—conventions that regulate forms and representations, parametric scripts that define the conditional logics of design, standards that govern the behavior of architects or the sequences of fabrications. The density of these external and internal codes and the fluidity of their presence have only increased in the digital restructuring of the contemporary city, and this in turn has only increased the urgency of a new architectural fluency in and a new architectural attention to the medium of codes.

The last in the sequence of core Architecture studios explored the design of codes and design through codes in order to carry forward the ongoing experiment that is architecture in the city. The work of the studio was to constitute a piece of urban fabric in New York City, understood and realized as a structure of coding, and to design architectural elements, also governed by explicit codes, within this structure. These elements are architectural objects that through their design are able to convey ramifications outward into the codes that structured them and into their relationships with other objects that surround them. To this end, the work undertaken in the studio was collaborative throughout, with each project realized in negotiation with other designed elements and codes. From the scale of collective urban configurations proceeding through to specificities of position, shape, and image, the mode of design was the formulation and manipulation of codes. The goal was not to confirm the priority of existing structures of code, but to produce, through architecture, new sequences of code that formulate a future of the city.

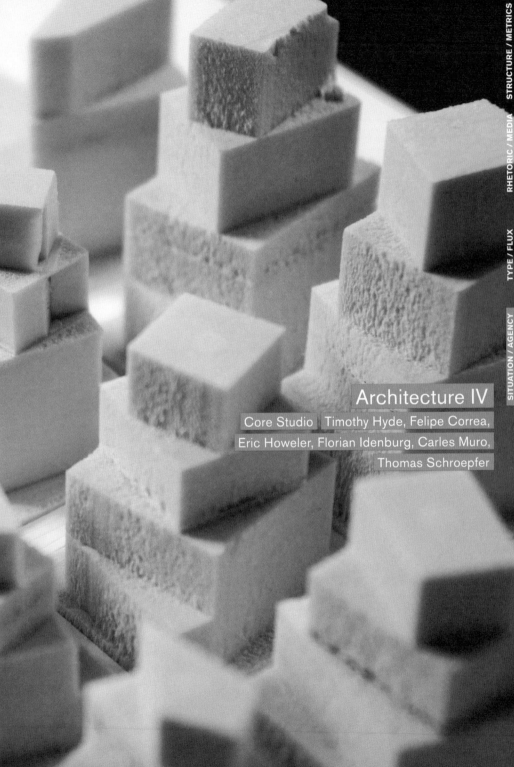

Architecture IV

Core Studio | Timothy Hyde, Felipe Correa,
Eric Howeler, Florian Idenburg, Carles Muro,
Thomas Schroepfer

Michael Smith

Taylor Dover, Tristie Tajima, Alison Von Glinow

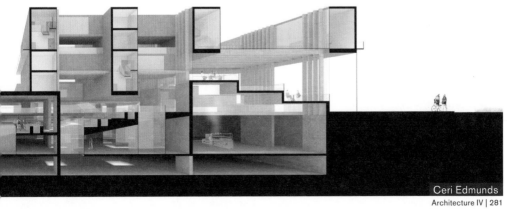

Ceri Edmunds

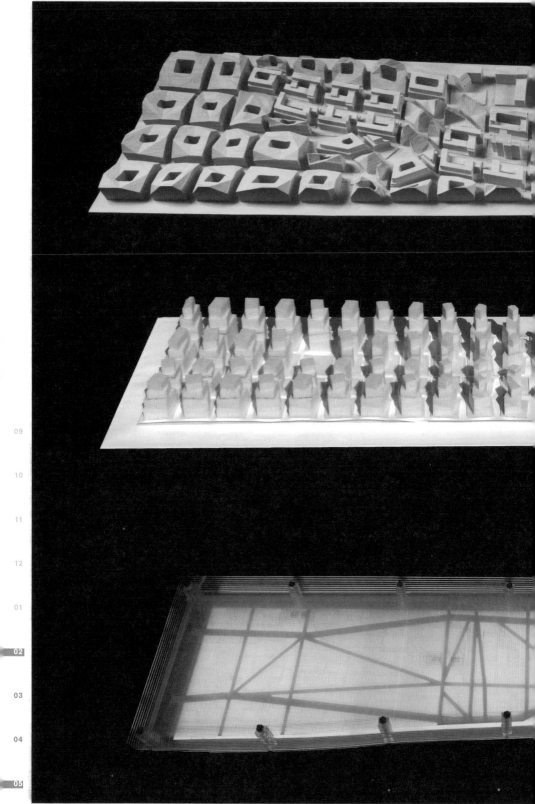

09

10

11

12

01

02

03

04

05

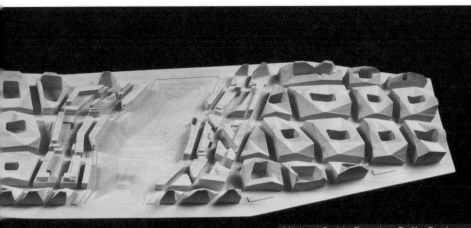

Michael Smith, Brandon Cuffy, Sookyung Chun

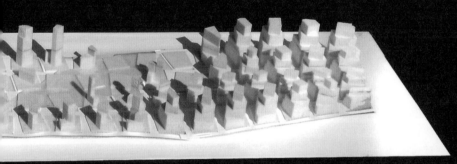

Jeung Eun Lee, Trey Kirk, Judy Fulton

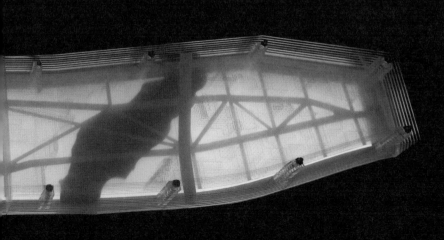

Arielle Assouline Lichten, Drew Cowdrey, Mark Pomarico

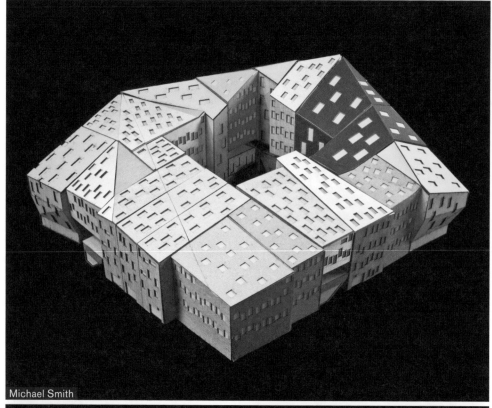

Michael Smith

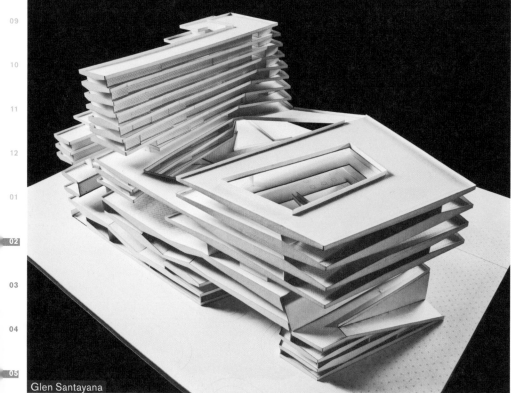

Glen Santayana

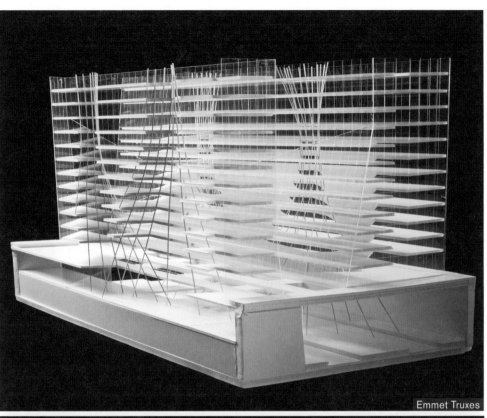

Emmet Truxes

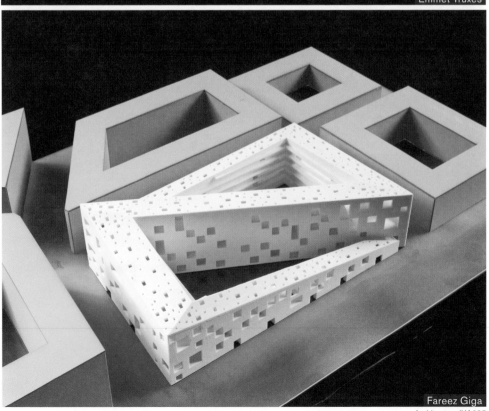

Fareez Giga

Glen Santayana

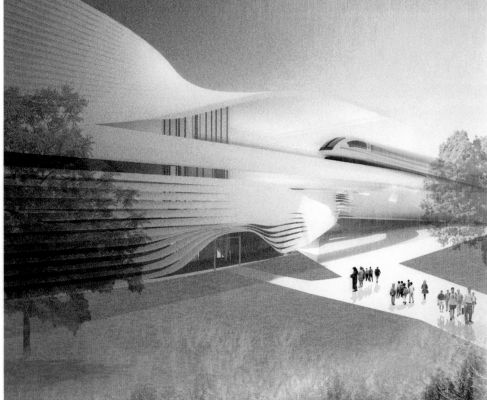

Conway Pedron

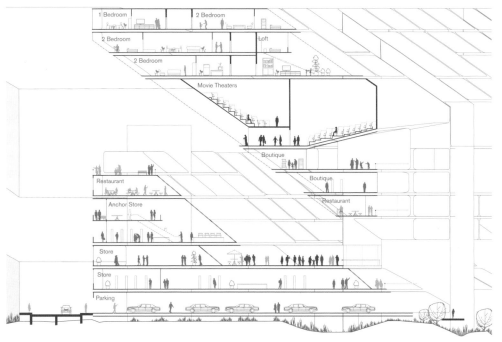

1 Bedroom
2 Bedroom
2 Bedroom
Loft
2 Bedroom
Movie Theaters
Boutique
Boutique
Restaurant
Restaurant
Anchor Store
Store
Store
Parking

Manuel Diaz

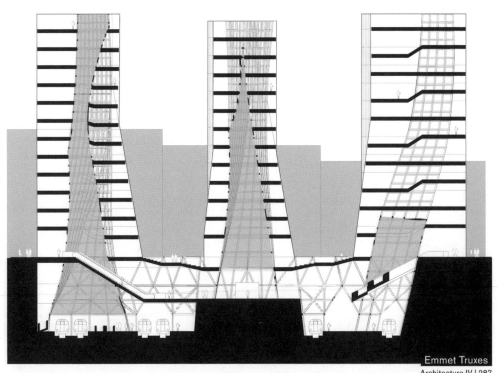

Emmet Truxes

The second semester Landscape Architecture core studio explored the research and design methods associated with interventions in complex urban conditions: sites layered with multiple interventions across a long span of history that present issues of connectivity, accessibility, identity, and need for contemporary programs. Students learned to apply various forms of research—historical, social, material, spatial, and technical—to the formulation of project arguments and strategies. The studio worked with two sites that have different scales, contexts, material expression, and organization, that are the result of different urban processes, and that contain different program.

The first site, City Hall Plaza in Boston, has been in an ongoing process of transformation since the founding of the city in 1630. Currently it is a 7.5 acre paved plaza, designed and built between 1963–68 by the Boston architecture firm Kallman McKinnell Wood, following a master plan by I.M. Pei. Forty years after its construction, the plaza remains a highly controversial space, inhospitable for the everyday user on the one hand, and one of very few event spaces in the city on the other.

The second site, a 70 acre golf course, is also part of a historic landscape, Frederick Law Olmsted's Franklin Park designed in 1885, at the confluence of three distinct neighborhoods: Jamaica Plain, Roxbury, and Dorchester. In their research, students explored the full range of processes that are at work on the site, describing its extent (surfaces), its depth (layers, literal and symbolic), and its flows (material, temporal, social, economic). Emphasis was placed on exploring the relationship between documentation, analytical research, and design through diverse conceptual frameworks that bridged between a retrospective understanding of the site (how it came to be the way it is now) and a projective attitude toward its future (how it could become something else). Strategic interventions, rather than complete erasure of the existing, opened a dialogue between past, present, and future, and between broad conceptual motivations and the instrumentality of specific design operations.

09

10

11

12

01

02

03

04

05

Landscape Architecture II

Core Studio | Anita Berrizbeitia

Holly Clarke, Jill Desimini

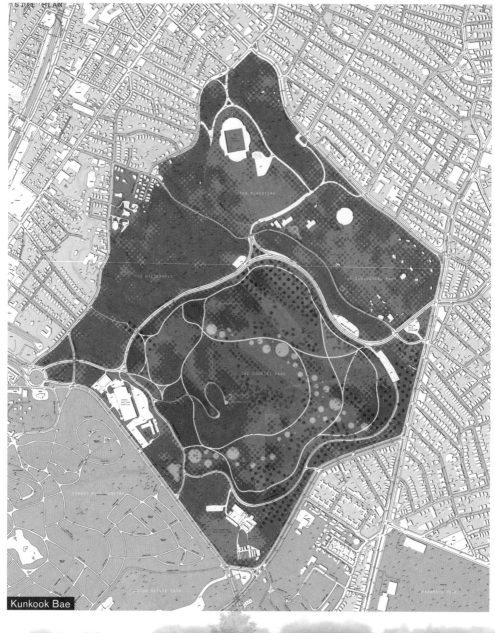

Kunkook Bae

Anne Weber

Yizhou Xu

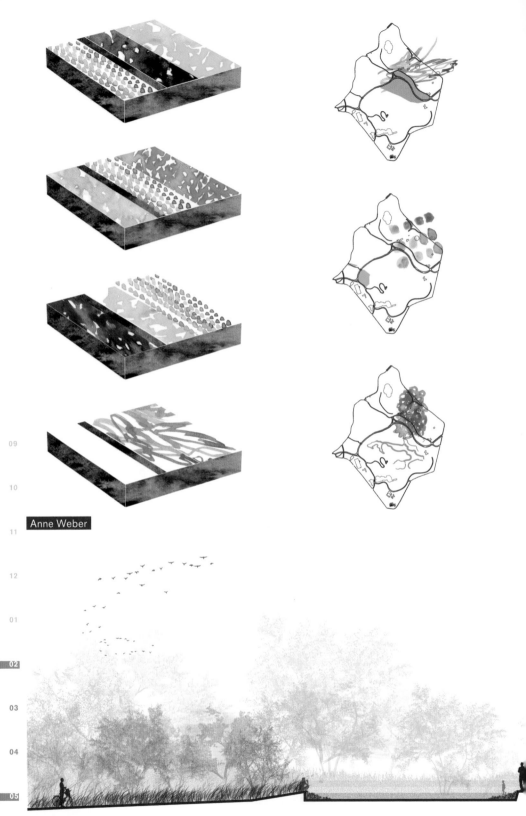

Anne Weber

09

10

11

12

01

02

03

04

05

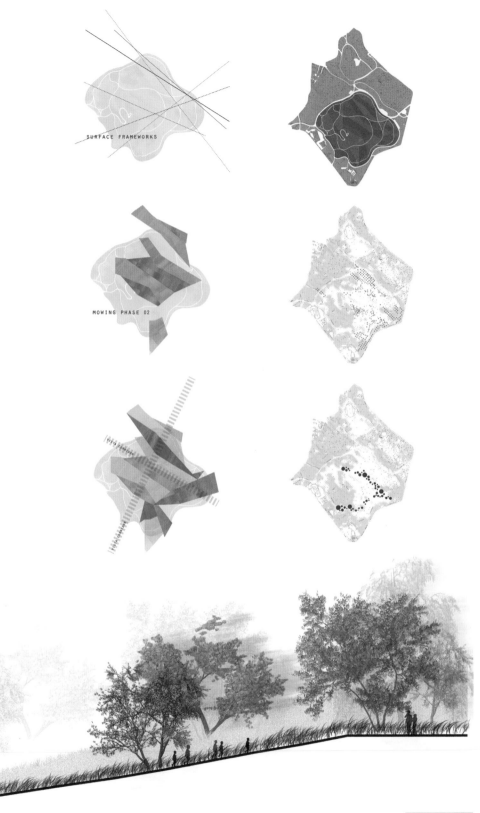

SURFACE FRAMEWORKS

MOWING PHASE 02

Kunkook Bae

Chuhan Zhang

Yizhou Xu

Kunkook Bae

Chuhan Zhang

Jacques Herzog: We are very glad to come back on a regular basis. [The GSD is] a place where we've always met interesting people and we've always had interesting discussions, sometimes hot discussions. We continue to have such discussions as, for instance, last night at the end of the dinner, we started to talk about books and I repeated what I said many times in the past that I don't believe in books on architecture and that they are bound to fail and disappear even faster than architecture.

Architecture sometimes lasts for a few generations, maybe sometimes even centuries, but as everything else, it goes. It disappears, which is also great to know somehow. What I wanted to say is not that I have no respect for people who write books because we have, since the beginning, written a lot and we have always felt the need to—for an intellectual and conceptual approach, which uses the word and involves the word, but we said it for totally different reasons.

Jacques Herzog

I want to point out once again how important it is that a discipline is just what it is. Poetry is poetry, architecture is architecture, literature is literature, painting is painting, photography is photography. We're not so interested in things about things, illustrative things, narrative things because they use something else to exist and—especially talking about architecture.

The great thing as everybody knows here, when you are facing a piece of architecture, a new one or an old one, the sheer experience, the immediate physical experience, is what counts and what makes this piece of architecture survive, whether it's fragile, made out of paper or wood like an old Japanese imperial palace, which lasts for centuries even if it's not very solid, or whether it's a contemporary building or an old medieval church. This immediate sensation, which involves all the senses we have—and that's very key today that we are not involving only visual senses, reading so to speak architecture, but really living it is what we continue to underscore and we try to teach also to the students and we try to realize in our work.

Kultur für den Norden

BMW.
HAUPTPARTNER DER
ELBPHILHARMONIE

HOCHTIEF

Herzog & de Meuron
Lecture | Jacques Herzog

Preston Scott Cohen: Tonight's conversation between Reinhold Martin and Jeff Kipnis: What Good Can Architecture Do? is part of an ongoing series of events in the architecture department that aim to elucidate divergences, different perspectives on the history and currency of modernism and post modernity. The aim is to elucidate tendencies and claims, whether they be apolitical or political, ironic or earnest, cynical or moral, decadent or righteous, and tonight matters of agency and effect will be our focus. Frequently, they are seen as opposite terms of commitment in the schools today.

In the summer of 2009, Reinhold Martin, the director of the Buell Center for the Study of American Architecture, held a one-day summit of sorts, though he pointedly did not call it that, of architects, theorists and leaders of architecture schools to discuss a number of current crises, made most conspicuous by the economic meltdown. He structured the day by dividing it in two, while expressing some reluctance to do so. Morning to confront architecture from the outside, so to speak, and afternoon to address those problems that emerge from within, recalling CIAM and Team 10 on the one hand and Charlottesville Tapes and ANY on the other, he proposed that whatever urgent questions and responsibilities facing our discipline quote, "We must insist that at best they represent only half the story, for architecture is also self-evidently an art form, as much as it is—or some would say more than it is—a technical or socioeconomic practice. Thus also the necessity of dealing with the intangible aesthetic questions, the esoteric, if you will, with which the discipline is notoriously plagued, but from which it also draws much of its internal energy and arguably its meaning," unquote.

If Martin expresses his skepticism of form, while finding himself extolling its irrefutable power, Jeff Kipnis is a more stalwart critic of the other side of the equation. Indeed, he can always be counted on to thwart the alliance of architecture with servitude or with science. Martin's books, *The Organizational Complex* and *Utopia's Ghost: Architecture and Post Modernism, Again*, delve deeply into crises in architecture outside moving

The Harvard GSD Symposia on Architecture: "What Good Can Design Do?"

Lecture Jeffrey Kipnis and Reinhold Martin

Destruction of Pruitt-Igoe. Harvard VIA KX1424.6

in, illuminating the beauty and havoc wrought on the post war landscape, Kipnis began inside, looking out in some of the most important texts to have done so and then turned it all on its head with his seminal work: Mood River, which has, to use Reinhold's term again "plagued" the discipline ever since. No longer is architectural discourse to be dominated by the problem of making buildings speak meaningfully, whether through defamiliarized symbols or abstract indices, instead it argues for the rigorous or approximate forms that merge with cultural politics, with inscrutable sensations. It is first and foremost about the production of affect.

Jeff Kipnis: The fundamental question I think we were asking is what model of knowledge should guide a contemporary architectural approach to new building? That's my interest. I'm interested in new building. I think there are three distinct models of architectural knowledge that we are now considering as it pertains to new building. One is that architecture is a service profession. The second is that it's a cultural practice or thirdly, that it's an applied human science based respectively on business for the professional practice, with the profit and client satisfaction as the basis of arbitration. The humanities have disciplinary discourse as the basis of arbitration, and the sciences have an idealized generic individual and collective beneficiary of measurable reproducible effects as the basis of arbitration.

I am obviously going to come down on the side of disciplinarity and I believe disciplinarity is better able to absorb the intelligence generated by both professional practice, legal practice, economic practices, and on the sciences rather than jettisoning the discipline, its histories, and its intelligence.

Reinhold Martin: Throughout Oscar Newman's analysis, *Defensible Space*, which integrates the territorial with the affective, with emotion and experience, Pruitt-Igoe stands as a representative example, possessed of an indefensible porosity and figural indeterminacy. So Newman critiques this building on essentially formal spatial terms, both inside and out. That what is physical here is equally psychical is reinforced by Newman's accounting of less tangible characteristics of the building, like what he calls "image and milieu" alongside the more tangible construction of physical boundaries to encourage what he calls "territoriality."

He tells this other story about a fence that's built as part of the constructional playground and that changes the dynamic of the place, so out of this series of kind of measurements that are done, Newman concludes that boundaries are necessary in order to kind of, let's say, mitigate the social and economic tensions that were expressing themselves in housing projects like this. So on the basis of this, he concludes, "This is an extreme example of territorial definition and is certainly not one which we are advocating, not necessarily building fences per se, but its accomplishments are significant in light of the Pruitt-Igoe failure. The question to be asked is how does one initially achieve through thoughtful building groupings rather than having to resort to barbed wire fences and locks after the fact?"

So, in other words, how to sublimate the fence into an architectural language that does its biopolitical work at the level of the spatial imaginary. In other words, thoughtful building groupings that inscribe a virtual territoriality, rather than through the raw power of barbed wire, that's essentially the question that Newman poses.

For more than 100 years, Chicago has managed its waterways with large-scale engineering solutions, the most famous of which is reversing the flow of the Chicago River. Despite the slowly falling levels of the Great Lakes (which constitute 20% of the world's surface fresh water), and the city's efforts to internationally brand itself as "green," contemporary municipal treatment and handling of stormwater and wastewater remain costly and unsustainable. Today, the unfolding crisis of invasive aquatic species moving toward the Great Lakes through the Chicago River (an unintended consequence of the river's reversal and subsequent connection with the Mississippi watershed) now offers an unprecedented opportunity to rethink the confluence of infrastructure, architecture, and ecology in the region.

Students were required to analyze and challenge the underlying premise of Chicago's approach to water in this option studio as they created design solutions to the invasive threat. Three interconnected design elements were included in the project: a physical barrier dividing the Chicago River from Lake Michigan, a new center for research on freshwater systems, and an urban land strategy that addressed flooding and water quality in the vicinity of the barrier.

Precedent research was drawn from such cities as Calcutta, India, and Xochimilco, Mexico, where wastewater is treated in a variety of ways and envisioned as a resource. The appeal of the project was its potential to have far-reaching significance for an entire metropolis while dealing with a very specific and viable site of intervention. Through their tri-part work, students were able to test architecture's ability to elevate the urban experience, discover untapped recreational and social value, and deploy strategic initiatives that resolve crucial contemporary transformations in cities.

Experts in ecology, engineering, and logistics, among others, consulted with the studio. National exposure of the work produced will be achieved though a print publication developed in collaboration between Studio Gang Architects and the National Resources Defense Council.

Center for Limnology:
Divided Waters in Chicago
Option Studio · Jeanne Gang

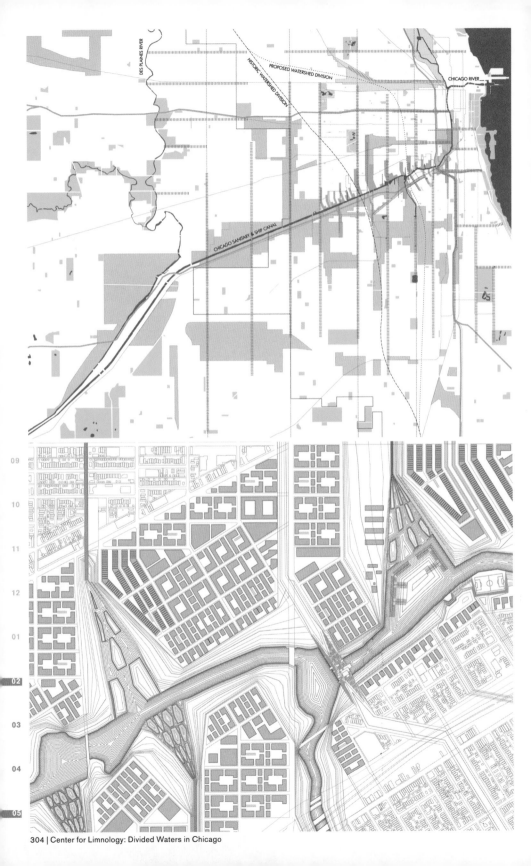

DES PLANES RIVER

PROPOSED WATERSHED DIVISION

HISTORIC WATERSHED DIVISION

CHICAGO RIVER

CHICAGO SANITARY & SHIP CANAL

09
10
11
12
01
02
03
04
05

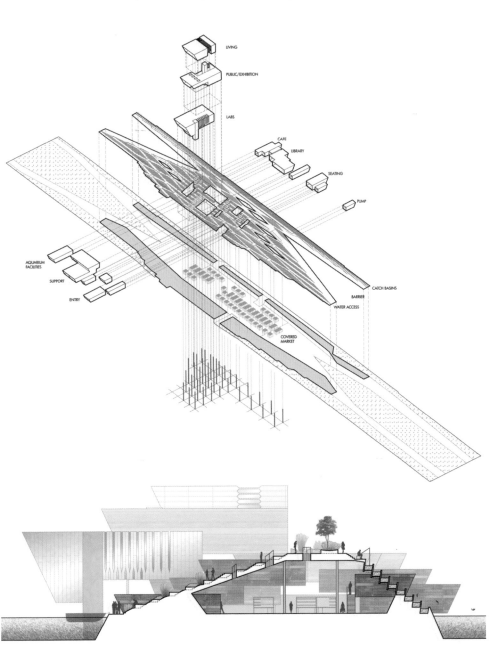

LIVING

PUBLIC/EXHIBITION

LABS

CAFE

LIBRARY

SEATING

PUMP

CATCH BASINS

BARRIER

WATER ACCESS

AQUARIUM
FACILITIES

SUPPORT

ENTRY

COVERED
MARKET

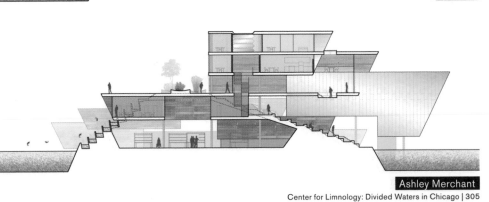

Ashley Merchant

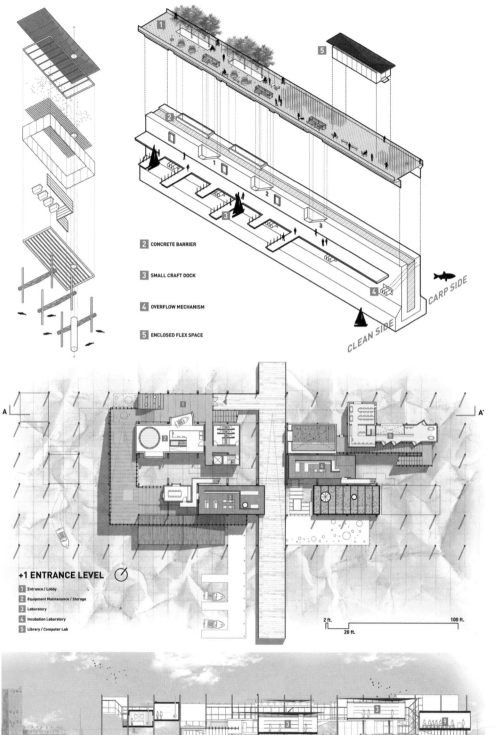

2 CONCRETE BARRIER

3 SMALL CRAFT DOCK

4 OVERFLOW MECHANISM

5 ENCLOSED FLEX SPACE

CARP SIDE

CLEAN SIDE

+1 ENTRANCE LEVEL

1 Entrance / Lobby
2 Equipment Maintenance / Storage
3 Laboratory
4 Incubation Laboratory
5 Library / Computer Lab

2 ft.   100 ft.
20 ft.

RHETORIC / MEDIA   STRUCTURE / METRICS

TYPE / FLUX

Andrew McGee

Center for Limnology: Divided Waters in Chicago | 307

RioStudio aimed to combine the creative experimentation of designers with the hard-nosed logic of business to evolve practical ideas that are socially, environmentally, and economically profitable.

Focusing on the problems and potentials of Rio de Janeiro, the studio generated ideas for how the imminent investments for the 2014 World Cup and the subsequent 2016 Olympic Games can be placed to catalyze long term improvements for the large local population, rather than merely servicing the temporary needs of tourists and the world press.

If we as designers are truly committed to addressing social issues, we need to design business models that improve the living conditions of the poor as a byproduct of profitable processes. We need to design ecosystems—systems of both economy and ecology—that operate like urban perpetual motion engines, independent of charity and state subsidies, triggered by private and public investment.

With the global attention and massive investment for the two upcoming mega events fueled by the roaring Brazilian economy, Rio is at a strategic moment to seize the situation and envision a millennium upgrade of its urban infrastructure. What if we could come up with ideas where profitable real estate development and improved living conditions for the favelas might be two sides of the same coin? What if the temporary swell in hotel capacity for the games would trigger better living conditions in the long term?

With the creation of Brasilia, Brazil has previously proven its capacity to pursue big ideas for order and progress. But rather than a tabula rasa where pure principles are projected on a clean canvas, this studio proposed an evolutionary model that interprets and intervenes in the existing conditions of Rio's urban landscape to breed new hybrids between the interests of investors and the interests of the people.

RioStudio

Option Studio   Bjarke Ingels, Paul Nakazawa

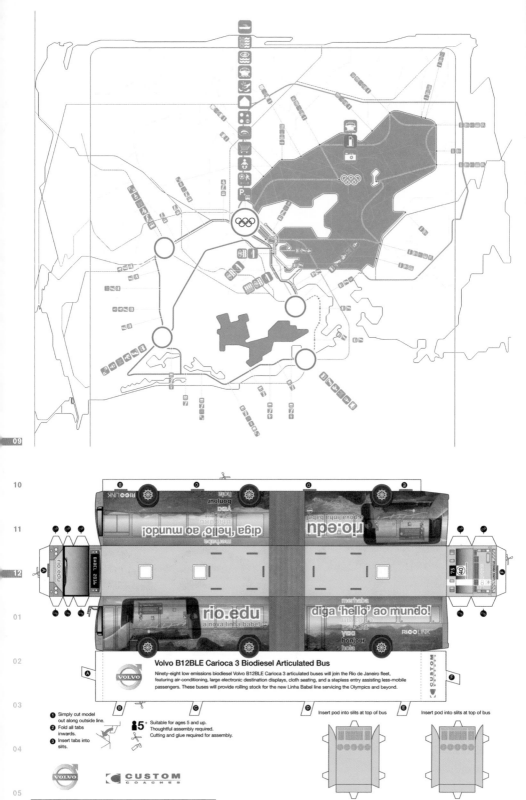

Volvo B12BLE Carioca 3 Biodiesel Articulated Bus

Ninety-eight low emissions biodiesel Volvo B12BLE Carioca 3 articulated buses will join the Rio de Janeiro fleet, featuring air-conditioning, large electronic destination displays, cloth seating, and a stepless entry assisting less-mobile passengers. These buses will provide rolling stock for the new Linha Babel line servicing the Olympics and beyond.

❶ Simply cut model out along outside line.
❷ Fold all tabs inwards.
❸ Insert tabs into slits.

5+ Suitable for ages 5 and up.
Thoughtful assembly required.
Cutting and glue required for assembly.

Insert pod into slits at top of bus

Insert pod into slits at top of bus

CUSTOM COACHES

Victor Munoz Sanz, Christopher Roach

Alix Beranger, Laura Janka Zires, Chan Youn

In no other community in America has the current economic recession wreaked more dislocation than Detroit. Over the last decade, Southeast Michigan has lost hundreds of thousands of highly paid manufacturing jobs through the contraction of the automotive industry. This crisis exacerbates the problems of an urban center that has experienced more than sixty years of disinvestment, flight, and blight. As a result, a city of 1.8 million people at its peak in the 1950s is now estimated to have just over 717,000 inhabitants, according to the 2010 U.S. Census.

So, what is to become of a regional urban center that is too large for its local government to manage, has too much land to return to near-term economic value, and is too spread out to maintain sustainable infrastructure, service delivery, neighborhoods. and communities? What must Detroit do to reposition itself as a new form of American city? If Detroit was known for its innovation in the auto industry in the twentieth century, what will Detroit be known for in the twenty-first century? And finally, how can we redefine the geographies of post-industrial cities to create stronger, healthier, and livelier regions?

Detroit Interrupted: Defining New Geographies for the American City explores new typologies for the twenty-first century American city. In part one of the studio, students examined Detroit's historic settlement patterns at multiple scales by mapping social and economic forces and the flux of formal and emergent landscapes. These maps, combined with an assessment of seminal urban form-making theories, were the basis for a video manifesto and a proposed new geography for Detroit—a physical framework that allows for contraction, expansion, and/or temporary or permanent development patterns. In part two, students developed informal and/or disruptive interventions that embodied their new geographical contexts. Projects engaged a variety of scales and timespans rather than a specific site, so that they may maximize their potential as didactic case studies that can be applied to other post-industrial shrinking cities. The intervention prototypes think big, operating at the system, neighborhood, and district scales so as to reposition Detroit as an important and still relevant American city.

09

10

11

12

01

02

03

04

05

Detroit, Interrupted

Option Studio | Toni Griffin, Andrea Hansen

Bailey Kinkel, Erin Kelly

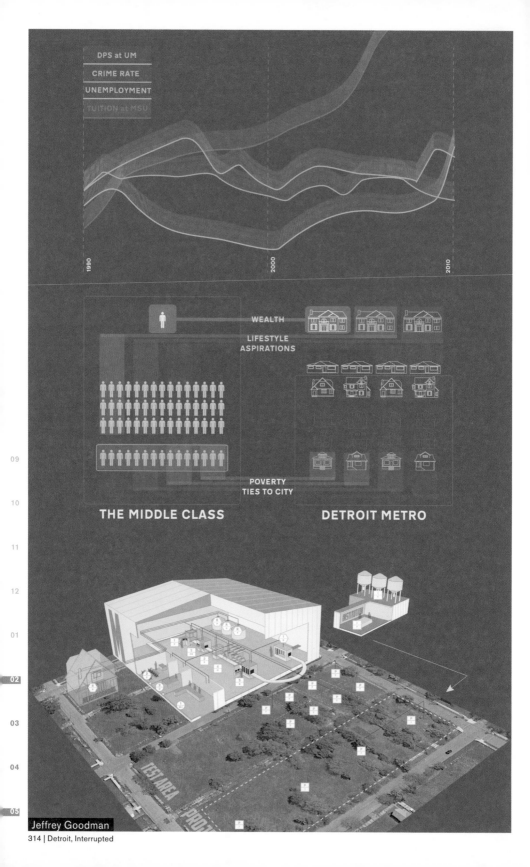

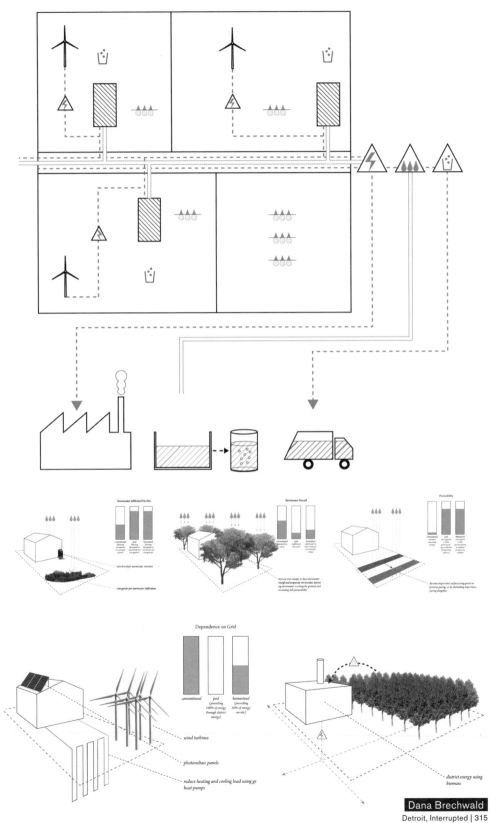

Stormwater Infiltrated On-Site

Stormwater Runoff

Permeability

Dependence on Grid

wind turbines

photovoltaic panels

reduce heating and cooling load using ge
heat pumps

district energy using
biomass

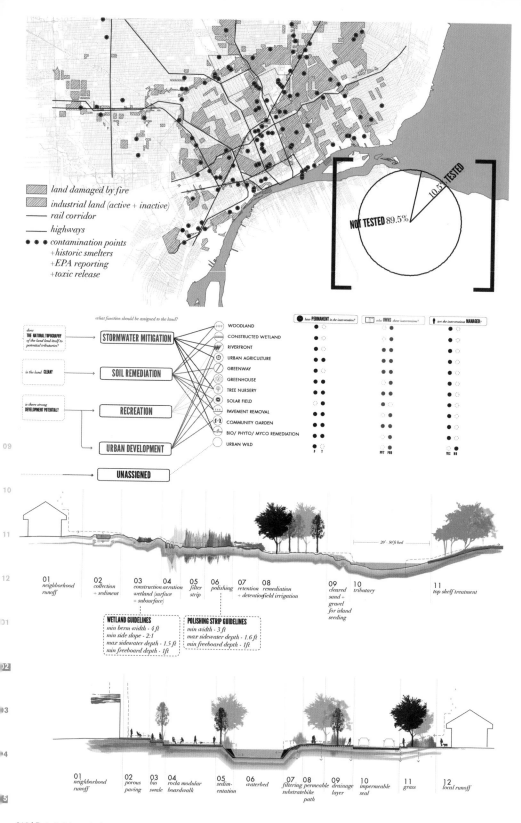

land damaged by fire

industrial land (active + inactive)

rail corridor

highways

contamination points
+historic smelters
+EPA reporting
+toxic release

NOT TESTED 89.5%

10.5 TESTED

what function should be assigned to the land?

does THE NATURAL TOPOGRAPHY of the land lend itself to potential tributaries?

STORMWATER MITIGATION

is the land CLEAR?

SOIL REMEDIATION

is there strong DEVELOPMENT POTENTIAL?

RECREATION

URBAN DEVELOPMENT

UNASSIGNED

WOODLAND
CONSTRUCTED WETLAND
RIVERFRONT
URBAN AGRICULTURE
GREENWAY
GREENHOUSE
TREE NURSERY
SOLAR FIELD
PAVEMENT REMOVAL
COMMUNITY GARDEN
BIO/ PHYTO/ MYCO REMEDIATION
URBAN WILD

how PERMANENT is the intervention?

who OWNS these interventions?

are the interventions MANAGED?

P T

PVT PUB

YES NO

01 neighborhood runoff

02 collection + sediment

03 construction aeration wetland (surface + subsurface)

05 filter strip

06 polishing

07 retention + detention

08 remediation field irrigation

09 cleared sand + gravel for island seeding

10 tributary

11 top shelf treatment

20'- 50'ft bed

WETLAND GUIDELINES
min berm width - 4 ft
min side slope - 2:1
max sidewater depth - 1.5 ft
min freeboard depth - 1ft

POLISHING STRIP GUIDELINES
min width - 3 ft
max sidewater depth - 1.6 ft
min freeboard depth - 1ft

01 neighborhood runoff

02 porous paving

03 bio swale

04 rocla modular boardwalk

05 sedimentation

06 waterbed

07 filtering permeable substrate

08 permeable bike path

09 drainage layer

10 impermeable seal

11 grass

12 local runoff

09
10
11
12
01
02
03
04
05

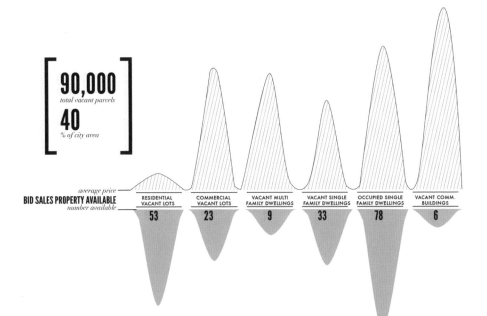

90,000
total vacant parcels

40
% of city area

BID SALES PROPERTY AVAILABLE
average price
number available

RESIDENTIAL VACANT LOTS	COMMERCIAL VACANT LOTS	VACANT MULTI FAMILY DWELLINGS	VACANT SINGLE FAMILY DWELLINGS	OCCUPIED SINGLE FAMILY DWELLINGS	VACANT COMM. BUILDINGS
53	23	9	33	78	6

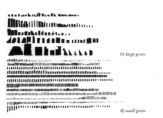

01 large grain

02 small grain

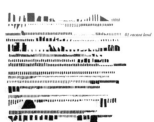

01 vacant land

02 non-vacant

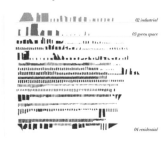

02 industrial

03 green space

04 residential

rebuild detroit
come together. build together. live together.

1,592,007 pieces included

The opportunities for urban development and advancement for Rio de Janeiro as it prepares for the impending global events of the 2014 FIFA World Cup and the 2016 Olympic Games are immense, real, and welcome. Events of this kind create great expectations for design innovation at all scales. Yet, the general path being followed to address those design opportunities still conforms to protocols already tried by other cities, involving well tested hierarchies of interventions with proven degrees of success but seldom acknowledged failures. In the best cases, careful thinking is devoted to planning the new interventions, in such a way as to become active and positive parts of daily urban life after the games are over. Yet, the very nature of the constraints imposed in the planning and implementation for world events of this kind (budget and schedules) and the monumental scale of its units of intervention, result in punctual time/space occurrences more than on continuous space/ time processes. This in turn tends to produce isolated solutions that resolve design issues only within precisely defined physical boundaries.

The results are duplicitous and contradictory: the creation of well-conceived, iconic high performance urban islands on the one hand, and on the other, the by-products of large "no man's land" interstitial urban spaces that operate by default as low performance connective urban tissue, a dichotomy that tends inevitably to exacerbate itself over time.

Such urban polarization, with its lack of both fluidity and reciprocal enrichment among its urban units, was the studio's concern as it focused on the Maracanã district of Rio–an area that would become central to both international sport events, and where lack of attention to these occurrences would be doubly hurting: some of the conditions described are already present due to the particular urban/ topographical history of Rio, where steep hills, cliffs, river beds, and narrow valleys have contributed to the city's distinctive image but also led to the creation of veritable archipelagos of disconnected fragments separated by freeways, railroad tracks, hills, and water bodies. In the Maracanã area it is possible to identify the following clearly isolated fragments:

a) the Maracanã Stadium;
b) the Museu Nacional and park;
c) the State University of Rio de Janeiro; and
d) the Federal Institute of Technology.

All of the above locations are surrounded by low density, low income, disconnected neighborhoods.

Considering the projected stadium improvements and the steady growth of the area in the next two decades, the conditions were ideal for the exploration of integrated, organic proposals that would address previously neglected opportunities by the design of high quality, high performance public urban spaces, buildings and services that created conditions of continuity and accessibility through the promotion of a balanced urban life.

This studio agenda also included the integration of the favela Mangueira, and the adjoining neighborhoods of Tijuca and São Cristovão, through the historically important Quinta da Boa Vista (formerly grounds of the royal palace, currently the National Museum and park).

The Architecture of Interstitial Urbanism

Option Studio | Jorge Silvetti, Paul Nakazawa

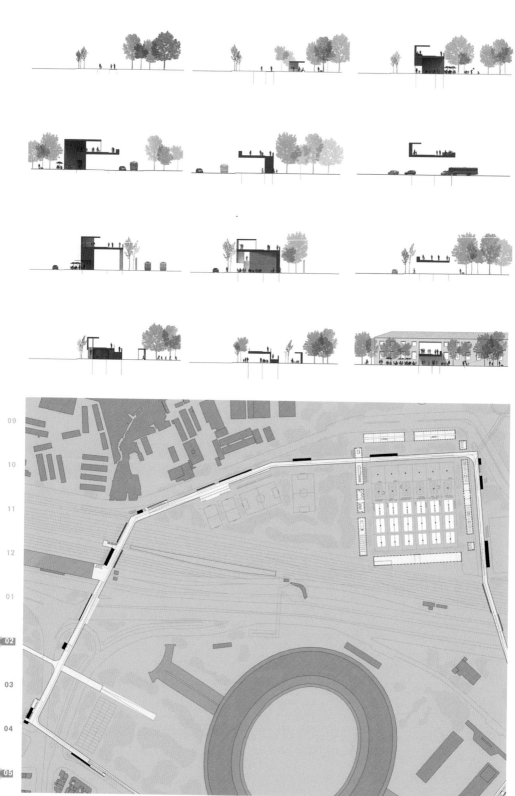

Jarrad Morgan

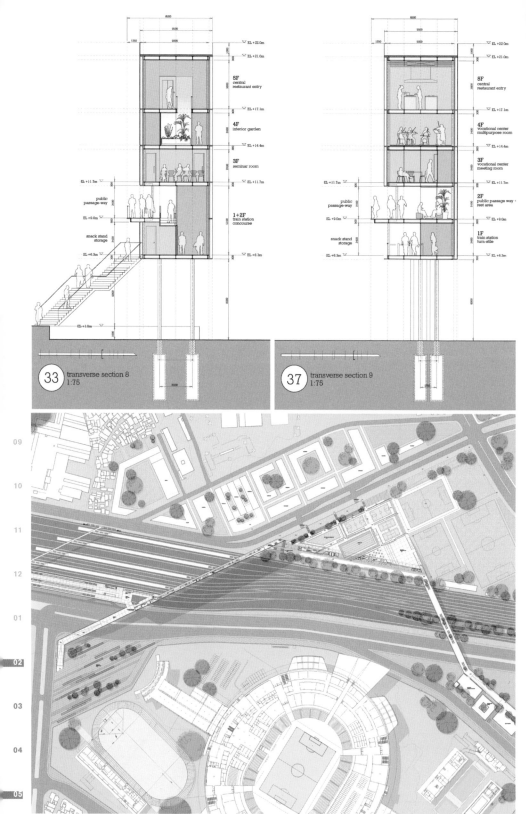

James Leng

The studio aims to unlock the architectural potential of the bridge as an infrastructural element by reconfiguring its status between system and object.

The site is the foot of the Ataturk Bridge in Istanbul and the adjacent navy dockyards that have been recently cleared for local public use. This newly available land will permit a series of improvements around the existing bridge, including enhancing the public space at the landing of the bridge and linking the nearby neighborhood of Kasimpasa to the waterfront.

The resurgent discussions on the future of infrastructure have focused primarily on the need to update it and reconceptualize it into integrated rather than isolated systems and networks. The main criticisms have focused on the modernist conceptions of infrastructure as isolated systems that have seriously ruptured the urban fabric and damaged the environment. As such, much of the bravura of early infrastructural feats and figures (the engineering of a span, the clover leaf) has been de-emphasized.

While bridges are one of the few infrastructural elements that have historically stood out as objects, this definition has nevertheless maintained too strong an engineering rendition and too sharp a separation from the immediately adjacent areas that they have also come under scrutiny and reconsideration.

The larger ambition of the studio was to find alternative ways of thinking about infrastructure, outside the systemic and technical polarity and towards a more edifying attitude towards the city and its elements. Through the bridge, the studio explored a range of possibilities for architecture between megaform and megastructure.

Istanbul's bridges over the relatively shallow Golden Horn are famous for the social and commercial activity that they carry across along with the traffic. Fishing, restaurants, markets, warehouses, and mooring docks, all happen on the bridge along with solicitors, trains, cars, and scooters. The intensity of bridge activity extends the street against the unfolding panoramas of the city. One is at once inside the city and viewing it from outside. The bridge is an optical device that magnifies, highlights, and orients. This suspension, the studio proposed, is but a heightening of the urban condition rather than its exception.

It is this possibility of object and flow, quasi-object or token, as Serres (and after him Bruno Latour) has imagined our relationship with artifacts that the studio aimed to explore: reconceiving infrastructure and architecture between dissolution and reification. These investigations extended from the geography of a bridge to the status of contemporary architecture.

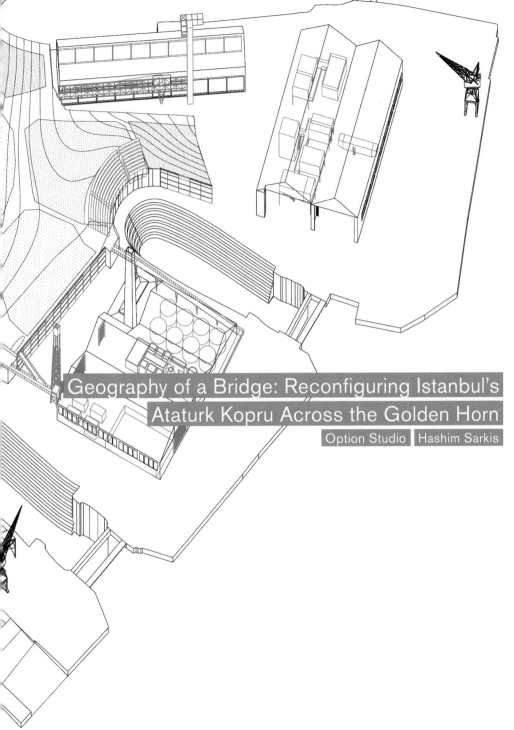

Geography of a Bridge: Reconfiguring Istanbul's Ataturk Kopru Across the Golden Horn

Option Studio | Hashim Sarkis

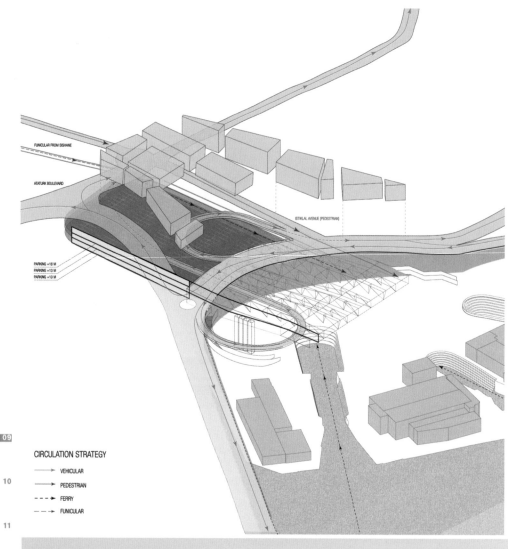

FUNICULAR FROM SISHANE

ATATURK BOULEVARD

ISTIKLAL AVENUE [PEDESTRIAN]

PARKING +16 M
PARKING +13 M
PARKING +10 M

CIRCULATION STRATEGY

→ VEHICULAR

→ PEDESTRIAN

---→ FERRY

---→ FUNICULAR

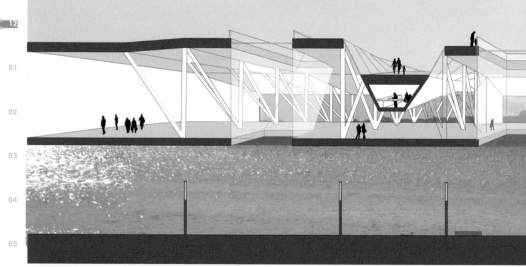

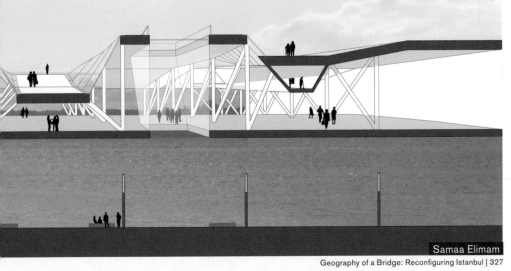

Samaa Elimam

The studio explored the condition of extreme urbanism in the form of social, cultural, and economic disparities and how these manifest themselves in the urban form. Social interactions, public space, and the broader issue of how architecture and urban design can facilitate the dissipation of polarities that exist in the urban landscape were the central themes of the studio.

Situated in Mumbai, the studio offered students the potential to engage with questions of housing, notions of public space and its correlation with specific local cultures, landscapes and ecology, as well as urban design questions at the city scale. Questions of real estate dynamics, climate change, and environmentalism in general drove concerns throughout the studio. In addition, the studio emphasized models and processes of implementation, forms of social engagement, and the challenges for advocacy at large—these were critical questions in the formulations for proposition for the site.

This studio was an advanced introduction to urbanism in Indian cities. Drawing on Mumbai's specific urban development experience from the past two decades, students considered how large-scale planning intervention could promote a plurality of visions for the city and how architects, planners, urban designers, and landscape architects can reconcile sharp dualities in city form. Furthermore, the studio explored how ecologically sensitive design can play a role in shifting the paradigms of urbanism for cities.

Extreme Urbanism
Option Studio | Rahul Mehrotra

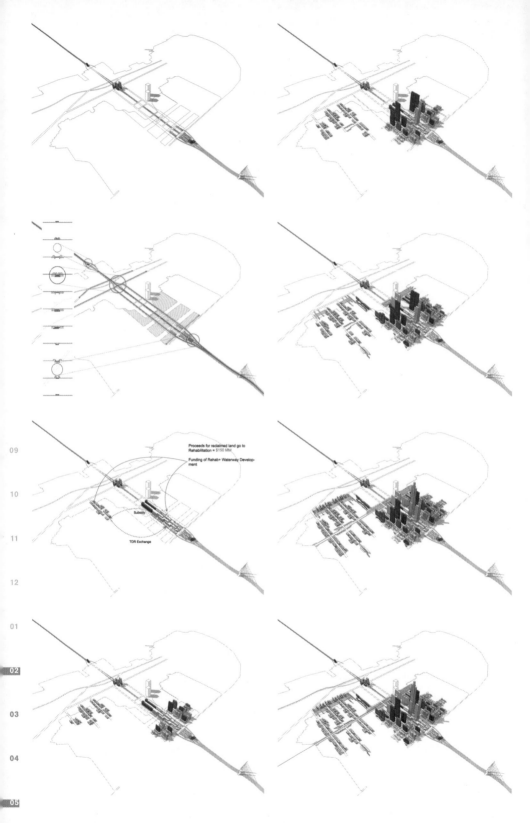

09

10

11

12

01

02

03

04

05

Proceeds for reclaimed land go to
Rehabilitation = $150 MM

Funding of Rehab+ Waterway Development

Subsidy

TDR Exchange

Robert Bracken

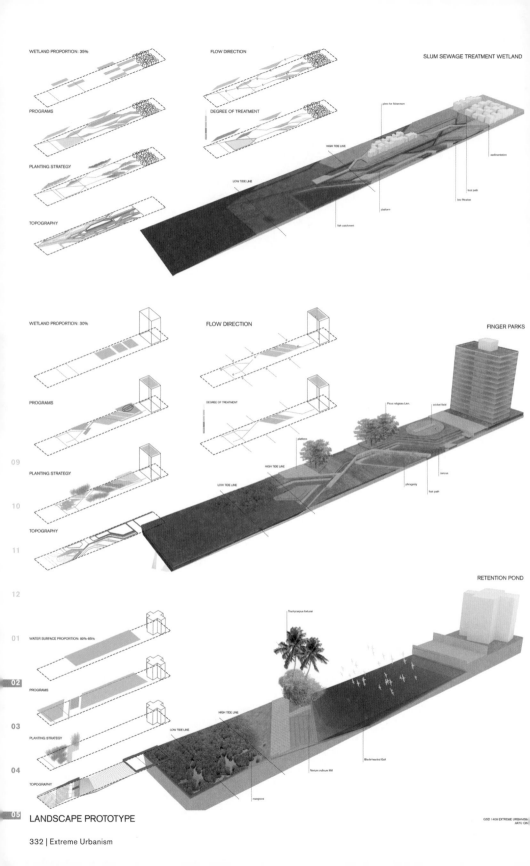

WETLAND PROPORTION: 35%

FLOW DIRECTION

SLUM SEWAGE TREATMENT WETLAND

PROGRAMS

DEGREE OF TREATMENT

PLANTING STRATEGY

TOPOGRAPHY

WETLAND PROPORTION: 30%

FLOW DIRECTION

FINGER PARKS

PROGRAMS

DEGREE OF TREATMENT

PLANTING STRATEGY

TOPOGRAPHY

WATER SURFACE PROPORTION: 90%-85%

RETENTION POND

PROGRAMS

PLANTING STRATEGY

TOPOGRAPHY

LANDSCAPE PROTOTYPE

GSD 1409 EXTREME URBANISM
JIAYU QIN

Jiayu Qin

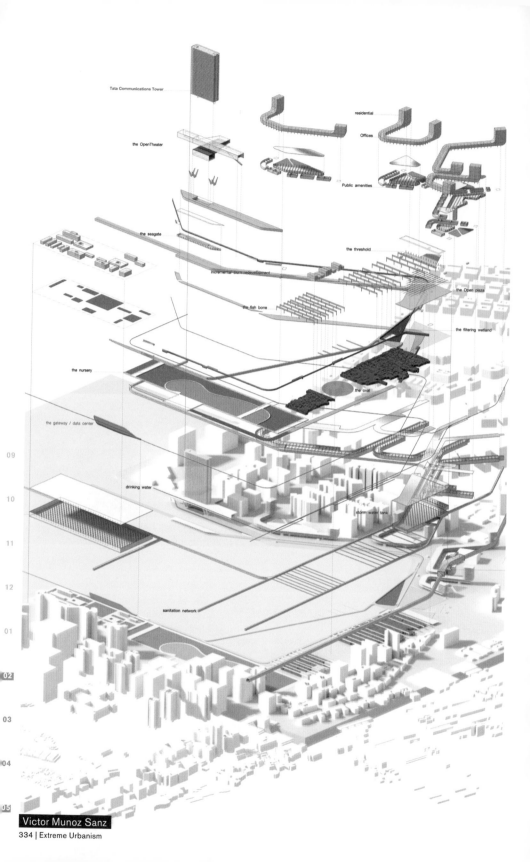

Tata Communications Tower

the OpenTheater

residential

Offices

Public amenities

the seagate

the threshold

incremental slum redevelopment

the Open plaza

the fish bone

the filtering wetland

the nursery

the oval

the gateway / data center

09

drinking water

10

11

storm water tank

12

sanitation network

01

02

03

04

05

Victor Munoz Sanz

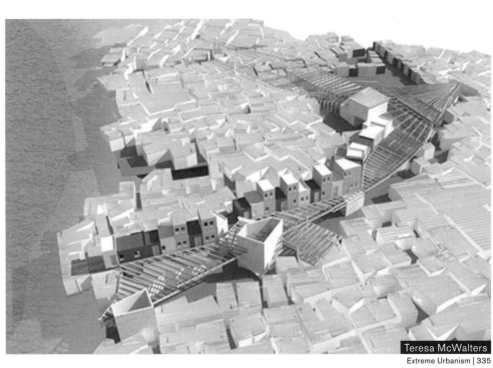

Philip Freelon: This evening, I'll set the stage for my friend and colleague David Adjaye as we share with you the current state of development of this wonderful project that we have been working on for the past year, the Smithsonian's National Museum of African American History and Culture, located on the Mall in Washington, D.C. I want to take a moment to put this incredible project into context, however. How it came about, its physical context, the site, and where we are in the process. Culturally specific museums have seen an increase in number and visitorship in recent years. As the U.S. population's median age increases, we see a heightened interest in cultural tourism and the exploration of family history and cultural heritage. Our approach to designs of institutions of this type is to fully integrate the building with the exhibits. And these exhibits tend to be long term if not permanent. That's first.

And secondly, we strive to meet the vision and express the vision of the institution in the architecture, and use the building to help convey the theme or the message as opposed to simply creating a beautiful building or vessel to house exhibits and galleries. Now, in the case of art museums, it's often appropriate to provide a backdrop-type building for the artwork.

David Adjaye

David Adjaye: We looked at a lot of things (for the competition). And what we said we wanted to do, in analyzing the incredible history of African American people, was to think "what do we want to say about this building, what was the message we want to say?" In the end, there are so many stories, but in a way, the unifying story we started to find, one that was continually kind of happening throughout, was one of incredible triumph, an incredible ability to overcome and move through these incredible adversities. In a way, this motif was something that kept occurring. We had one room where we placed lots of images, and we reflected on these. Continually, the celebratory motif, a kind of spiritual motif of a victory over certain adversities that come, kept appearing, and we were very moved by that as a form. At the same time, we were doing very specific didactic research into a kind of trajectory into an architectural specificity that we could try and locate, to work with. [It involved] Going back to the beginnings of the civilization of African people and trying to look at the roots of specifically where the community comes from.

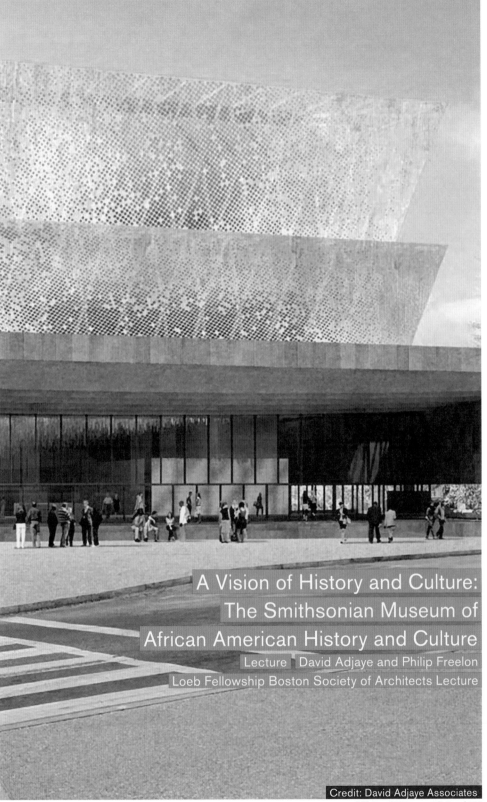

A Vision of History and Culture:
The Smithsonian Museum of
African American History and Culture
Lecture David Adjaye and Philip Freelon
Loeb Fellowship Boston Society of Architects Lecture

Credit: David Adjaye Associates

The central focus of the seminar is the relationship between urbanism and oil. Baku, the capital of Azerbaijan, formerly part of the Russian Empire and Soviet Union, is now one of the most dynamic and rapidly changing urban territories in the world. Located at a critical geopolitical nexus between Europe, the Middle East, and Central Asia, Baku has strong historical, cultural, and economic ties to all three. Today, the city is undergoing its second major oil boom (the first was at the turn of the twentieth century) and Baku is poised to become a major player in the global economy. For Baku's city planners and business elites, that future includes the capital's aspiration to be a twenty-first century first: "the oil city that goes green."

The modern history of Baku is inextricably bound up with oil, so is its economic future. The purpose of the seminar is to analyze the historical development of the city from late nineteenth century bourgeois boom town, to Soviet industrial center, to capital of independent republic and capitalist powerhouse with vast reserves of oil and natural gas. Emphasis is on how urban design, planning, and architecture have dealt with the issue of oil under different political conditions over the course of Baku's modern development.

Photo: Arhitektura SSSR

Research topics include: Infrastructure at urban, regional, national, and international scales: networks, pipelines, railways, trade routes past and future. Planned and unplanned urban growth. Urban formations directly connected to oil extraction: the late nineteenth '"Black City," early twentieth "White City," and mid-century "Oily Rocks" in the Caspian Sea, as well as current plans for remediation and off-shore extraction. Architecture: Imperial Russian and Stalinist public building, Khrushchev and Brezhnev era Soviet housing, current public projects, and strategies for recladding and optimizing space and energy use in Soviet-era building.

Structured in collaboration with the Architecture University in Baku, the seminar involved a site visit to Baku in late February and early March 2011. Students worked with documents (maps, plans, archival photographs, etc.) from city archives and planning offices, and with planners, preservationists, and historians in Baku—analyzing sites, buildings, contemporary and historical urban fabric, executed and unexecuted plans to understand the evolution of the city, its urban morphologies and architectural typologies, infrastructure conditions, and distinctive dynamics.

Baku: Oil City

Seminar | Eve Blau

Photo: Shelby Doyle

In recent years, the pace of research on women in landscape architecture has accelerated. Many monographs, anthologies, and scholarly books on their contributions to the field have appeared, such that we now have the beginnings of a detailed picture of the role of women in design at both the start and the conclusion of the twentieth century. But one aspect of this story is unexamined: the place of women in the emergence of modernist landscape architecture in the decades just after the Second World War. The Department of Landscape Architecture convened a one-day colloquium in the spring semester of 2011 to address this gap in scholarship.

In 1964, when the Museum of Modern Art organized the exhibition and published the book *Modern Gardens and the Landscape*, it included no women, beyond a glancing reference to Gertrude Jekyll. When an expanded version of the book appeared in 1984, it still included no women. When the anthology *Modern Landscape Architecture: A Critical Review* appeared, it included the work of only one woman designer—of a decidedly later generation. Yet we know women were active in the formations of modernism in the decades after the war, as designers, academics, and writers, especially in the United States, Europe, and South America.

The colloquium featured presentations by and about some of the leading women designers of the time: Cornelia Oberlander, Rosa Kliass, and Carol Johnson, among others. Leading historians of the era provided an overview, presenting some of the professional challenges facing women in the years after the war and the various ways that women contributed to the emergence of modernism in different countries and contexts. Scholars were invited to talk specifically about particular designers, and the designers themselves participated in a moderated discussion.

Speakers included Thaisa Way on the role of women in post-war practice in the United States; Sonja Dumpelmann on post-war practice in Europe; Maria Cecilia Gorski on the work of Rosa Kliass in the context of Brazilian modernism; Susan Herrington on Cornelia Oberlander and modernism in North America; and Kelly Comras on Ruth Shellhorn and the Southern California commercial landscape. Cornelia Oberlander, Rosa Kliass, and Carol Johnson also spoke on their own work.

Women and Modernism in Landscape Architecture
Conference ▪ Various Speakers

The traumatic process of displacement carves a spatio-temporal placelessness that prompts investigation into architecture's agency in providing reconciliation through normalcy and lived experience. Yet, the UNHCR continues to regard settlement in refugee camps as the interim between displacement and resettlement, rather than conditions of real duration that may require such considerations for the potential role of emplacement.

In looking at repatriation trends, it becomes more relevant to approach, not within the framework of disaster relief, but as population migrations. What happens when you consider that these camps become cities, and what are the long-term implications of these constructs in the evolution of refugee communities?

Currently, with minimal initial planning for expected growth, the camps develop as un-densified and spontaneous sprawl, void of the potential for maturing as an active urban organization with charged spaces for interaction, and essentially lingering in a state of temporal suspension both politically and spatially.

Accepting that the camp scenario is not ideal, that integration into existing urban developments is preferred, I would argue that the UNHCR's limited definition of durability to include only repatriation is detrimental to the development of camps in the face of more realistic camp timelines, and should be broadened in scope to consider processes of placemaking that will facilitate a transition to future growth. Given the global scale of existing camp landscapes, this project accepts the camp as its given site and proposes a system of interventions to facilitate emplacement in the midst of indeterminate duration.

The necessity of emplacement for these camps, now "humanitarian bubbles, non-places...which could be everywhere and which are nowhere," is severely disrupted by the UNHCR focus on refugee aid as a shortsighted process of categorization and standardization, neglecting individual narrative in the name of disaster relief and further radicalizing this suspended state. Within the discourse of post-traumatic rehabilitation, the architectural process of emplacement aims to provide a sense of continuum within fragment through sensorial and corporal engagement. This critique of the UNHCR's neutral approach to refugee camp design questions roles of the experiential, having little to do with the distribution of these basic service programs and more to do with creating an infrastructure for movement and experience in efforts to recover lost memory and place-associated collective identity.

Taking the stance that the present camp model falls short of accessing true potential for placemaking in its failure to address the "in between," currently treating the camp as a set of discreet objects, the proposal is situated at several levels in the interstitial: spatially as occurring within the framework of existing structures and amenities, between the code itself and specificities of time and place, and within the liminal space that is the state of displacement itself. In addressing the shortcomings of the UNHCR code, including its irresolution of the state of temporal suspension, disarticulation, and social categorization, this proposal aims towards creating a network of interventions that focus on the neglected liminal space of existing camp developments in efforts towards hosting everyday life in a landscape of chronic disruption.

The Liminal Space of Emplacement:
Redefining Durability in the City-Camp Paradigm

| MArch Thesis | Kathryn Soven |
| Advisor | Hashim Sarkis |

DAILY OCCUPANCY PATTERNS

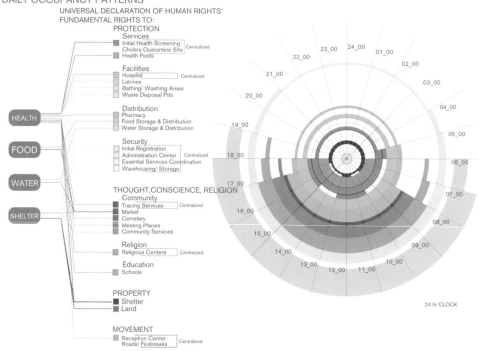

UNIVERSAL DECLARATION OF HUMAN RIGHTS'
FUNDAMENTAL RIGHTS TO:

PROTECTION

Services
- Initial Health Screening — Centralized
- Cholera Quarantine Site
- Health Posts

Facilities
- Hospital — Centralized
- Latrines
- Bathing/ Washing Areas
- Waste Disposal Pits

Distribution
- Pharmacy
- Food Storage & Distribution
- Water Storage & Distribution

Security
- Initial Registration
- Administration Center — Centralized
- Essential Services Coordination
- Warehousing/ Storage

THOUGHT, CONSCIENCE, RELIGION

Community
- Tracing Services — Centralized
- Market
- Cemetery
- Meeting Places
- Community Services

Religion
- Religious Centers — Centralized

Education
- Schools

PROPERTY
- Shelter
- Land

MOVEMENT
- Reception Center
- Roads/ Firebreaks — Centralized

HEALTH

FOOD

WATER

SHELTER

23_00 24_00 01_00
22_00   02_00
21_00   03_00
20_00   04_00
19_00   05_00
18_00   06_00
17_00   07_00
16_00   08_00
15_00   09_00
14_00   10_00
13_00 12_00 11_00

24 hr CLOCK

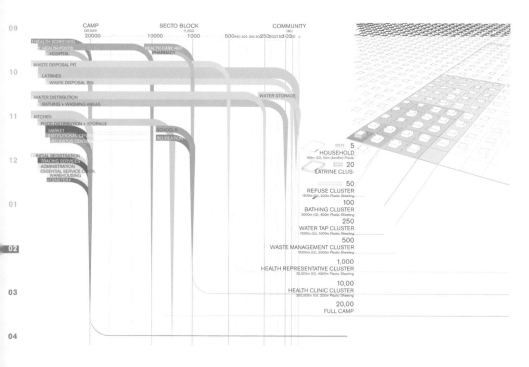

CAMP (20,000) 20000 · 10000 · 1000
SECTO BLOCK (1,250)
COMMUNITY (90)
500 480 400 350 300 250 200 150 100 50 2

09
1 HEALTH SCREENING
2 HEALTH POSTS
3 HOSPITAL
HEALTH CARE REF.
PHARMACY

10
WASTE DISPOSAL PIT
LATRINES
WASTE DISPOSAL BIN

WATER DISTRIBUTION
BATHING + WASHING AREAS
WATER STORAGE

11
KITCHEN
FOOD DISTRIBUTION + STORAGE
MARKET
INSTITUTIONAL CENTER
RELIGIOUS CENTERS
SCHOOLS
RECREATION

12
INITIAL REGISTRATION
TRACING SERVICES
ADMINISTRATION
ESSENTIAL SERVICE COOR.
WAREHOUSING
CEMETERY

01

02

03

04

05

5
HOUSEHOLD
150m (G), 20m (4mx5m) Plastic

20
LATRINE CLUS-

50
REFUSE CLUSTER
1600m (G), 200m Plastic Sheeting

100
BATHING CLUSTER
3600m (G), 400m Plastic Sheeting

250
WATER TAP CLUSTER
7500m (G), 1000m Plastic Sheeting

500
WASTE MANAGEMENT CLUSTER
15000m (G), 2000m Plastic Sheeting

1,000
HEALTH REPRESENTATIVE CLUSTER
30,000m (G), 4000m Plastic Sheeting

10,00
HEALTH CLINIC CLUSTER
300,000m (G), 200m Plastic Sheeting

20,00
FULL CAMP

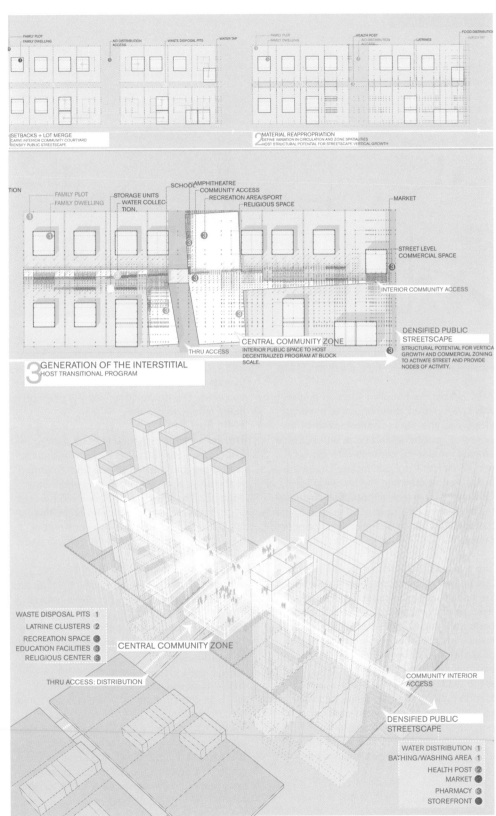

The aim of this thesis is to set up a camouflage strategy for an already developed territory located in the north of Italy, close to Milano.

After almost five hundred years of mapping, and one hundred years of active planning strategies, the site is characterized by a series of unused, abandoned, unfunctional spaces, fragments generated by physical and administrative boundaries. These areas are never mapped into the planning tools, as GIS layers. This lack of precision happens because maps are abstractions, and it affects the spatial qualities of the areas that people inhabit.

The first part of the thesis focuses on the analysis of abandoned spaces in the continuous generic landscape, called dystopias. Using descriptions, pictures, and handmade maps of gradients of biological invasion and dystopic potential, a pattern of abandoned infrastructure, leftovers, and emerging woodlands emerges. This condition is the result of the unquestioned use of standard anthropogenic planning tools, which prevent any reinterpretation of the space outside of the logic of industrial development and real estate market. On top of this existing condition, a camouflage strategy is set.

A regional camouflage strategy is designed to operate simultaneously at the strategic, visual, and ecological levels by inserting disturbances that affect the way land is traditionally planned and seen. The goal is to rethink the perception of the space from within.

The selected disturbance is bees. Since 2006, because of Colony Collapse Disorder (a disease that prevents bees from returning to their hives), one third of the world's bee population has been lost. Almost 75 percent of global food sources depend on pollination to exist, and bees are the main pollinators. It is evident why design for bees can influence human existence.

The overlap of the dystopic potential map and the gradient of human use define a pattern of spaces in which beehives and gardens are located. These constitute the main structure for a multifunctional light and weak regional infrastructure.

Because pollinators can see ultraviolet patterns, the infrastructure is a guide both for humans and bees. The blue color creates a hybrid: objects designed to be functional for people, such as playgrounds and benches, when painted in blue, will also serve as a guide for bees and the pollination process, contributing to the densification and spread of selected vegetation over time.

Crossing Boundaries:
The Aesthetic of Fragments
An Operation of Regional Camouflage

| MLA Thesis | Paola Sturla |
| Advisor | Holly Clarke |

bees' vision
multimodal stimulation
chromatic vision: UV patterns perception

gradient   contra

BEES' visible spectrum

humans' visible spectrum

400nm   700nm

light spectrum

light s

Gamma rays   10-3nm   10-1nm   101nm   103nm   105nm   107nm   109nm   1011nm   1013nm   1015nm
                         X rays   ultraviolet visible infrared rays   radar   radio FM   television   radio AM   AC circuits

COBALT BLUE
HYBRID CONDITION
OVERLAP OV BEES' AND HUMANS' PERCEPTIBLE RANGE OF WAVELENGHTS

BEES' REAL MOVEMENT

BLUE STONE EXPERIMENT
HYBRIDIZATION OF VIEWS

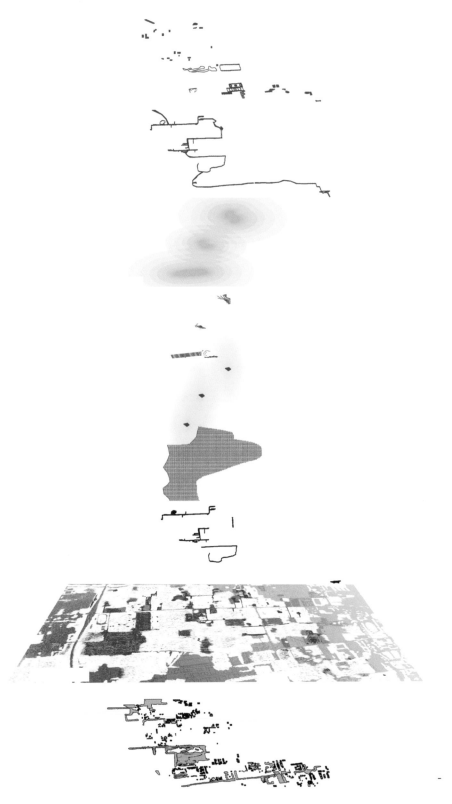

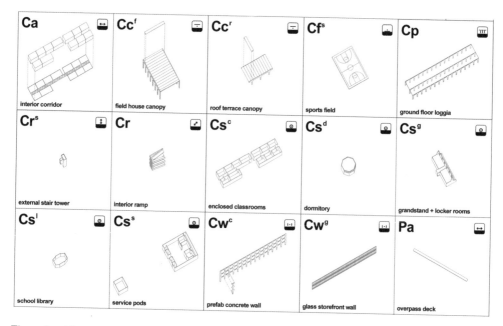

Ca — interior corridor
Cc^f — field house canopy
Cc^r — roof terrace canopy
Cf^s — sports field
Cp — ground floor loggia
Cr^s — external stair tower
Cr — interior ramp
Cs^c — enclosed classrooms
Cs^d — dormitory
Cs^g — grandstand + locker rooms
Cs^l — school library
Cs^s — service pods
Cw^c — prefab concrete wall
Cw^g — glass storefront wall
Pa — overpass deck

The school is not merely an autonomous typology that appears within the urban fabric, but is the expression of an educational system that, like a utility or mobility system, can be analyzed and understood in terms of how it organizes territory and shapes urbanism. This relationship between city and school was codified in Clarence Perry's concept of the neighborhood unit, subsequently deployed as the basic unit of urbanism in the modernist city planning of CIAM and its offspring.

But as the neatly ordered and nested scales of the neighborhood unit have given way to the realities of the heterogeneous and multi-centered modern city, the syntax that is generated between the school and other urban elements (dwellings, public buildings, parks, roads, etc.) remains relevant to the problems of scale and interconnectedness that face contemporary cities. Moreover, equally as important as this syntax is the Utopian desire that underlies the idea of the neighborhood unit, and arguably, any school system. This is to say that embodied within any model of education is an alternative vision for the ordering of society, and because of the close association of citizenship to urbanity, this is also an alternative proposal for ordering the urban environment.

Education Superinfrastructure recovers the instrumentality of the neighborhood unit, the diagrammatic association it makes between school and urbanism, while emptying it of the ideological baggage that limits its applicability to the modern city. It is a search for a new model for understanding and projecting urban form against the backdrop of the increasing instability and illegibility of the contemporary city. This search begins in Rio de Janeiro, where a series of model secondary schools and teacher training facilities are hybridized with bus rapid transit stations. These are deployed in the interstitial spaces of the city to overcome its particularly fragmented urban condition, and rescale the existing infrastructure to propose an alternative physical and social order.

Edutopias: The Utopian Geography of Education is a manifesto for reconceiving our cities around the exchange of knowledge, and for giving shape to urban form as the emplacement of that exchange.

passarela 10

passarela 07

passarela 03

Edutopias:
The Utopian Geography of Education

MAUD Thesis	Christopher Roach
Advisor	Hashim Sarkis

2011 Urban Planning and Design Thesis Prize

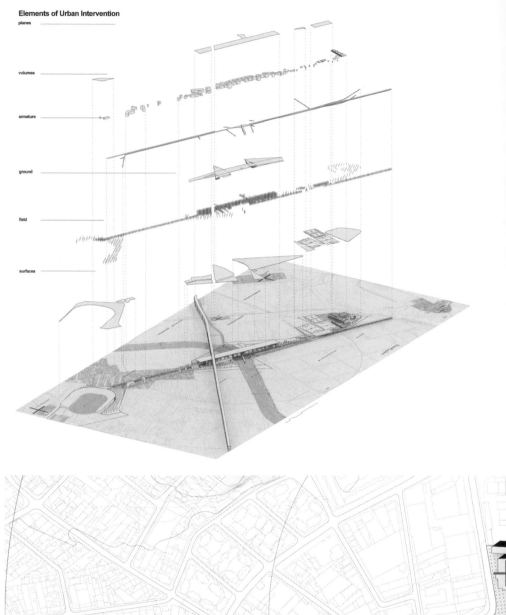

Elements of Urban Intervention

planes

volumes

armature

ground

field

surfaces

09

10

11

12

01

02

03

04

05

favela vila santo antônio

igreja evangelho quadrangular

igreja sta. cruz

igreja universal

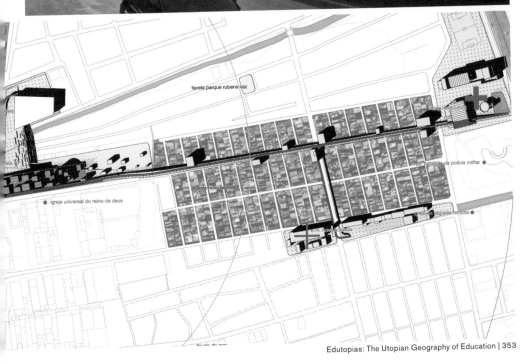

What might American education look like in the year 2030? By that time, today's newborns will become college freshmen. The task of looking ahead at today's American educational system was an opportunity to think about the long-range future through a collaboration between the disciplines of Design and Education.

In the first part of the seminar, Hashim Sarkis, Chair of the Research Advancement Initiative (RAI Labs), as well as Lewis Spence, Co-Director of the Harvard Graduate School of Education, organized a series of lectures addressing the future of education in relation to school facility typologies, community models, technology, and sustainability.

In the last part of the seminar, students from the Graduate School of Design and the Graduate School of Education collaborated as "designers" and "clients" in a pedagogical exercise on the design of a new school facility to be developed in a site at Boston.

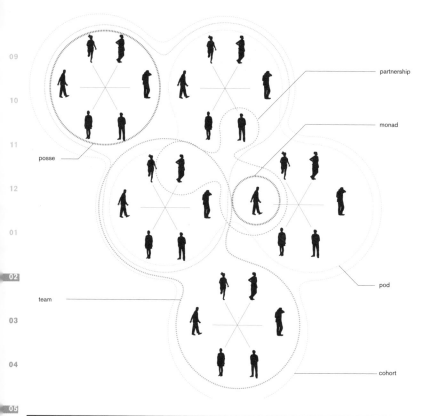

09
10
11
12
01
02
03
04
05

partnership

monad

posse

team

pod

cohort

F. Izquierd, T. Money, C. Roach, L. Suxo, S. Cohen, Y. Cohen. J. Doctor, T. Henderson

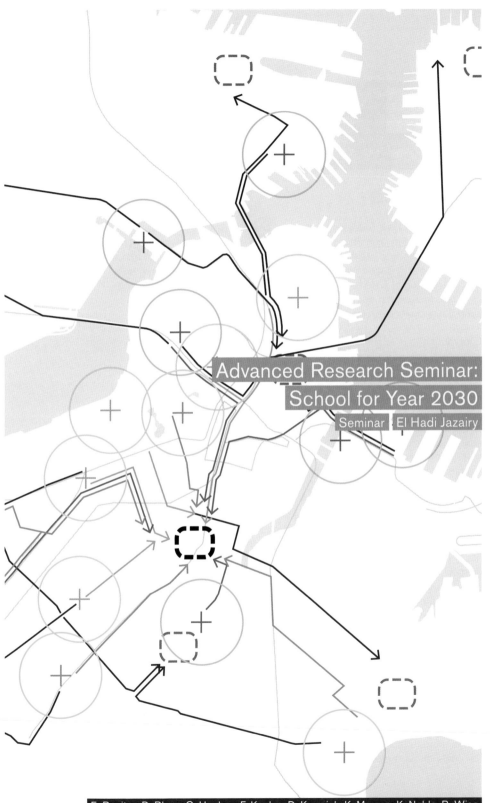

Advanced Research Seminar:
School for Year 2030

Seminar | El Hadi Jazairy

E. Benitez, D. Blase, C. Hughes, F. Kaplan, D. Kumnick, K. Moreno, K. Noble, R. Wise

Mohsen Mostafavi: Today and tomorrow are the celebrations of our fiftieth anniversary of the urban design program. This is obviously a very special moment, after fifty years when the main discipline and practices of urban design were introduced here at the GSD by Jose Luis Sert, building on a sort of tradition of CIAM and yet differentiating it in terms of the specifics of urban design as it became one of the key aspects of the work that the school has been involved with for the past fifty years.

One thing about urban design is that historically at the GSD it has been very much about urban design's relationship to planning, urban design's relationship to landscape architecture, urban design's relationship to architecture. These kinds of relationships are very important, and in a way, it's not something, as I said earlier, that is new. Quoting from one of our speakers, Eric Mumford's book on *Defining Urban Design*, there's a little quote from Jose Luis Sert. Eric is quoting Sert's sort of discussion of the challenges for architects that, according to Sert, would be "carrying out of large civic complexes, the integration of city planning, architecture, and landscape architecture, the building of a complete environment." Sert was saying these things fifty years ago, that what we need is integration. It's not a new thing for us to then be thinking about integrating architecture and urban design and urban planning and landscape architecture, when we hear Jose Luis Sert talk about the notion of complete environments. It's really necessary, given the kind of incredible transformations that we are seeing across the globe, for us to be thinking in this kind of holistic fashion. We have the realities of unbelievable forms of extreme growth in many of our cities. We have incredible challenges in terms of resources. We have incredible challenges in terms of questions of climate change. Many of these things need to be thought of in a bigger way than we have ever thought before. Urban design, under Jose Luis Sert was really focusing very much on the concept of urban fragments, on the idea that one really deals with parts of the city that are bigger than a piece of architecture, but they're really not looking beyond the ideas of core or the notion of the heart of the city or the pedestrianization. The reality today is that the scale of the things that we have to look at are very different than the scale of the urban fragment, and so the challenge today is precisely the challenge of the relationship of the specificity of urban design and its relationship to this concept of the phenomena, which is larger than simply the scale of the territory.

Territories of Urbanism:
Urban Design at 50
Conference | Various Speakers

Appendix

**Beijing: The Tsinghua University
Campus as an Operative Device to
Reshape the Metropolis**
Joan Busquets
Harvard Graduate School of Design

A View on Harvard GSD, Vol. 3
Harvard GSD (Editor)
Mohsen Mostafavi (Dean)
Tank

**Nieuw Centrum = New Civic Center:
Nesselande/Rotterdam**
Joan Busquets
Harvard Graduate School of Design

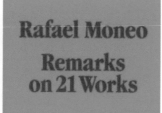

**Catalunya Continental: infrastructura
ferroviaria com a espina dorsal del
territori**
Joan Busquets
Felipe Correa & GSD Students (Co-Authors)
Harvard Graduate School of Design

Remarks on 21 Works
Rafael Moneo
The Monacelli Press

**Material Design: Informing
Architecture by Materiality**
Thomas Schröpfer
Birkhäuser Architecture

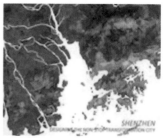

Made to Measure
Leers Weinzapfel Associates
Marion Weiss (preface), Joan Busquets
(foreword)
Princeton Architectural Press

**Beyond Paris: A New Campus for the
University of Paris South XI at Saclay**
Andrea Leers
Harvard Graduate School of Design

**Shenzhen: Designing the Non-stop
Transformation City**
Joan Busquets/Doreen Heng Liu
University of Hong Kong / Harvard University
Harvard Graduate School of Design

New Geographies, 3: Urbanisms of Color
Gareth Doherty (Editor)
Harvard Graduate School of Design

Harvard Design Magazine 32
William Saunders
Harvard Graduate School of Design

The Just City
Susan S. Fainstein
Cornell University Press

Spoorzone Delft : ontwerp openbare ruimte = public space project
Joan Busquets
Harvard Graduate School of Design

Requiem For the City at the End of the Millennium
Sanford Kwinter
Actar

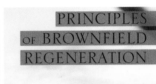

Implicate and Explicate: Aga Khan Award for Architecture
Mohsen Mostafavi (Editor)
Lars Muller Publishers

A City and its Stream: An Appraisal of the Cheonggyecheon Restoration Project and its Environs in Seoul, South Korea
Peter G. Rowe
Seoul Development Institute

Landscape and Ecological Urbanism Alternatives for Sujiatuo, Beijing
Kongjian Yu, Stephen Ervin
Turenscape

Principles of Brownfield Regeneration: Cleanup, Design, and Reuse of Derelict Land
Justin Hollander and Niall Kirkwood
Island Press

Platform 3
Emily Waugh (Editor)
Mohsen Mostafavi (Dean)
Actar

Landscape Infrastructure Primer
Pierre Belanger (Editor)
Harvard Graduate School of Design

Krzysztof Wodiczko
Duncan McCorquodale, Krzysztof
Wodiczko (Editors), Dick Hebdige,
Denis Hollier, Lisa Saltzman (contributing)
Black Dog Publishing

New Geographies, 4: Scales of the Earth
El Hadi Jazairy (Editor)
Harvard Graduate School of Design

Moving Forward: The Future of Consumer Credit and Mortgage Finance
Nicolas P. Retsinas, Eric S. Belsky (Editors)
Brookings Institution Press

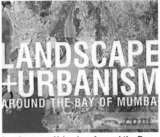

Landscape + Urbanism Around the Bay of Mumbai
Rahul Mehrotra (Editor)
MIT Press

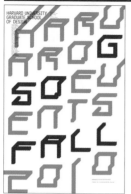

Fall Lecture Series

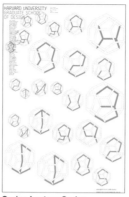

Spring Lecture Series

Deconstruction/Construction
The Cheonggyecheon River
Project in Seoul
The Tenth Veronica Rudge Green
Prize in Urban Design

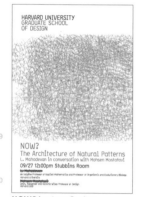

NOW? Lecture Series
09.07.10 / Material Computation
09.27.10 / The Architecture of Natural
Patterns
10.13.10 / What is Structural Design?

Critical and Strategic Conservation
Colloquium

Discussions in Architecture
09.14.10 / Neil Denari
11.10.10 / Bjarke Ingels
04.12.10 / Rafael Moneo

World Economic Forum at Harvard:
Design and Global Challenges

The Structural Engineering
of a Metaphor:
The UK Pavilion at the 2010
World Expo

Science & Democracy Lecture Series
11.30.10 / Michael Crow
04.12.11 / David Brooks

Women and Modernism in Landscape Architecture

In the Life of Cities...Parallel Narratives of the Urban

The Harvard GSD Symposia on Architecture: The Eclipse of Beauty
03.09.11 / Parametric Beauty
03.29.11 / Taste
04.20.11 / Unsettling Beauty or Ugliness?

Digital Culture, Technology Platform Visualizations : Realizations

The Divine Comedy Exhibition and Artists' Talk

A New Innocence: Emerging Trends in Japanese Architecture
02.19.11 / Sou Fujimoto
03.22.11 / Junya Ishigami
03.31.11 / Kazuyo Sejima & Ryue Nishizawa
04.25.11 / Toyo Ito

Student Groups

American Society of Landscape Architects
Asia GSD
Beer n' Dogs
Build Club
Canada GSD
China GSD
Club MEDINA
Critical Digital
Design Agent
Design with Animals
DIY (Design Initiative for Youth)
European Design Circle
Greece GSD
Green Design
Group for the Philosophy of Architecture
GSD Christian Community
GSD Real Estate Development Club
Harvard Urban Planning Organization

Housing GSD
India GSD
Inflatables
International Development and Urbanism
Italian Society at Harvard GSD
Japan GSD
Korea GSD
Land GSD
Landscape Lunchbox
Latin GSD
MDesS Club
The Mediterranean Society
Midwest GSD
My City, My Future
Nat'l Organization of Minority Arch. Students (NOMAS)
New Geographies
Out Design
Planners Network

Repurpose Group
Student Lecture Series
SoCA (Social Change and Activism)
Student Wall
Trays
Tourism Club
Urban Mobilities
Village Link
Women in Design
"YES NO" Student Journal
Yoga GSD

Harvard Graduate School of Design

Mohsen Mostafavi, Dean of the Graduate School of Design
Martin Bechthold, Co-Director of the Master in Design Studies Program
Eve Blau, Director of the Master in Architecture Programs
Preston Scott Cohen, Chair of the Department of Architecture
Felipe Correa, Director of the Master of Architecture in Urban Design Degree Program
K. Michael Hays, Associate Dean for Academic Affairs, Co-Director of Doctoral Programs
Rahul Mehrotra, Chair of the Department of Urban Planning and Design
Judith Grant Long, Director of the Master in Urban Planning Degree Program
Sanford Kwinter, Co-Director of the Master in Design Studies Program
Antoine Picon, Co-Director of Doctoral Programs
Charles Waldheim, Chair of the Department of Landscape Architecture
Christian Werthmann, Director of the Master in Landscape Architecture Degree Programs

Faculty of Design

Alan Altshuler, Ruth and Frank Stanton Professor of Urban Policy and Planning and Harvard University Distinguished Service Professor
John Beardsley, Adjunct Professor of Landscape Architecture
Martin Bechthold, Professor of Architectural Technology, Co-Director of Master in Design Studies Program, Technology Platform Coordinator
Pierre Belanger, Associate Professor of Landscape Architecture
Anita Berrizbeitia, Professor of Landscape Architecture
Eve Blau, Adjunct Professor of Architectural History, Director of the Master in Architecture Programs
Joan Busquets, Martin Bucksbaum Professor in Practice of Urban Planning and Design
Holly Clarke, Associate Professor of Landscape Architecture
Preston Scott Cohen, Gerald M. McCue Professor in Architecture, Chair of the Department of Architecture
Felipe Correa, Assistant Professor of Urban Planning and Design
Jill Desimini, Assistant Professor of Landscape Architecture
Danielle Etzler, Assistant Professor of Architecture
Susan Fainstein, Professor of Urban Planning
Richard T.T. Forman, Professor of Advanced Environmental Studies in the Field of Landscape Ecology
Jose Gomez-Ibanez, Derek Bok Professor of Urban Planning and Public Policy
Toni Griffin, Adjunct Associate Professor of Urban Planning and Design
K. Michael Hays, Eliot Noyes Professor in Architectural Theory, Associate Dean for Academic Affairs, Co-Director of Doctoral Programs
Gary Hilderbrand, Adjunct Professor of Landscape Architecture
John Hong, Adjunct Associate Professor of Architecture
Michael Hooper, Assistant Professor of Urban Planning and Design
Timothy Hyde, Assistant Professor of Architecture
Mariana Ibanez, Assistant Professor of Architecture
Jerold S. Kayden, Frank Backus Williams Professor of Urban Planning and Design
Niall Kirkwood, Professor of Landscape Architecture
Remment Koolhaas, Professor in Practice of Architecture and Urban Design
Alex Krieger, Professor in Practice of Urban Design
Sanford Kwinter, Professor of Architectural Theory and Criticism, Co-Director of the Master in Design Studies Program
Mark Laird, Senior Lecturer in Landscape Architecture
Andrea Leers, Adjunct Professor of Architecture and Urban Planning and Design
Jonathan Levi, Adjunct Professor of Architecture
Judith Grant Long, Associate Professor of Urban Planning and Design
Rahul Mehrotra, Professor of Urban Planning and Design, Chair of the Department of Urban Planning and Design
Paula Meijerink, Assistant Professor of Landscape Architecture
Michael Meredith, Associate Professor of Architecture
Rafael Moneo, Josep Lluis Sert Professor in Architecture
Toshiko Mori, Robert P. Hubbard Professor in the Practice of Architecture
Mohsen Mostafavi, Dean of the Graduate School of Design, Alexander and Victoria Wiley Professor of Design
Farshid Moussavi, Professor in Practice of Architecture
Mark Mulligan, Adjunct Associate Professor of Architecture
Erika Naginski, Associate Professor of Architecture
Richard Peiser, Michael D. Spear Professor of Real Estate Development
Antoine Picon, G. Ware Travelstead Professor of the History of Architecture and Technology, Co-Director of Doctoral Programs
Spiro Pollalis, Professor of Architecture
Chris Reed, Adjunct Associate Professor of Landscape Architecture
Christoph Reinhart, Associate Professor of Architectural Technology
Ingeborg Rocker, Assistant Professor of Architecture
Joyce Rosenthal, Assistant Professor of Urban Planning and Design
Peter G. Rowe, Raymond Garbe Professor of Architecture and Urban Design and Harvard University Distinguished Service Professor
A. Hashim Sarkis, Aga Khan Professor of Landscape Architecture and Urbanism in Muslim Societies
Daniel L. Schodek, Kumagai Research Professor of Architectural Technology, Emeritus

Thomas Schroepfer, Associate Professor of Architecture

Matthias Schuler, Adjunct Professor of Architecture

Martha Schwartz, Professor in Practice of Landscape Architecture

Mack Scogin, Kajima Professor in Practice of Architecture

Jorge Silvetti, Nelson Robinson Jr. Professor in Architecture

Christine Smith, Robert C. and Marian K. Weinberg Professor of Architectural History

John R. Stilgoe, Robert and Lois Orchard Professor in the History of Landscape Development

Kostas Terzidis, Associate Professor of Architecture

Maryann Thompson, Adjunct Professor of Architecture

Michael Van Valkenburgh, Charles Eliot Professor in Practice of Landscape Architecture

Charles Waldheim, John E. Irving Professor of Landscape Architecture, Chair of the Department of Landscape Architecture

Christian Werthmann, Associate Professor of Landscape Architecture, Director of the Master in Landscape Architecture Degree Programs

T. Kelly Wilson, Adjunct Associate Professor of Architecture

Krzysztof Wodiczko, Professor of Architecture

Cameron Wu, Assistant Professor of Architecture

Visiting Faculty

Inaki Abalos, Design Critic in Urban Planning and Design

Sahel Al Hiyari, Design Critic in Architecture

Simon Allford, Design Critic in Architecture

Steven Apfelbaum, Design Critic in Landscape Architecture

Leire Asensio Villoria, Design Critic in Architecture

Bridget Baines, Design Critic in Landscape Architecture

Daniel Barber, Design Critic in Landscape Architecture

Eric Belsky, Lecturer in Urban Planning and Design

Brian Blaesser, Lecturer in Urban Planning and Design

Sibel Bozdogan, Lecturer in Architecture

Paola Cannavo, Visiting Associate Professor of Landscape Architecture

Stephen Cassell, Design Critic in Landscape Architecture

Lucien Castaing-Taylor, Visiting Associate Professor of Architecture

Shane Coen, Design Critic in Landscape Architecture

Philippe Coignet, Design Critic in Landscape Architecture

Betsy Colburn, Lecturer in Landscape Architecture

Janne Corneil, Design Critic in Urban Planning and Design

Paul Cote, Lecturer in Urban Planning and Design

James Dallman, Design Critic in Architecture

Tim Dekker, Lecturer in Landscape Architecture

Peter Del Tredici, Lecturer in Landscape Architecture

Philip Demokritou, Visiting Assistant Professor of Architecture

Neil Denari, Visiting Professor of Architecture

Richard Dimino, Lecturer in Urban Planning and Design

Daniel D'Oca, Design Critic in Urban Planning and Design

Gareth Doherty, Lecturer in Architecture

Susannah Drake, Design Critic in Landscape Architecture

Angus Eade, Design Critic in Architecture

Stephen Ervin, Lecturer in Urban Planning and Design

Michael Flynn, Lecturer in Landscape Architecture

Peter Galison, Visiting Professor in Architecture, Landscape Architecture and Urban Planning

David Gamble, Design Critic in Urban Planning and Design

Jeanne Gang, Design Critic in Architecture

Anton Garcia-Abril, Design Critic in Architecture

Andreas Georgoulias, Lecturer in Architecture

Christopher Gordon, Lecturer in Architecture

Oscar Grauer, Lecturer in Urban Planning and Design

Gregory Halpern, Lecturer in Landscape Architecture

David Hamilton, Jr., Lecturer in Urban Planning and Design

Andrea Hansen, Lecturer in Landscape Architecture

Sonia Hirt, Lecturer in Urban Planning and Design

Eelco Hooftman, Design Critic in Landscape Architecture

Hiromi Hosoya, Visiting Professor in Architecture

Eric Howeler, Design Critic in Architecture

Christopher Hoxie, Lecturer in Architecture

John Dixon Hunt, Visiting Professor in Landscape Architecture

Jane Hutton, Lecturer in Landscape Architecture

Florian Idenburg, Design Critic in Architecture

Bjarke Ingels, Design Critic in Architecture

Lisa Iwamoto, Design Critic in Architecture

Visiting Faculty (cont.)

El Hadi Jazairy, Lecturer in Urban Planning and Design

Richard Jennings, Lecturer in Architecture, Landscape Architecture

Joseph Kalt, Visiting Professor in Urban Planning and Design

Kenneth Kao, Lecturer in Architecture

Hanif Kara, Lecturer in Architecture

Ernst Karel, Lecturer in Architecture

Brian Kenet, Lecturer in Architecture, Landscape Architecture

Kathryn Kennen, Instructor in Landscape Architecture

Matthew Kiefer, Lecturer in Urban Planning and Design

Nico Kienzl, Lecturer in Architecture

Wooyoung Kimm, Lecturer in Architecture

Varun Kohli, Lecturer in Architecture

Eugene Kohn, Lecturer in Architecture

Grace La, Design Critic in Architecture

George L. Legendre, Design Critic in Architecture

Nina-Marie Lister, Visiting Associate Professor of Landscape Architecture

Peter Lynch, Lecturer in Architecture

John Macomber, Lecturer in Architecture

David Mah, Lecturer in Landscape Architecture

Edward Marchant, Lecturer in Urban Planning and Design

Wilson Martin, Lecturer in Landscape Architecture

Miho Mazereeuw, Design Critic in Landscape Architecture

Anne McGhee, Lecturer in Landscape Architecture

Michael McGough, Lecturer in Architecture

Achim Menges, Visiting Professor of Architecture

Panagiotis Michalatos, Lecturer in Architecture

Joshua Mosley, Visiting Associate Professor of Landscape Architecture

Lars Muller, Lecturer in Architecture

Carles Muro, Design Critic in Architecture

Nashid Nabian, Lecturer in Architecture, Urban Planning and Design

Ciro Najle, Design Critic in Urban Planning and Design

Paul Nakazawa, Lecturer in Architecture

Erik Olsen, Lecturer in Architecture

Piet Oudolf, Lecturer in Landscape Architecture

Katharine Parsons, Lecturer in Landscape Architecture

Dennis Pieprz, Design Critic in Urban Planning and Design

Anna Pla Catala, Design Critic in Architecture

Nicolas Retsinas, Lecturer in Urban Planning and Design

Matthias Rudolph, Lecturer in Architecture

Allen Sayegh, Lecturer in Architecture

Jeffrey Schnapp, Visiting Professor of Architecture, Landscape Architecture and Urban Planning

Michael Shroeder, Lecturer in Architecture

Craig Scott, Design Critic in Architecture

Rafael Segal, Design Critic in Urban Planning and Design

Jesse Shapins, Instructor in Architecture

Laura Solano, Lecturer in Landscape Architecture

John Spengler, Visiting Professor of Architecture

Kathy Spiegelman, Design Critic in Urban Planning and Design

James Stockard, Lecturer in Urban Planning and Design

Belinda Tato, Design Critic in Urban Planning and Design

Matthew Urbanski, Lecturer in Landscape Architecture

Jose Luis Vellejo, Design Critic in Urban Planning and Design

Ben Van Berkel, Visiting Professor of Architecture

Alexander von Hoffman, Lecturer in Urban Planning and Design

Michael Wang, Design Critic in Architecture

Bing Wang, Lecturer in Urban Planning Design

Julia Watson, Design Critic in Landscape Architecture

Emily Waugh, Lecturer in Landscape Architecture

Elizabeth Whittaker, Design Critic in Architecture

Jay Wickersham, Lecturer in Architecture

Andrew Witt, Lecturer in Architecture

Kongjian Yu, Visiting Professor of Urban Planning and Design

Darina Zlateva, Lecturer in Landscape Architecture

Loeb Fellows

Bryan Bell

Andy Cao

Herbert Dreiseitl

Ana Maria Duran

Theaster Gates

Ana Gelabert-Sanchez

Brent Leggs

Chee Pearlman

Tim Stonor

Staff

Jane Acheson, Dean's Office
Joseph Amato, Building Services
Robert Angilly, Frances Loeb Library
Nader Ardalan, Architecture
Alla Armstrong, Academic Finance
Lauren Baccus, Human Resources
Kermit F. Baker, Joint Center for Housing Studies
Pamela H. Baldwin, Joint Center for Housing Studies
Lauren L. Beath, Finance Office
P. Todd Belton, Computer Resources
Allison Benedetti, Frances Loeb Library
Sue Boland, Computer Resources
Dan F. Borelli, Exhibitions
Stacy Buckley, Academic Services
Kevin Cahill, Building Services
Bonnie Campbell, External Relations
Susie Chung, Joint Center for Housing Studies
Anna Cimini, Computer Resources
Doug F. Cogger, Computer Resources
Ellen Colleran, Landscape Architecture, UPD
Sean Kelliher Conlon, Student Services
Anne Creamer, Career Services
Andrea Croteau, Architecture
Maria Tina T. da Rosa, Frances Loeb Library
Mary Daniels, Special Collections
Zhu Xiao Di, Joint Center for Housing Studies
Sarah Dickinson, Collections
Kerry Donahue, Joint Center for Housing Studies
Barbara Elfman, Advanced Studies Programs
Angela Flynn, Joint Center for Housing Studies
Jennifer Friedman, Frances Loeb Library
Heather Gallagher, Executive Education
Suneeta Gill, Dean's Office
Keith A. Gnoza, Financial Assistance
Meryl Golden, Academic and Student Services
Desiree Goodwin, Public Services
Irina Gorstein, Frances Loeb Library
Hal Gould, Computer Resources
Norton Greenfeld, Development and Alumni Relations
Arin Gregorian, Academic Finance
Deborah L. Grohe, Building Services
Gail Gustafson, Admissions
Mark Hagen, Computer Resources
Jennifer Halloran, Development and Alumni Relations
Barry J. Harper, Building Services
Jill Harrington, Admissions
Amanda Heighes, Publications
Cynthia Henshall, Real Estate Academic Initiative
Chris Herbert, Joint Center for Housing Studies
Jackie B. Hernandez, Joint Center for Housing Studies
Megan Homan, Development and Alumni Relations
Joanna Hurier, Human Resources
Maggie Janik, User Services
Anne Jeffko, Human Resources
Nancy Jennings, Executive Education
Pilar Jordan, Academic Finance Office
Johanna Kasubowski, Visual Resources
Adam Kellie, Frances Loeb Library
Brooke Lynn King, Events
Linda Ruth Kitch, Frances Loeb Library
Karen Kittredge, Finance Office
Beth Kramer, Development and Alumni Relations
Mary Lancaster, Joint Center for Housing Studies
Ameilia Latham, Finance Office
Kevin Lau, Frances Loeb Library

Justin Lavallee, Shop
Sharon Lembo, Real Estate Academic Initiative
Mary MacLean, Finance Office
Daniel McCue, Joint Center for Housing Studies
Mike A. McGrath, Faculty Planning
Megan McHugh, Human Resources
Margaret Moore de Chicojay, Executive Education
Corlette Moore McCoy, Executive Education
Maria Moran, Advanced Studies Programs
Jerry Mui, Computer Resources
Maria Murphy, Student Services
Geri Sue Nederhoff, Admissions
Page Nelson, Technical Services
Caroline Newton, Landscape Architecture, UPD
Meg Nipson, Joint Center for Housing Studies
Trevor D. O'Brien, Building Services
Robert Ochshorn, Administration and Academic
Programs
Jackie Piracini, Administration and Academic Programs
Cecily Pollard, Development and Alumni Relations
Benjamin Prosky, Communications
Alix Reiskind, Visual Resources
Ann Renauer, Finance Office
Carlos Reyes, Student Services
Patricia J. Roberts, Administration and Academic
Programs
Kate Ryan, External Relations
Meghan Sandberg, Harvard Design Magazine
Nicole Sander, Landscape Architecture and UPD
Ronee Saroff, Communications
William S. Saunders, Harvard Design Magazine
Paul Scannell, Building Services
Emily Scudder, Technical Services
Laura S. Snowdon, Dean of Students
Shannon Stecher, Exhibitions
Jennifer Swartout, Architecture
Aimee Taberner, Administration and Academic
Programs
Kelly Teixeira, Student Services
Julia Topalian, Development
Ashley Torr, Architecture
Jennifer Vallone, Finance Office
Edna Van Saun, Landscape Architecture
Melissa Vaughn, Publications
Rachel Vroman, Shop
Ciel Wendel, Student Services
Ann Whiteside, Frances Loeb Library
Sara J. Wilkinson, Human Resources
Abbe Will, Joint Center for Housing Studies
Cameron Willard, Shop
Janet Wysocki, Executive Education
Sally Young, Loeb Fellowship
Ines Maria Zalduendo, Frances Loeb Library
David Zimmerman-Stuart, Exhibitions

Harvard Graduate School of Design

Mohsen Mostafavi, Dean of the Graduate School of Design
Martin Bechthold, Co-Director of the Master in Design Studies Program
Mark Mulligan, Director of the Master in Architecture Programs
Preston Scott Cohen, Chair of the Department of Architecture
Felipe Correa, Director of the Master of Architecture in Urban Design Degree Program
K. Michael Hays, Associate Dean for Academic Affairs, Co-Director of Doctoral Programs
Rahul Mehrotra, Chair of the Department of Urban Planning and Design
Jerold S. Kayden, Director of the Master in Urban Planning Degree Program
Sanford Kwinter, Co-Director of the Master in Design Studies Program
Antoine Picon, Co-Director of Doctoral Programs
Charles Waldheim, Chair of the Department of Landscape Architecture
Christian Werthmann, Director of the Master in Landscape Architecture Degree Programs

Melissa Vaughn, Director of Publications
Eric Howeler, Assistant Professor of Architecture and Faculty Editor
Andrew Domnitz (MArch AP 2011), Editor
James Leng (MArch AP 2012), Editor
Drew Cowdrey (MArch 1 2013), Editor
Aisling O'Carroll (MLA AP 2012)
Scottie McDaniel (MLA AP 2012)
Amanda Heighes, Copy Editor
Anita Kan, Model Photography (unless otherwise noted)
Shannon Stecher, Art Collector

Photo Credits

Jacob Belcher
Lian Chang
Bradley Crane
Anita Kan
Trey Kirk
Justin Knight
Evangelos Kotsioris
Carl Koepcke
James Leng
Stephanie Lin
Ricardo Munoz
Aaron Orenstein
Shanshan Qi
Levi Stolove
Dan Sullivan
Ken Yip

Special Thanks

We would like to thank the following individuals, for without their efforts this publication would not have been possible:

Emily Waugh, Michael Kubo, Dan Borelli, David Zimmerman-Stuart, Gabrielle Piazza Patawaran, Tom Cakuls, John R. Stilgoe, Stephen Ervin, David Turturo, Iñaki Ábalos.

We are particularly grateful to Lian Chang for her help.

Imprint

Published by
Harvard University Graduate School of Design, Actar

Graphic design and production
ActarBirkäuserPro

GSD Platform 4 represents selected studios, seminars, research, events, and exhibitions from the 2010-2011 academic year.

For additional information and a more comprehensive selection of student work, see www.gsd.harvard.edu/studioworks.

The Harvard Graduate School of Design is a leading center for education, information, and technical expertise on the built environment. Its Departments of Architecture, Landscape Architecture, and Urban Planning and Design offer masters and doctoral degree programs, and provide the foundation for the school's Advanced Studies and Executive Education Programs.

© Of this edition, President and Fellows of Harvard College and Actar, 2011
© Of the works, 2011 President and Fellows of Harvard College
All rights reserved

ISBN: 978-84-15391-00-5
DL B-34.501-2011

Distribution

ActarBirkhäuserD
Barcelona-Basel-New York
www.actarbikhauser-d.com

Roca I Batlle 2
E-08023 Barcelona
T +34 93 417 49 93
F +34 93 418 67 07
salesbarcelona@actarbikhauser.com

Viaduktsrasse 42
CH-4051 Basel
T +41 61 5689 800
F +41 61 5689 899
salesbasel@actarbikhauser.com

151 Grand Street, 5th floor
New York, NY 10013
T +1 212 966 2207
F +1 212 966 2214
salesnewyork@actarbikhauser.com